Routledge Revivals

The Handbook of British Regiments

Since the creation of the standing army in 1661, when each regiment was known by the name of its current colonel, there have been many reforms and rationalizations of the British army. From 31 cavalry regiments and 113 infantry regiments in 1881, at the time of this title's first publication in 1988, the army had reduced to just 16 regiments of armour and 39 regiments of infantry through processes of absorption and amalgamation. *The Handbook of British Regiments* provides insight into the lineage and history of the approximately 85 regiments and corps which formed the British army towards the end of the 1980s. Comprehensive in coverage, each has a separate entry giving factual details in a layout standardized for easy comparison, including current title, colonel-in-chief, uniform and history, amongst others.

A key reference title amongst Routledge reissues, this handbook provides an accessible guide to specialists as well as lay enthusiasts, and illustrates a sense of the continuity and inherited tradition of each regiment and corps.

The Handbook of British Regiments

Christopher Chant

First published in 1988
by Routledge

This edition first published in 2013 by Routledge
2 Park Square, Milton Park, Abingdon, Oxon, OX14 4RN

Simultaneously published in the USA and Canada
by Routledge
711 Third Avenue, New York, NY 10017

Routledge is an imprint of the Taylor & Francis Group, an informa business

© 1988 Christopher Chant

All rights reserved. No part of this book may be reprinted or reproduced or utilised in any form or by any electronic, mechanical, or other means, now known or hereafter invented, including photocopying and recording, or in any information storage or retrieval system, without permission in writing from the publishers.

Publisher's Note
The publisher has gone to great lengths to ensure the quality of this reprint but points out that some imperfections in the original copies may be apparent.

Disclaimer
The publisher has made every effort to trace copyright holders and welcomes correspondence from those they have been unable to contact.

A Library of Congress record exists under LC control number: 87003009

ISBN 13: 978-0-415-71076-3 (hbk)
ISBN 13: 978-1-315-88482-0 (ebk)
ISBN 13: 978-0-415-71079-4 (pbk)

The Handbook of British Regiments

Christopher Chant

Routledge
London and New York

First published in 1988 by
Routledge
11 New Fetter Lane, London EC4P 4EE

Published in the USA by
Routledge Inc.
in association with Methuen Inc.
29 West 35th Street, New York, NY 10001

Set in Linotron Rockwell Light 10/12pt
by Input Typesetting Ltd, London
and printed in Great Britain
by T J Press (Padstow) Ltd
Padstow, Cornwall

© Imp Publishing Services Ltd 1988

No part of this book may be reproduced in
any form without permission from the publisher
except for the quotation of brief passages
in criticism

Library of Congress Cataloging in Publication Data

Chant, Christopher.
The handbook of British regiments.
Includes index.
1. Great Britain. Army—History. I. Title.
UA649.C47 1988   355.3'1'0941   87-3009

British Library CIP Data also available
ISBN 0-415-00241-9

For My Parents
John and Jean Chant

CONTENTS

ix

Introduction

xi

The precedence of corps and regiments
of the regular British Army

1

The *Handbook of British Regiments*

310

Index

INTRODUCTION

Reduced overseas commitments, financial constraints, altered social conditions, and greater reliance on technology than manpower in modern warfare – these and other factors have all played decisive parts in the reduction of the British army from its heyday in late Victorian times to its present modest strength. A force that in 1881 numbered 31 regiments of cavalry and 113 regiments of infantry has been trimmed to a mere 16 regiments of armour and 39 regiments of infantry (including four of Gurkhas). Yet most of the regiments current in 1881 are still present in today's army, thanks to a process of amalgamation rather than disbandment. In such a way the traditions, nicknames and customs of older regiments survive (even if this survival is only in truncated form) in the regiments of today, much to the delight of those concerned with the history and continuity of the British army.

The welter of amalgamations in 1881, the early 1920s, the late 1950s and the late 1960s therefore preserved older regiments and their traditions, but also made it difficult to discern the precise origins of much that is still with us. The object of this book, therefore, is to trace the order of battle and antecedents of the regular corps and regiments of the current British army, and thus to provide an insight into the lineage of the corps and 55 regiments still on the list of the British army. There are many ways in which this information can be organized and presented, but that chosen for the present book concentrates on information set out in uniform manner to show comparable details for each corps and regiment:

1. Corps or regimental badge
2. Current name, and the number(s) of the 1881 regiment(s) that went into the present regiment
3. Current colonel-in-chief and colonel
4. Battle honours
5. Headquarters (administrative) and museum
6. March(es)
7. Motto(es)
8. Nickname(s)
9. Full dress uniform (full dress uniform was officially banned after World War I except for the Household Cavalry and the Regiments of Foot Guards, but is generally maintained on an individual regimental basis for use on special occasions, and reflects more closely the ancestry of the corps or regiment than does the more utilitarian modern uniform)
10. Allied and affiliated regiments (current alliances and imperial affiliations of the period immediately after World War I)

11. Regimental history with basic details of the regiment's creation and subsequent changes of name, together with comparable information for the regiments that have been amalgamated into the present regiment, these predecessor regiments being treated in order of seniority.

When the standing army was created in 1661, shortly after the restoration of Charles II, each regiment was known by the name of its colonel, a situation fraught with confusion for the army of the time and for interested parties of later generations. In 1751 it was decided, therefore, that each regiment should be known by its number (or rank) in the line, a system already instituted in 1694 but which now excluded rather than complemented the system of colonels' names. In this revision of 1751 some regiments were permitted to maintain other distinctive names, and in 1782 most regiments were given an additional territorial or county title. Then in 1881 the Cardwell army reforms grouped the original regiments in pairs as two-battalion regiments. Names were generally revised in the aftermath of World War I, and in the 1950s and 1960s further rationalization reduced the number of regiments still further.

I must express my great indebtedness to a number of publications dealing with this basic topic, most notably *The Army List*, *The Army Quarterly and Defence Journal*, David Ascoli's *A Companion to the British Army 1669–1983*, Michael Barthorp's *The Armies of Britain 1485–1980*, J. M. Brereton's *A Guide to the Regiments and Corps of the British Army*, J. B. M. Frederick's *Lineage Book of the British Army: Mounted Corps and Infantry 1660–1980*, C. B. Norman's *Battle Honours of the British Army*, and Paymaster Lieutenant-Commander E. C. Talbot-Booth's *The British Army: Its History, Traditions and Uniforms* (arranged alphabetically by author). Together with other works and a host of regimental histories too numerous to list, these have been a pleasure to read and use, and valuable sources of information of all types. Finally, any errors in this book are inevitably those of the author alone.

Regiments and corps are presented in order of military precedence. Within the lists of battle honours, original contemporary spellings have been retained for the sake of historical accuracy. Mascots are mentioned only for regiments where they are officially recognized; in most cases the source of nicknames given is clear or has been explained, but other nicknames have been included for the sake of completeness and interest.

Christopher Chant

Swayfield
Grantham
Lincolnshire
December 1986

PRECEDENCE OF CORPS AND REGIMENTS OF THE REGULAR BRITISH ARMY

1. Household Cavalry
2. Royal Horse Artillery*
3. Royal Armoured Corps
4. Royal Regiment of Artillery
5. Corps of Royal Engineers
6. Royal Corps of Signals
7. Regiments of Foot Guards
8. Regiments of Infantry
9. Special Air Service Regiment
10. Army Air Corps
11. Royal Army Chaplains' Department
12. Royal Corps of Transport
13. Royal Army Medical Corps
14. Royal Army Ordnance Corps
15. Corps of Royal Electrical and Mechanical Engineers
16. Corps of Royal Military Police
17. Royal Army Pay Corps
18. Royal Army Veterinary Corps
19. Small Arms School Corps
20. Military Provost Staff Corps
21. Royal Army Educational Corps
22. Royal Army Dental Corps
23. Royal Pioneer Corps
24. Intelligence Corps
25. Army Physical Training Corps
26. Army Catering Corps
27. Army Legal Corps
28. General Service Corps (a pool for unattached officers, and not covered here)
29. Queen Alexandra's Royal Army Nursing Corps
30. Women's Royal Army Corps

* *See p.65*

HOUSEHOLD CAVALRY: ORDER OF PRECEDENCE

1. The Life Guards
2. The Blues and Royals

HOUSEHOLD CAVALRY REGIMENTS 1

The Life Guards

Colonel-in-Chief
HM The Queen

Colonel
Major-General Lord Fitzalan Howard

Battle honours
Dettingen Peninsula Waterloo Tel-el-Kebir Egypt 1882 Relief of Kimberley Paardeberg South Africa 1899–1900 Mons Le Cateau Retreat from Mons Marne 1914 Aisne 1914 Messines 1914 Armentieres 1914 Ypres 1914, '15, '17 Langemarck 1914 Gheluvelt Nonne Boschen St Julien Frezenberg Somme 1916, '18 Albert 1916 Arras 1916, '18 Scarpe 1917, '18 Broodseinde Poelcappelle Passchendaele Bapaume 1918 Hindenburg Line Selle France and Flanders 1914–18 Mont Pincon Souleuvre Noireau Crossing Amiens 1944 Brussels Neerpelt Nederrijn Nijmegen Lingen Bentheim North-West Europe 1944–45 Baghdad 1941 Iraq 1941 Palmyra Syria 1941 El Alamein North Africa 1942–43 Arezzo Advance to Florence Gothic Line Italy 1944

Regimental headquarters
RHQ Household Cavalry, Horse Guards, Whitehall, London.

Regimental museum

Household Cavalry Museum, Combermere Barracks, Windsor, Berkshire.

Regimental marches

(slow) Anonymous (attributed to the Duchess of Kent), and Men of Harlech (traditional)
(quick) Milanollo (Val Hamm)

Regimental motto

Honi Soit Qui Mal y Pense (Evil be to Him who Evil Thinks)

Nicknames

The Bangers, The Gallopers, The Tins, The Tin Bellies, The Patent Safeties, The Cheeses, The Cheesemongers

Uniform

Scarlet with blue velvet facings

Allied regiments

none

Regimental history

This is the senior regiment of the Household Cavalry, and can be traced to the body of noblemen and gentlemen who accompanied King Charles II on his exile in France and the Low Countries. In 1660 these were His Majesty's 1st, 2nd and 3rd Troops of Horse Guards (or Life Guards of Horse), and they escorted the king on his return to London after his restoration in that same year. In 1661 these troops became part of the new Standing Army, and were supplemented by the Scottish (or 4th) Troop of Horse Guards, which was raised in Edinburgh. The establishment was further increased in 1678, when three troops of Horse Grenadier Guards were raised, one being attached to each of the three troops of Horse Guards on the English establishment; a 4th (Scottish) Troop of Horse Grenadier Guards was raised in 1686 and attached to the 4th (Scottish) Troop of Horse Guards. A short-lived expansion was the Dutch Troop of Horse Guards (4th Troop of Horse Guards) which was raised in 1689 on the English establishment but disbanded in 1699. A reorganization was undertaken in 1709, when the 1st, 2nd and 3rd Troops of Horse Grenadier Guards were redesignated the 1st Troop of Horse Grenadier Guards, and the 4th (Scottish) Troop of Horse Grenadier Guards became the 2nd Troop of Horse Grenadier Guards. Thereafter a measure of stability returned until 1746, when the 3rd and 4th Troops of Horse Guards were disbanded. A major alteration came in 1788, however, when the 1st Troop of Horse Guards and the 1st Troop of Horse Grenadier Guards were amalgamated as the 1st Regiment of Life Guards, and the 2nd Troop of Horse Guards and the 2nd Troop of Horse Grenadier Guards were combined as the 2nd Regiment of Life Guards. There followed a period of some 130 years before the equilibrium was again disturbed in the aftermath of World War I, when the 1st and 2nd Regiments of Life Guards were amalgamated as The Life Guards (1st and 2nd), the regiment's title being changed to The Life Guards in 1928 and remaining unaltered thereafter to the present day. The nicknames given above were associated with The Life Guards in its older forms although they have never achieved any currency within the regiment or its predecessors.

HOUSEHOLD CAVALRY REGIMENTS 2

The Blues and Royals

Colonel-in-Chief

HM The Queen

Colonel

General Sir Desmond Fitzpatrick

Battle honours

Tangier 1662–80   Dettingen   Warburg   Beaumont   Willems   Fuentes d'Onor   Peninsula   Waterloo   Balaklava   Sevastopol   Tel-el-Kebir   Egypt 1882   Relief of Kimberley   Paardeberg   Relief of Ladysmith   South Africa 1899–1902   Mons   Le Cateau   Retreat from Mons   Marne 1914   Aisne 1914   Messines 1914   Armentieres 1914   Ypres 1914, '15, '17   Langemarck 1914   Gheluvelt   Nonne Bosschen   St Julien   Frezenberg   Loos   Arras 1917   Scarpe 1917   Broodseinde   Poelcappelle   Passchendaele   Somme 1918   Amiens   Hindenburg Line   Cambrai 1918   Sambre   Pursuit to Mons   France and Flanders 1914–18   Mont Pincon   Souleuvre   Noireau Crossing   Amiens 1944   Brussels   Neerpelt   Nederrijn   Nijmegen   Rhine   Lingen   Bentheim   North-West Europe 1944–45   Baghdad   Iraq 1941   Palmyra   Syria 1941   Knightsbridge   El Alamein   Advance on Tripoli   North Africa 1941–43   Sicily 1943   Arezzo   Advance to Florence   Gothic Line   Italy 1943–44   Falkland Islands 1982

Regimental headquarters

Horse Guards, Whitehall, London.

Regimental museum

Household Cavalry Museum, Combermere Barracks, Windsor, Berkshire.

Regimental marches

(slow) Anonymous (attributed to the Duchess of Kent)
(quick) Grand March from Aïda (Verdi), and
Regimental March of the Royal Dragoons
(Blankenburg, quick version)

Regimental motto

Honi Soit Qui Mal y Pense (Evil be to Him who Evil Thinks)

Nicknames

see below

Uniform

Blue with scarlet facings

Allied regiments

The Royal Canadian Dragoons
The Governor General's Horse Guards (Canada)

Regimental history

This second component of the Household Cavalry was formed in March 1969 by the amalgamation of two historic regiments, namely the Royal Horse Guards (The Blues) and The Royal Dragoons (1st Dragoons). The Royal Horse Guards date to 1661, when Colonel Unton Crook's Regiment of Horse in the disbanded parliamentary army was taken into the royal service under the command of the Earl of Oxford, whose blue livery was used by the new regiment, known initially as The Royal Regiment of Horse or the Earl of Oxford's Regiment of Horse. In 1685 the title changed to the Royal Regiment of Horse (Guards), this being modified slightly in 1714 to the Royal Regiment of Horse Guards. The regiment continued unaltered until 1875, when it became the Royal Horse Guards. In 1891 it became the Royal Horse Guards (The Blues), the regiment's long-lasting nickname finally being incorporated into the official title. The regiment's long and notable history is reflected by the battle honours it brought into the amalgamated regiment in 1969:

Dettingen   Warburg   Beaumont   Willems   Peninsula   Waterloo   Tel-el-Kebir   Egypt 1882   Relief of Kimberley   Paardeberg   South Africa 1899–1902   Mons   Le Cateau   Retreat from Mons   Marne 1914   Aisne 1914   Messines 1914   Armentieres 1914   Ypres 1914, '15, '17   Langemarck 1914   Gheluvelt   Nonne Bosschen   St Julien   Frezenberg   Loos   Arras 1917   Scarpe 1917   Broodseinde   Poelcappelle   Passchendaele   Somme 1918   Amiens   Hindenburg Line   Cambrai 1918   Sambre   France and Flanders 1914–18   Mont Pincon   Souleuvre   Noireau Crossing   Amiens 1944   Brussels   Neerpelt   Nederrijn   Nijmegen   Lingen   Bentheim   North-West Europe 1944–45   Baghdad   Iraq 1941   Palmyra   Syria 1941   El Alamein   North Africa 1942–43   Arezzo   Advance to Florence   Gothic Line   Italy 1943–44

The motto of the regiment was 'Honi Soit Qui Mal y Pense' (Evil be to Him who Evil Thinks), and the regimental marches were 'Anonymous' (attributed to the Duchess of Kent) and the 'Grand March from Aïda' (Verdi). The uniform was blue with scarlet facings, and the nicknames associated with The Royal Horse Guards were 'The Oxford Blues' and 'The Blues'.

The other component of The Blues and Royals was The Royal Dragoons (1st Dragoons), whose history runs back to 1661, when The Tangier Horse was raised by the Earl of Peterborough as the cavalry within the garrison of Tangier. The regiment returned to England in 1684 and, with the expansion provided by two new troops of dragoons, became The King's Own Royal Regiment of Dragoons, this title being modified during 1690 to The Royal Regiment of Dragoons. Some 60 years later, in 1751, the regiment became the 1st (Royal) Dragoons, and this title remained current for almost 170 years, until the regiment became the 1st The Royal Dragoons in 1920. Eight years before the regiment's amalgamation with the Royal Horse Guards, the regiment became The Royal Dragoons (1st Dragoons) during 1961. The regiment had enjoyed a career comparable to that of the Royal Horse Guards, and the battle honours it brought to the amalgamation were the following:

Tangier 1662–80   Dettingen   Warburg   Beaumont   Willems   Fuentes d'Onor   Peninsula   Waterloo   Balaklava   Sevastopol   Relief of

Ladysmith   South Africa 1899–1902   Ypres 1914, '15   Langemarck 1914   Gheluvelt   Nonne Bosschen   St Julien   Frezenberg   Loos   Arras 1917   Scarpe 1917   Somme 1918   St Quentin   Avre   Amiens   Hindenburg Line   Beaurevoir   Cambrai 1918   Pursuit to Mons   France and Flanders 1914–18   Veghel   Rhine   North-West Europe 1944–45   Syria 1941   Msus   Gazala   Knightsbridge   Defence of El Alamein Line   El Alamein   El Agheila   Advance on Tripoli   North Africa 1941–43   Sicily 1943   Italy 1943

The motto of the regiment was 'Spectemur Agendo' (Let us be Judged by Our Deeds), and the regimental marches were slow and quick versions of 'The Regimental March of the Royal Dragoons' (Blankenburg). The uniform was scarlet with blue facings, and nicknames associated with the Royal Dragoons were 'The Royals' and 'The Birdcatchers'. The only imperial regiment affiliated to The Royal Dragoons was The Royal Canadian Dragoons.

ROYAL ARMOURED CORPS: ORDER OF PRECEDENCE

1. 1st The Queen's Dragoon Guards
2. The Royal Scots Dragoon Guards (Carabiniers and Greys)
3. 4th/7th Royal Dragoon Guards
4. 5th Royal Inniskilling Dragoon Guards
5. The Queen's Own Hussars
6. The Queen's Royal Irish Hussars
7. 9th/12th Royal Lancers (Prince of Wales's)
8. The Royal Hussars (Prince of Wales's Own)
9. 13th/18th Royal Hussars (Queen Mary's Own)
10. 14th/20th King's Hussars
11. 15th/19th The King's Royal Hussars
12. 16th/5th The Queen's Royal Lancers
13. 17th/21st Lancers
14. Royal Tank Regiment

ROYAL ARMOURED CORPS REGIMENTS 1

1st The Queen's Dragoon Guards

Colonel-in-Chief

HM Queen Elizabeth The Queen Mother

Colonel

Major-General D. H. G. Rice

Battle honours

Blenheim Ramillies Oudenarde Malplaquet Dettingen Warburg Beaumont Willems Waterloo Sevastopol Lucknow Taku Forts Pekin 1860 South Africa 1879 South Africa 1901–02 Mons Le Cateau Retreat from Mons Marne 1914 Aisne 1914 Messines 1914 Armentieres 1914 Ypres 1914, '15 Frezenberg Bellewaarde Somme 1916, '18 Flers-Courcelette Morval Arras 1917 Scarpe 1917 Cambrai 1917, '18 St Quentin Bapaume 1918 Rosieres Amiens Albert 1918 Hindenburg Line St Quentin Canal Beaurevoir Pursuit to Mons France and Flanders 1914–18 Somme 1940 Withdrawal to the Seine North-West Europe 1940 Beda Fomm Defence of Tobruk Tobruk 1941 Tobruk Sortie Relief of Tobruk Msus Gazala Bir el Aslagh Bir Hacheim Cauldron Knightsbridge Via Balbia Mersa Matruh Defence of Alamein Line Alam el Halfa El Alamein El Agheila Advance on Tripoli Tebaga Gap Point 201 (Roman Wall) El Hamma Akarit El Kourzia Djebel Kournine Tunis Creteville Pass North Africa 1941–43

Capture of Naples   Scafati Bridge   Monte Camino   Garigliano Crossing
Capture of Perugia   Arezzo   Gothic Line   Coriano   Carpineta
Lamone Crossing   Defence of Lamone Bridgehead   Rimini Line
Ceriano Ridge   Cesena   Argenta Gap   Italy 1943–45   Athens
Greece 1944–45

Regimental headquarters

Maindy Barracks, Whitchurch Road, Cardiff, Wales.

Regimental museum

Clive House, College Hill, Shrewsbury, Shropshire.

Regimental marches

(slow) The Queen's Dragoon Guards
(quick) Radetsky March (J. Strauss), and Rusty Buckles (traditional)

Regimental motto

Pro Rege et Patria (For King and Country)

Nicknames

see below

Uniform

Scarlet with blue facings

Allied regiments

The Governor General's Horse Guards (Canada)
1st/15th Royal New South Wales Lancers (Australia)
11th Cavalry (Frontier Force) (Pakistan)
1st Reconnaissance Regiment (Sri Lanka)

Regimental history

The 1st The Queen's Dragoon Guards is the senior of the 14 regiments that constitute the Royal Armoured Corps, which ranks third in the overall list of precedence of regiments and corps in the British army. The RAC was formed in April 1939 to group together the mechanized regiments of the erstwhile Cavalry of the Line and the regiments of The Royal Tank Corps, which then became the Royal Tank Regiment. (It should be noted that though the two regiments of Household Cavalry are now armoured, they are not part of the RAC.)

This regiment was formed in January 1959 by the amalgamation of the 1st King's Dragoon Guards and The Queen's Bays (2nd Dragoon Guards). The origins of the 1st King's Dragoon Guards can be traced back to the accession of James II in 1685, when Sir John Lanier raised The Queen's Regiment of Horse (ranked as the 2nd Horse), which was in 1714 renamed The King's Own Regiment of Horse. In 1746 George II ordered that the title be altered to the 1st (or King's) Regiment of Dragoon Guards. This title was retained in essence for the rest of the regiment's life as an individual unit, the only modifications being changes of name in 1856 to the 1st (King's) Dragoon Guards and in 1920 to the 1st King's Dragoon Guards. In a varied career the regiment served extensively overseas, and its battle honours were the following:

Blenheim Ramillies Oudenarde Malplaquet Dettingen Warburg Beaumont Waterloo Sevastopol Taku Forts Pekin 1860 South Africa 1879 South Africa 1901–02 Somme 1916 Morval France and Flanders 1914–18 Beda Fomm Defence of Tobruk Tobruk 1941 Tobruk Sortie Relief of Tobruk Gazala Bir Hacheim Defence of Alamein Line Alam el Halfa El Agheila Advance on Tripoli Tebaga Gap Point 201 (Roman Wall) El Hamma Akarit Tunis North Africa 1941–43 Capture of Naples Scafati Bridge Monte Camino Garigliano Crossing Capture of Perugia Arezzo Gothic Line Italy 1943–44 Athens Greece 1944–45

The mottoes of the regiment were 'Honi Soit Qui Mal y Pense' (Evil be to Him who Evil Thinks) and 'Dieu et Mon Droit' (God and My Right), and the regimental marches were 'The King's Dragoon Guards' (Mercadente, slow) and 'The Radetsky March' (J. Strauss, quick, in celebration of the appointment in 1896 of Emperor Franz-Josef of Austria-Hungary as colonel-in-chief of the regiment). The nicknames associated with the 1st King's Dragoon Guards were 'The Trades Union', 'Bland's Horse' and 'The KDGs'. Imperial regiments affiliated to the 1st King's Dragoon Guards were the Mississauga Horse (Canada) and the 1st/21st Light Horse (Australia).

The Queen's Bays (2nd Dragoon Guards) was also raised in 1685, in this instance as The Earl of Peterborough's Regiment of Horse, the title then changing in accordance with the names of the regiment's various colonels. However, in 1715 it became The Princess of Wales's Own Regiment of Horse, and this association with female royalty has been maintained since that time. Thus in 1727 the regiment became The Queen's Own Regiment of Horse, in 1747 the 2nd or Queen's Own Royal Regiment of Horse, in 1870 (having in 1766 adopted the exclusive use of bay horses) the 2nd

Dragoon Guards (Queen's Bays) and in 1921 The Queen's Bays (2nd Dragoon Guards). Up to the time of World War I the regiment was deployed overseas less frequently than the 1st King's Dragoon Guards, but then saw greater service in World War I and roughly similar service in World War II. The battle honours of the regiment were the following:

Warburg   Willems   Lucknow   South Africa 1901–02   Mons   Le Cateau   Retreat from Mons   Marne 1914   Aisne 1914   Messines 1914   Armentieres 1914   Ypres 1914, '15   Frezenberg   Bellewaarde   Somme 1916, '18   Flers-Courcelette   Arras 1917   Scarpe 1917   Cambrai 1917, '18   St Quentin   Bapaume 1918   Rosieres   Amiens   Albert 1918   Hindenburg Line   St Quentin Canal   Beaurevoir   Pursuit to Mons   France and Flanders 1914–18   Somme 1940   Withdrawal to the Seine   North-West Europe 1940   Msus   Gazala   Bir el Aslagh   Cauldron   Knightsbridge   Via Balbia   Mersa Matruh   El Alamein   Tebaga Gap   El Hamma   El Kourzia   Djebel Kournine   Tunis   Creteville Pass   North Africa 1941–43   Coriano   Carpineta   Lamone Crossing   Lamone Bridgehead   Rimini Line   Ceriano Ridge   Cesena   Argenta Gap   Italy 1943–45

The motto of the regiment was 'Pro Rege et Patria' (For King and Country), and the regimental marches were 'The Queen's Bays' (slow) and 'Rusty Buckles' (quick). The nicknames associated with The Queen's Bays were 'The Bays' and 'The Rusty Buckles'. Imperial regiments affiliated to The Queen's Bays were The Governor-General's Bodyguard (Canada) and the 7th Light Horse (Australia).

ROYAL ARMOURED CORPS REGIMENTS 2

The Royal Scots Dragoon Guards (Carabiniers and Greys)

Colonel-in-Chief

HM The Queen

Colonel

Lieutenant-General Sir Norman Arthur

Battle honours

Blenheim   Ramillies   Oudenarde   Malplaquet   Dettingen   Warburg   Beaumont   Willems   Waterloo   Talavera   Albuhera   Vittoria   Peninsula   Balaklava   Sevastopol   Delhi 1857   Abyssinia   Afghanistan 1879–80   Relief of Kimberley   Paardeberg   South Africa 1899–02   Mons   Le Cateau   Retreat from Mons   Marne 1914   Aisne 1914   Messines 1914   Armentieres 1914   Ypres 1914, '15   Nonne Bosschen   Gheluvelt   Neuve Chapelle   St Julien   Frezenberg   Bellewaarde   Loos   Arras 1917   Scarpe 1917   Cambrai 1917, '18   Lys   Hazebrouck   Somme 1918   St Quentin   Avre   Amiens   Albert 1918   Bapaume   Hindenburg Line   Canal du Nord   St Quentin Canal   Beaurevoir   Selle   Sambre   Pursuit to Mons   France and Flanders 1914–18   Caen   Hill 112   Falaise   Venlo Pocket   Hochwald   Aller   Bremen   North-West Europe 1944–45   Merjayun   Syria 1941   Alam el Halfa   El Alamein   El Agheila   Nofilia   Advance on Tripoli

North Africa 1942–43   Salerno   Battipaglia   Volturno Crossing
Italy 1943   Imphal   Tamu Road   Nunshigum   Bishenpur
Kanglatongbi   Kennedy Peak   Shwebo   Sagaing   Mandalay   Ava
Irrawaddy   Yenangyaung 1945   Burma 1944–45

Regimental headquarters

The Castle, Edinburgh, Scotland.

Regimental museums

(3rd Carabiniers) The Castle, Chester, Cheshire.
(Royal Scots Greys) The Castle, Edinburgh, Scotland.

Regimental marches

(slow) In the Garb of Old Gaul (Reid)
(quick) 3rd DG

Regimental motto

Nemo Me Impune Lacessit (No one Provokes me with Impunity)

Nicknames

none

Uniform

Scarlet with yellow facings

Allied regiments

The Windsor Regiment (Canada)
12th/16th Hunter River Lancers (Australia)
1st and 2nd Squadrons, New Zealand and Scottish, RNZAC

Regimental history

Formed in July 1971, The Royal Scots Dragoon Guards (Carabiniers and Greys) is an amalgamation of two very famous regiments, the 3rd Carabiniers (Prince of Wales's Dragoon Guards) and The Royal Scots Greys (2nd Dragoons). The official mascot of the regiment is a drum horse.

The 3rd Carabiniers (Prince of Wales's Dragoon Guards) was itself the result of a 1928 title change for another amalgamation, namely that of 1922 between the 3rd Dragoon Guards (Prince of Wales's Own) and The Carabiniers (6th Dragoon Guards) as the 3rd/6th Dragoon Guards. The battle honours of this combined regiment were the following:

> Blenheim Ramillies Oudenarde Malplaquet Warburg Beaumont Willems Talavera Albuhera Vittoria Peninsula Sevastopol Delhi 1857 Abyssinia Afghanistan 1879–80 Relief of Kimberley Paardeberg South Africa 1899–1902 Mons Le Cateau Retreat from Mons Marne 1914 Aisne 1914 Messines 1914 Armentieres 1914 Ypres 1914, '15 Nonne Bosschen St Julien Frezenberg Bellewaarde Loos Arras 1917 Scarpe 1917 Cambrai 1917, '18 Somme 1918 St Quentin Avre Lys Hazebrouck Amiens Bapaume 1918 Hindenburg Line Canal du Nord Beaurevoir Selle Sambre France and Flanders 1914–18 Imphal Tamu Road Nunshigum Bishenpur Kanglatongbi Kennedy Peak Shwebo Sagaing Mandalay Ava Irrawaddy Yenangyaung 1945 Burma 1944–45

The motto of the regiment was 'Ich Dien' (I Serve), and the regimental marches were '6th DG' (slow) and '3rd DG' (quick). The uniform was scarlet with yellow facings, and the nicknames associated with the regiment were 'The Carbs' and 'The Old Canaries'. There were no imperial regiments affiliated to The Carabiniers.

Both components of this initial 1922 amalgamation had been raised in 1685 on the accession of James II and the threat of Monmouth's Rebellion, the senior being the 3rd Dragoon Guards (Prince of Wales's), which had been raised as The Earl of Plymouth's Regiment of Horse (ranked as the 4th Horse) and subsequently underwent a number of title changes in accordance with the name of the current colonel. In 1746 the title 3rd Regiment of Dragoon Guards was adopted, this changing in 1765 to the 3rd (The Prince of Wales's) Dragoon Guards, and in 1921 to the 3rd Dragoon Guards (Prince of Wales's) just before its amalgamation with The Carabiniers (6th Dragoon Guards). The battle honours of the regiment were the following:

> Blenheim Ramillies Oudenarde Malplaquet Warburg Beaumont Willems Talavera Albuhera Vittoria Peninsula Abyssinia South Africa 1901–02 Ypres 1914, '15 Nonne Bosschen Frezenberg Loos Arras 1917 Scarpe 1917 Somme 1918 St Quentin Avre Amiens Hindenburg Line Beaurevoir Cambrai 1918 Pursuit to Mons France and Flanders 1914–18

The motto of the regiment was 'Ich Dien' (I Serve), and the regimental marches were 'March of the Men of Harlech' (traditional, slow) and 'God Bless the Prince of Wales' (Richards, quick). The regimental uniform was scarlet with yellow facings, and the nickname was 'The Old Canaries'. There were no imperial regiments affiliated to the 3rd Dragoon Guards.

As noted above, The Carabiniers (6th Dragoon Guards) was also raised in 1685, in this instance by Lord Lumley as The Queen Dowager's Regiment of Horse (ranked as the 9th Horse, and also known as Lumley's Horse). In 1691 the regiment became The Carabiniers, though it was also known as the 1st Carabiniers and The King's Carabineers (ranked as the 8th Horse). In 1746 the regiment was moved onto the Irish establishment as the 3rd Regiment of Horse, in 1756 becoming the 3rd Horse or Carabineers. The year 1788 saw a considerable change, the regiment being renamed the 6th Dragoon Guards, this being modified in 1826 to the 3rd Dragoon Guards (Carabineers), which by 1855 had been modified to 3rd Dragoon Guards (Carabiniers). Two years before the amalgamation with the 3rd Dragoon Guards, the regiment was in 1920 restyled The Carabiniers (6th Dragoon Guards). The battle honours of the regiment were the following:

Blenheim   Ramillies   Oudenarde   Malplaquet   Warburg   Willems   Sevastopol   Delhi 1857   Afghanistan 1879–80   Relief of Kimberley   Paardeberg   South Africa 1899–1902   Mons   Le Cateau   Retreat from Mons   Marne 1914   Aisne 1914   Messines 1914   Armentieres 1914   Ypres 1915   St Julien   Bellewaarde   Arras 1917   Scarpe 1917   Cambrai 1917, '18   Somme 1918   St Quentin   Lys   Hazebrouck   Amiens   Bapaume 1918   Hindenburg Line   Canal du Nord   Selle   Sambre   France and Flanders 1914–18

The motto of the regiment was 'Honi Soit Qui Mal y Pense' (Evil be to Him who Evil Thinks), and the regimental marches were '6th Dragoon Guards' (slow) and 'God Bless the Prince of Wales' (Richards, quick). The uniform was blue with white facings, and nicknames associated with the Carabiniers were 'The Carbs' and 'Tichborne's Own'. Imperial regiments affiliated to The Carabiniers were the 1st and 2nd Royal Natal Carabiniers (South Africa).

The other half of the amalgam that went into The Royal Scots Dragoon Guards (Carabiniers and Greys) was The Royal Scots Greys (2nd Dragoons). This regiment can be traced back to 1681, when Lieutenant-General Thomas Dalyell of The Carbiniers combined several independent troops of Scottish dragoons into the Royal Regiment of Scots Dragoons (ranked as the 2nd Dragoons in 1688). In 1700 the regiment decided to use only grey horses, a practice continued up to the present day, though it should be noted that in the 2nd Boer War and World War I the horses were dyed other colours to disguise the precise identity of the regiment. In 1707 the regiment was retitled The Royal Regiment of North British Dragoons, but was also known as The Scots Regiment of White Horses. Further changes in the regiment's title followed in 1751 as the 2nd (or Royal North British) Regiment of Dragoons, in 1866 as the 2nd (Royal North

British) Dragoons (Royal Scots Greys), in 1877 as the 2nd Dragoons (Royal Scots Greys) and in 1921 as The Royal Scots Greys (2nd Dragoons). As a separate regiment The Royal Scots Greys had enjoyed a formidable reputation, and the battle honours of the regiment were the following:

Blenheim   Ramillies   Oudenarde   Malplaquet   Dettingen   Warburg   Willems   Waterloo   Balaklava   Sevastopol   Relief of Kimberley   Paardeberg   South Africa 1899–1902   Mons   Retreat from Mons   Marne 1914   Aisne 1914   Messines 1914   Ypres 1914, '15   Gheluvelt   Neuve Chapelle   St Julien   Bellewaarde   Arras 1917   Scarpe 1917   Cambrai 1917, '18   Lys   Hazebrouck   Amiens   Somme 1918   Albert 1918   Bapaume 1918   Hindenburg Line   St Quentin Canal   Beaurevoir   Pursuit to Mons   France and Flanders 1914–18   Caen   Hill 112   Falaise   Venlo Pocket   Hochwald   Aller   Bremen   North-West Europe 1944–45   Merjayun   Syria 1941   Alam el Halfa   El Alamein   El Agheila   Nofilia   Advance on Tripoli   North Africa 1942–43   Salerno   Battipaglia   Volturno Crossing   Italy 1943

The motto of the regiment was 'Nemo Me Impune Lacessit' (No one Provokes me with Impunity), and the regimental marches were slow and quick versions of 'In the Garb of Old Gaul' (Reid). The uniform was scarlet with blue facings, and the nicknames associated with The Royal Scots Greys were 'The Greys', 'The Bubbly Jocks' and 'The Birdcatchers', the second in reference to the eagle on the regiment's badge ('bubbly jock' being a Scots name for a turkey cock), and the last in reference to the regiment's capture of a French eagle at the Battle of Waterloo (1814). Imperial regiments affiliated to The Royal Scots Greys were the 2nd Dragoons (Canada), the New Brunswick Dragoons (Canada), the 12th Light Horse (Australia), and the North Auckland Mounted Rifles (New Zealand).

ROYAL ARMOURED CORPS REGIMENTS 3

4th/7th Royal Dragoon Guards

Colonel-in-Chief
Honorary Major-General HRH The Duchess of Kent

Colonel
General Sir Robert Ford

Battle honours

Blenheim Ramillies Oudenarde Malplaquet Dettingen Warburg Peninsula South Africa 1846–47 Balaklava Sevastopol Tel-el-Kebir Egypt 1882 South Africa 1900–02 Mons Le Cateau Retreat from Mons Marne 1914 Aisne 1914 La Bassee 1914 Messines 1914 Armentieres 1914 Ypres 1914, '15 Givenchy 1914 St Julien Frezenberg Bellewaarde Somme 1916, '18 Bazentin Flers-Courcelette Arras 1917 Scarpe 1917 Cambrai 1917, '18 St Quentin Rosieres Avre Lys Hazebrouck Amiens Albert 1918 Hindenburg Line St Quentin Canal Beaurevoir Pursuit to Mons France and Flanders 1914–18 Dyle Dunkirk 1940 Normandy Landing Odon Mont Pincon Seine 1944 Nederrijn Geilenkirchen Roer Rhineland Cleve Rhine Bremen North-West Europe 1940, '44–45

Regimental headquarters
3 Tower Street, York, Yorkshire.

Regimental museum

3 Tower Street, York, Yorkshire.

Regimental marches

(slow) 4th/7th Royal Dragoons (anonymous)
(quick) St Patrick's Day (traditional)

Regimental motto

Quis Separabit? (Who Shall Separate?)

Nickname

The First and the Last

Uniform

Scarlet with royal blue facings

Allied regiments

The Fort Garry Horse (Canada)
4th/9th Prince of Wales's Light Horse (Australia)
Queen Alexandra's (Waikato/Wellington East Coast) Squadron, RNZAC
15th Lancers (Pakistan)

Regimental history

The 4th/7th Royal Dragoon Guards was formed in April 1922 by the amalgamation of two older regiments, the 4th Royal Irish Dragoon Guards and the 7th Dragoon Guards (Princess Royal's). The new regiment was at first known as the 4th/7th Dragoon Guards, the 'Royal' prefix being granted in 1936 by Edward VIII in recognition of the long associations with the British monarchy enjoyed by the two components of the amalgamated regiment.

The 4th Royal Irish Dragoon Guards was raised in 1685 by the Earl of Arran as Arran's Horse (or Cuirassiers) and ranked as the 6th Horse for two years until 1687, when it became the 5th Horse. The name of the regiment changed in accordance with the names of the colonels until 1715, when it became The Prince of Wales's Own Regiment of Horse. In 1746 the regiment became the 1st Horse on the Irish establishment, in 1788 becoming the 4th (Royal Irish) Dragoon Guards. This latter title remained unaltered until 1921, when the regiment became the 4th Royal Irish

Dragoon Guards just before the 1922 amalgamation which produced the 4th/7th Dragoon Guards. The battle honours of the regiment were the following:

Peninsula   Balaklava   Sevastopol   Tel-el-Kebir   Egypt 1882   Mons   Le Cateau   Retreat from Mons   Marne 1914   Aisne 1914   La Bassee 1914   Messines 1914   Armentieres 1914   Ypres 1914, '15   St Julien   Frezenberg   Bellewaarde   Somme 1916, '18   Bazentin   Flers-Courcelette   Arras 1917   Scarpe 1917   Cambrai 1917, '18   St Quentin   Rosieres   Avre   Lys   Hazebrouck   Amiens   Albert 1918   Hindenburg Line   St Quentin Canal   Beaurevoir   Pursuit to Mons   France and Flanders 1914–18

The motto of the regiment was 'Quis Separabit?' (Who Shall Separate?), and the regimental marches were '4th Royal Irish Dragoon Guards' (anonymous, slow) and 'St Patrick's Day' (traditional, quick). The uniform was scarlet with blue facings, and the several nicknames associated with the 4th Royal Irish Dragoon Guards included 'The Blue Horse', 'Virgin Mary's Guards', 'The Mounted Micks' and 'The Buttermilks'. There were no imperial regiments affiliated with the 4th Royal Irish Dragoon Guards.

The 7th Dragoon Guards (Princess Royal's) began life in 1688 as The Earl of Devonshire's Horse (ranked as the 10th Horse), which was also known as Cavendish's Horse after the Earl of Devonshire, William Cavendish. In 1692 the regiment was re-ranked as the 8th Horse, and like other regiments of the period suffered title changes in accordance with the names of its various colonels. In 1746 the regiment became the 4th Horse on the Irish establishment, becoming the 7th (Princess Royal's) Dragoon Guards in 1788. There followed only one other title change before the 1922 amalgamation with the 4th Royal Irish Dragoon Guards, when in 1921 the regiment became for a short time the 7th Dragoon Guards (Princess Royal's). The battle honours of the regiment were the following:

Blenheim   Ramillies   Oudenarde   Malplaquet   Dettingen   Warburg   South Africa 1846–47   Tel-el-Kebir   Egypt 1882   South Africa 1900–02   La Bassee 1914   Givenchy 1914   Somme 1916, '18   Bazentin   Flers-Courcelette   Cambrai 1917, '18   St Quentin   Avre   Lys   Hazebrouck   Amiens   Hindenburg Line   St Quentin Canal   Beaurevoir   Pursuit to Mons   France and Flanders 1914–18

The motto of the regiment was 'Quo Fata Vocant' (Whither the Fates Lead), and the regimental march was '7th (Princess Royal's) Dragoon Guards' (anonymous, slow). The uniform was scarlet with black facings, and the nicknames associated with the 7th (Princess Royal's) Dragoon Guards were 'The Blacks', 'The Black Horse' and 'The Strawboots', the first in reference to the colour of the regiment's facings. Imperial regiments affiliated to the 7th (Princess Royal's) Dragoon Guards were the Fort Garry Horse

(Canada), the 4th Light Horse (Australia) and the Waikato Mounted Rifles (New Zealand).

ROYAL ARMOURED CORPS REGIMENTS 4

5th Royal Inniskilling Dragoon Guards

Colonel-in-Chief

HRH The Prince of Wales

Colonel

Major-General R. C. Keightley

Battle honours

Blenheim Ramillies Oudenarde Malplaquet Dettingen Warburg Beaumont Willems Salamanca Vittoria Toulouse Peninsula Waterloo Balaklava Sevastopol Defence of Ladysmith South Africa 1899–1902 Mons Le Cateau Retreat from Mons Marne 1914 Aisne 1914 La Bassee 1914 Messines 1914 Armentieres 1914 Ypres 1914, '15 Frezenberg Bellewaarde Somme 1916, '18 Flers-Courcelette Morval Arras 1917 Scarpe 1917 Cambrai 1917, '18 St Quentin Rosieres Avre Lys Hazebrouck Amiens Albert 1918 Hindenburg Line St Quentin Canal Beaurevoir Pursuit to Mons France and Flanders 1914–18 Withdrawal to Escaut St Omer-La Bassee Dunkirk 1940 Mont Pincon St Pierre la Vielle Lisieux Risle Crossing Lower Maas Roer Ibbenburen North-West Europe 1940, '44–45 The Hook 1952 Korea 1951–52

Regimental headquarters

The Castle, Chester, Cheshire.

Regimental museums

(5th Dragoon Guards) The Castle, Chester, Cheshire.
(The Inniskillings) Carrickfergus Castle, Co. Antrim, Northern Ireland.

Regimental marches

(slow) Soldiers' Chorus from Faust (Gounod)
(quick) Fare Thee Well Inniskilling (traditional)

Regimental motto

Vestigia Nulla Retrorsum (We do not Retreat)

Nickname

The Skins

Uniform

Scarlet with royal blue facings

Allied regiments

The British Columbia Dragoons (Canada)
3rd/9th South Australian Mounted Rifles

Regimental history

The 5th Royal Inniskilling Dragoon Guards resulted from the amalgamation in April 1922 of the 5th Dragoon Guards (Princess Charlotte of Wales's) and The Inniskillings (6th Dragoons). The original designation of the amalgamated regiment was the 5th/6th Dragoons, this being changed in 1927 to the 5th Inniskilling Dragoon Guards and in 1935 (to celebrate the silver jubilee of George V) to the 5th Royal Inniskilling Dragoon Guards.

The senior of the two components was the 5th Dragoon Guards (Princess Charlotte of Wales's), which had been raised in 1685 as The Earl of Shrewsbury's Horse, and ranked as the 7th Horse. In 1698 the regiment was re-ranked at the 6th Horse, and in the period up to 1746 the regiment's title changed in accordance with the name of the colonel. In 1746, however, the regiment became part of the Irish establishment as the 2nd Horse, a title maintained up to 1788, when it became the 5th Dragoon Guards. In 1894 the regiment was 'adopted' into the royal family as the 5th (Princess Charlotte of Wales's) Dragoon Guards, and this latter title was maintained up to 1920, when for the short period before its amalgamation with The Inniskillings it became the 5th Dragoon Guards (Princess Charlotte of Wales's). The battle honours of the regiment were the following:

Blenheim   Ramillies   Oudenarde   Malplaquet   Warburg   Willems   Sevastopol   Delhi 1857   Afghanistan 1879–80   Relief of Kimberley   Paardeberg   South Africa 1899–02   Mons   Le Cateau   Retreat from Mons   Marne 1914   Aisne 1914   La Bassee 1914   Messines 1914   Armentieres 1914   Ypres 1914, '15   Frezenberg   Bellewaarde   Somme 1916, '18   Flers-Courcelette   Arras 1917   Scarpe 1917   Cambrai 1917, '18   St Quentin   Rosieres   Amiens   Albert 1918   Hindenburg Line   St Quentin Canal   Beaurevoir   Pursuit to Mons
France and Flanders 1914–18

The motto of the regiment was 'Vestigia Nulla Retrorsum' (We do not Retreat), and the regimental marches were the 'Soldiers' Chorus from Faust' (Gounod, slow) and 'The Gay Cavalier' (quick). The uniform was scarlet with dark green facings, and the nicknames associated with the 5th Dragoon Guards were 'The Green Horse' and 'The Old Farmers'.

The Inniskillings had been raised in 1690 as Conyngham's Dragoons (ranked as the 6th Dragoons), Colonel Sir Albert Conyngham regularizing the various troops of horse that had been levied to hold the town of Enniskillen against the forces of ex-King James II. For the next 60 years the title of the regiment changed in accordance with the name of its colonel, but in 1751 it became the 6th (Inniskilling) Dragoons, a designation that remained unaltered until 1921, when the regiment became the Inniskillings (6th Dragoons) in the year before the amalgamation with the 5th Dragoon Guards. The battle honours of the regiment were the following:

Dettingen   Warburg   Willems   Waterloo   Balaklava   Sevastopol   South Africa 1899–1902   Somme 1916, '18   Morval   Cambrai 1917, '18   St Quentin   Avre   Lys   Hazebrouck   Amiens   Hindenburg Line   St Quentin Canal   Beaurevoir   Pursuit to Mons
France and Flanders 1914–18

The motto of the regiment was 'Honi Soit Qui Mal y Pense' (Evil be to Him who Evil Thinks), and the regimental marches were 'The Inniskilling Dragoons' (anonymous, slow) and 'Fare Thee Well Inniskilling' (traditional, quick). The uniform was scarlet with primrose facings, and the nicknames associated with The Inniskillings were 'The Skins', 'The Black Dragoons', 'The Old Inniskillings' and 'The Skillingers'. Imperial regiments affiliated to The Inniskillings were the 10th Brant Dragoons (Canada), the 9th Light Horse (Australia), and the Manawatu Mounted Rifles (New Zealand).

ROYAL ARMOURED CORPS REGIMENTS 5

The Queen's Own Hussars

Colonel-in-Chief
HM Queen Elizabeth The Queen Mother

Colonel
Lieutenant-General Sir Robin Carnegie

Battle honours

Dettingen Warburg Beaumont Willems Salamanca Vittoria Orthes Toulouse Peninsula Waterloo Cabool 1842 Mookdee Ferozeshah Sobraon Chillianwallah Goojerat Punjaub Lucknow South Africa 1901–02 Mons Le Cateau Retreat from Mons Marne 1914 Aisne 1914 Messines 1914 Armentieres 1914 Ypres 1914, '15 Gheluvelt St Julien Bellewaarde Arras 1917 Scarpe 1917 Cambrai 1917, '18 Somme 1918 St Quentin Lys Hazebrouck Amiens Bapaume 1918 Hindenburg Line Canal du Nord Selle Sambre France and Flanders 1914–18 Khan Baghdadi Sharqat Mesopotamia 1917–18 Egyptian Frontier 1940 Sidi Barrani Buq Buq Beda Fomm Sidi Suleiman Sidi Rezegh 1941 El Alamein North Africa 1940–42 Citta della Pieve Ancona Citta di Castello Rimini Line Italy 1944–45 Crete Pegu Paungde Burma 1942

Regimental headquarters
28 Jury Street, Warwick, Warwickshire.

Regimental museum

The Lord Leycester Hospital, High Street, Warwick, Warwickshire.

Regimental marches

(slow) In the Garb of Old Gaul (Reid)
(quick) Light Cavalry (Suppe)

Regimental motto

Nec Aspera Terrent (Neither do Difficulties Deter)

Nickname

see below

Uniform

Blue with garter blue facings

Allied regiments

The Sherbrooke Hussars (Canada)
3rd/9th South Australian Mounted Rifles
Queen Alexandra's (Waikato/Wellington East Coast) Squadron, RNZAC

Regimental history

The Queen's Own Hussars was formed in November 1958 by the amalgamation of the 3rd The King's Own Hussars and the 7th Queen's Own Hussars. The official mascot of the regiment is a drum horse.

The 3rd The King's Own Hussars had been raised in 1685 from three troops of royal dragoons, and was initially designated The Queen Consort's Regiment of Dragoons. In common with comparable regiments of the period, it was also known by the name of its colonel (the first such titling being The Duke of Somerset's Regiment of Dragoons), but it was as soon as 1714 that it acquired a more permanent designation, in this instance the 3rd King's Own Regiment of Dragoons. In 1818 the regiment became the 3rd King's Own Light Dragoons, but a more radical modification followed in 1861 when it became the 3rd King's Own Hussars, this being modified slightly in 1921 to produce the 3rd The King's Own Hussars. The regiment served overseas with distinction on a number of occasions, and the battle honours brought to the amalgamation by the regiment were the following:

Dettingen   Salamanca   Vittoria   Toulouse   Peninsula   Cabool 1842   Mookdee   Ferozeshah   Sobraon   Chillianwallah   Goojerat   Punjab   South Africa 1902   Mons   Le Cateau   Retreat from Mons   Marne 1914   Aisne 1914   Messines 1914   Armentieres 1914   Ypres 1914, '15   Gheluvelt   St Julien   Bellewaarde   Arras 1917   Scarpe 1917   Cambrai 1917, '18   Somme 1918   St Quentin   Lys   Hazebrouck   Amiens   Bapaume 1918   Hindenburg Line   Canal du Nord   Selle   Sambre   France and Flanders 1914–18   Sidi Barrani   Buq Buq   Beda Fomm   Sidi Suleiman   El Alamein   North Africa 1940–42   Citta della Pieve   Citta di Castello   Rimini Line   Italy 1944   Crete

The motto of the regiment was 'Nec Aspera Terrent' (Neither do Difficulties Deter), and the regimental marches were 'The Third Hussars Slow March' (anonymous, slow) and 'Robert the Devil' (Meyerbeer, quick). The uniform was blue with a garter blue busby bag, and the nicknames associated with the 3rd The King's Own Hussars were 'The Mookdee Wallahs' and 'Lord Adam Gordon's Life Guards'. Imperial regiments affiliated to the 3rd The King's Own Hussars were the King's Canadian Dragoons (Canada), the 19th Alberta Light Horse (Canada), the 3rd Light Horse (Australia), the Auckland Mounted Rifles (New Zealand), and the Natal Mounted Rifles (South Africa).

The 7th Queen's Own Hussars had been raised in 1690 by Colonel Richard Cunningham from a number of independent troops of Scottish dragoons, and was initially known as Cunningham's Dragoons. In accordance with the practice of the period, the regiment's name changed with each colonel, but in 1715 the association with female royalty was established as the regiment became The Princess of Wales's Own Royal Regiment of Dragoons. Thereafter the regiment underwent a number of title changes, to The Queen's Own Royal Regiment of Dragoons in 1727, the 7th (or Queen's Own) Regiment of Dragoons in 1751, the 7th (or Queen's Own) Light Dragoons in 1783, the 7th (or The Queen's Own) Regiment of (Light) Dragoons (Hussars) in 1807, the 7th (The Queen's Own) Regiment of Hussars in 1861, the 7th (Queen's Own) Hussars in 1880, and the 7th Queen's Own Hussars in 1921. The battle honours brought into the amalgamated regiment by the 7th Queen's Own Hussars were the following:

Dettingen   Warburg   Beaumont   Willems   Orthes   Peninsula   Waterloo   Lucknow   South Africa 1902–02   Khan Baghdadi   Sharqat   Mesopotamia 1917–18   Egyptian Frontier 1940   Beda Fomm   Sidi Rezegh 1941   North Africa 1940–41   Ancona   Rimini Line   Italy 1944–45   Pegu   Paungde   Burma 1942

The motto of the regiment was 'Honi Soit Qui Mal y Pense' (Evil be to Him who Evil Thinks), and the regimental marches were 'In the Garb of Old Gaul' (Reid, slow) and 'Bannocks o'Barley Meal' (traditional, quick). The uniform was blue with a scarlet busby bag, and the nicknames associated with the 7th Queen's Own Hussars were 'The Saucy Seventh', 'The Lillywhite Seventh', 'The Old Straws', 'The Strawboots' and 'The Young Eyes'. Imperial regiments affiliated with the 7th Queen's Own Hussars were the 7th/11th Hussars (Canada), the Wellington East Coast Mounted Rifles (New Zealand), and the Umvoti Mounted Rifles (South Africa).

ROYAL ARMOURED CORPS REGIMENTS 6

The Queen's Royal Irish Hussars

Colonel-in-Chief
Field-Marshal HRH The Prince Philip Duke of Edinburgh

Colonel
Lieutenant-General Sir Brian Kenny

Battle honours

Dettingen Leswarree Hindoostan Talavera Albuhera Salamanca Vittoria Toulouse Peninsula Ghuznee 1839 Affghanistan 1839 Alma Balaklava Inkerman Sevastopol Central India Afghanistan 1879–80 South Africa 1900–02 Mons Le Cateau Retreat from Mons Marne 1914 Aisne 1914 Messines 1914 Armentieres 1914 Ypres 1914, '15 Langemarck 1914 Gheluvelt Givenchy 1914 St Julien Bellewaarde Somme 1916, '18 Bazentin Flers-Courcelette Arras 1917 Scarpe 1917 Cambrai 1917, '18 St Quentin Bapaume 1918 Rosieres Amiens Albert 1918 Hindenburg Line Canal du Nord St Quentin Canal Beaurevoir Pursuit to Mons France and Flanders 1914–18 Villers Bocage Mont Pincon Dives Crossing Nederrijn Best Lower Maas Roer Rhine North-West Europe 1944–45 Egyptian Frontier 1940 Sidi Barrani Buq Buq Sidi Rezegh 1941 Relief of Tobruk Gazala Bir el Igela Mersa Matruh Defence of Alamein Line Ruweisat Alam el Halfa El Alamein North Africa 1939–42 Coriano San Clemente Senio Pocket Rimini Line Conventello-Comacchio Senio

Santerno Crossing Argenta Gap Italy 1944–45 Proasteion Corinth Canal
Greece 1941 Seoul Hill 327 Imjin Kowang-San Korea 1950–51

Regimental headquarters

Regent's Park Barracks, Albany Street, London.

Regimental museum

Carrickfergus Castle, Carrickfergus, Co. Antrim, Northern Ireland.

Regimental marches

(slow) Litany of Loretto (anonymous), and
March of the Scottish Archers
(quick) Arrangement of Berkeley's Dragoons and
St Patrick's Day (traditional)

Regimental motto

Mente et Manu (With Mind and Hand)

Nicknames

see below

Uniform

Blue

Allied regiments

The Royal Canadian Mounted Hussars
8th Canadian Hussars
2nd/14th Queensland Mounted Infantry (Australia)
8th/13th Victorian Mounted Rifles (Australia)
3rd Battalion The Royal Australian Regiment

Regimental history

The Queen's Royal Irish Hussars came into existence in October 1958 as a result of the amalgamation of the 4th Queen's Own Hussars and the 8th King's Royal Irish Hussars.

The 4th Queen's Own Hussars had been raised in 1685 by Colonel John

Berkeley, who combined a number of independent dragoon troops to make The Princess Anne of Denmark's Regiment of Dragoons, also known as Berkeley's Dragoons. The regiment escaped the standard practice of adopting the names of successive colonels, and the first change of name came in 1751, when it became the 4th Dragoons. The regiment then underwent a number of title changes, in 1788 to the 4th (or Queen's Own) Regiment of Dragoons, in 1818 to the 4th Regiment of Light Dragoons, in 1819 to the 4th (or The Queen's Own) Light Dragoons, in 1861 to the 4th (Queen's Own) Hussars, and in 1921 to the 4th Queen's Own Hussars. The battle honours of the regiment are clear evidence of extensive and successful overseas service, and were the following:

Dettingen   Talavara   Albuhera   Salamanca   Vittoria   Toulouse   Peninsula   Ghuznee 1839   Affghanistan 1839   Alma   Balaklava   Inkerman   Sevastopol   Mons   Le Cateau   Retreat from Mons   Marne 1914   Aisne 1914   Messines 1914   Armentieres 1914   Ypres 1914, '15   Langemarck 1914   Gheluvelt   St Julien   Bellewaarde   Arras 1917   Scarpe 1917   Cambrai 1917   Somme 1918   Amiens   Hindenburg Line   Canal du Nord   Pursuit to Mons   France and Flanders 1914–18   Gazala   Defence of Alamein Line   Ruweisat   Alam el Halfa   El Alamein   North Africa 1942   Coriano   San Clemente   Senio Pocket   Rimini Line   Conventello-Comacchio   Senio   Santerno Crossing   Argenta Gap   Italy 1944–45   Proasteion   Corinth Canal   Greece 1941

The motto of the regiment was 'Mente et Manu' (With Mind and Hand), and the regimental marches were 'Litany of Loretto' (anonymous, slow) and 'Berkeley's Dragoons' (anonymous, quick). The uniform was blue with a yellow busby bag, and the nickname associated with the 4th Queen's Own Hussars was 'Paget's Irregular Horse'. Imperial regiments affiliated to the 4th Queen's Own Hussars were the British Columbia Hussars (Canada), the 4th Hussars (Canada), the 2nd Light Horse (Australia), and the Imperial Light Horse (South Africa).

The 8th King's Royal Irish Hussars had been raised from Irish protestants in 1693 by Colonel Conyngham of the Inniskilling Dragoons, and the regiment was initially known as Conyngham's Regiment of Irish Dragoons, a variation being Cunningham's Regiment of Irish Dragoons. Thereafter the title of the regiment changed in accordance with the names of its colonels until 1751, when it became the 8th Regiment of Dragoons. This set the pattern for future changes to the 8th Regiment of Light Dragoons in 1775, to the 8th (or The King's Royal Irish) Regiment of Light Dragoons in 1777, to the 8th (or King's Royal Irish) Regiment of Light Dragoons (Hussars) in 1822, to the 8th (King's Royal Irish) Hussars in 1861 and to the 8th King's Royal Irish Hussars in 1920. The regiment saw considerable service overseas, and the battle honours brought to the amalgamation were the following:

Leswarree Hindoostan Alma Balaklava Inkerman Sevastopol Central India Afghanistan 1879–80 South Africa 1900–02 Givenchy 1914 Somme 1916, '18 Bazentin Flers-Courcelette Cambrai 1917, '18 St Quentin Bapaume 1918 Rosieres Amiens Albert 1918 Hindenburg Line St Quentin Canal Beaurevoir Pursuit to Mons France and Flanders 1914–18 Villers Bocage Mont Pincon Dives Crossing Nederrijn Best Lower Maas Roer Rhine North-West Europe 1944–45 Egyptian Frontier 1940 Sidi Barrani Buq Buq Sidi Rezegh 1941 Relief of Tobruk Gazala Bir el Igela Mersa Matruh Alam el Halfa El Alamein North Africa 1939–42 Seoul Hill 327 Imjin Kowang-San Korea 1950–51

The motto of the regiment was 'Pristinae Virtutis Memores' (Mindful of Former Valour), and the regimental marches were 'Scottish Archers' (anonymous, slow) and 'St Patrick's Day' (traditional, quick). The uniform was blue with a scarlet busby bag, and the nicknames associated with the 8th King's Royal Irish Hussars were 'The Cross-Belts', 'St George's', 'The Twenty-Fives', 'The King's' and 'The Dirty 8th'. There were no imperial regiments affiliated to the 8th King's Royal Irish Hussars.

ROYAL ARMOURED CORPS REGIMENTS 7

9th/12th Royal Lancers (Prince of Wales's)

Colonel-in-Chief
HM Queen Elizabeth The Queen Mother

Colonel
Colonel M. ff. Woodhead

Battle honours

Egypt (with the Sphinx)   Salamanca   Peninsula   Waterloo   Punniar   Sobraon   Chillianwallah   Goojerat   Punjaub   South Africa 1851–53   Sevastopol   Delhi 1957   Central India   Lucknow   Charasiah   Kabul 1879   Kandahar 1880   Afghanistan 1878–80   Modder River   Relief of Kimberley   Paardeberg   South Africa 1899–1902   Mons   Le Cateau   Retreat from Mons   Marne 1914   Aisne 1914   La Bassee 1914   Messines 1914   Armentieres 1914   Ypres 1914, '15   Neuve Chapelle   Gravenstafel   St Julien   Frezenberg   Bellewaarde   Somme 1916, '18   Pozieres   Flers-Courcelette   Arras 1917   Scarpe 1917   Cambrai 1917, '18   St Quentin   Rosieres   Lys   Hazebrouck   Amiens   Albert 1918   Hindenburg Line   St Quentin Canal   Beaurevoir   Sambre   Pursuit to Mons   France and Flanders 1914–18   Dyle   Defence of Arras   Arras Counter-Attack   Dunkirk 1940   Somme 1940   Withdrawal to Seine   North-West Europe 1940   Chor es Sufan   Saunnu   Gazala

Bir el Aslagh   Sidi Rezegh 1942   Defence of Alamein Line   Ruweisat   Ruweisat Ridge   Alam el Halfa   El Alamein   Advance on Tripoli   Tebaga Gap   El Hamma   Akarit   El Kourzia   Djebel Kournine   Tunis   Creteville Pass   North Africa 1941–43   Citerna   Gothic Line   Coriano   Capture of Forli   Lamone Crossing   Pideura   Defence of Lamone Bridgehead   Conventello-Comacchio   Argenta Gap   Bologna   Sillaro Crossing   Idice Bridgehead   Italy 1944–45

Regimental headquarters

Glen Parva Barracks, Wigston, Leicestershire.

Regimental museum

Derby Museum and Art Gallery, The Strand, Derby, Derbyshire.

Regimental marches

(slow) Men of Harlech (traditional), and Cobourg (anonymous)
(quick) God Bless the Prince of Wales (Richards)

Regimental motto

Honi Soit Qui Mal y Pense (Evil be to Him who Evil Thinks)

Nicknames

see below

Uniform

Blue with scarlet facings

Allied regiments

The Prince Edward Island Regiment (Canada)
12th Cavalry (Pakistan)

Regimental History

The 9th/12th Royal Lancers (Prince of Wales's) came into existence in September 1960 through the amalgamation of the 9th Queen's Royal Lancers and the 12th Royal Lancers (Prince of Wales's).

The 9th Queen's Royal Lancers had originated in 1715 when Major-

General Owen Wynn raised Wynn's Dragoons. Thereafter the title of the regiment changed with its colonels, until in 1751 it was designated the 9th Regiment of Dragoons, becoming the 9th Regiment of (Light) Dragoons in 1783. The Napoleonic wars brought the concept of lighter, more mobile cavalry regiments into Western Europe, and in 1816 the regiment became the 9th Regiment of (Light) Dragoons (Lancers), a change formalized in 1830 when the title was changed once more, this time to the 9th (The Queen's Royal) Lancers. Further modification of this then followed in 1878 and 1921, the earlier year seeing the retitling of the regiment as the 9th (Queen's Royal) Lancers and the later year witnessing the regiment's definitive title, the 9th Queen's Royal Lancers. The battle honours of the regiment were the following:

Peninsula   Punniar   Sobraon   Chillianwallah   Goojerat   Punjaub   Delhi 1857   Lucknow   Charasiah   Kabul 1879   Kandahar 1880   Afghanistan 1878–80   Modder River   Relief of Kimberley   Paardeberg   South Africa 1899–1902   Mons   Le Cateau   Retreat from Mons   Marne 1914   Aisne 1914   La Bassee 1914   Messines 1914   Armentieres 1914   Ypres 1914, '15   Gravenstafel   St Julien   Frezenberg   Bellewaarde   Somme 1916, '18   Pozieres   Flers-Courcelette   Arras 1917   Scarpe 1917   Cambrai 1917, '18   St Quentin   Rosieres   Avre   Amiens   Albert 1918   Hindenburg Line   Pursuit to Mons   France and Flanders 1914–18   Somme 1940   Withdrawal to Seine   North-West Europe 1940   Saunnu   Gazala   Bir el Aslagh   Sidi Rezegh 1942   Defence of Alamein Line   Ruweisat   Ruweisat Ridge   El Alamein   Tebaga Gap   El Hamma   El Kourzia   Tunis   Creteville Pass   North Africa 1942–43   Coriano   Capture of Forli   Lamone Crossing   Pideura   Defence of Lamone Bridgehead   Argenta Gap   Italy 1944–45

The regiment's motto was 'Honi Soit Qui Mal y Pense' (Evil be to Him who Evil Thinks), and the regimental marches were 'Soldiers' Chorus from Faust' (Gounod, slow) and 'March of the Men of Harlech' (traditional, quick). The uniform was blue with scarlet facings, and the nicknames associated with the 9th Queen's Royal Lancers were 'The Delhi Spearmen' and 'The Queen's', the former in reference to the regiment's punishment of mutineers in the Indian Mutiny (1857–58). Imperial regiments affiliated with the 9th Queen's Royal Lancers were the Prince Edward Island Light Horse (Canada), the Saskatchewan Mounted Rifles (Canada), and the 22nd Light Horse (Australia).

The 12th Royal Lancers (Prince of Wales's) had been raised in 1715 by Colonel Phineas Bowles as Bowles's Dragoons, and the regiment's title thereafter changed with its colonels until 1751, when it became the 12th Regiment of Dragoons. In 1768 it received royal patronage in the form of a revised title, the 12th (or The Prince of Wales's) Regiment of (Light)

Dragoons. In 1816 the regiment fell to the vogue for light cavalry, becoming the 12th (or The Prince of Wales's) Regiment of Lancers in 1817, the 12th (Prince of Wales's Royal) Lancers in 1856, and the 12th Royal Lancers (Prince of Wales's) in 1921. The battle honours of the regiment were the following:

    Salamanca   Peninsula   Waterloo   South Africa 1851–53   Sevastopol   Central India   Relief of Kimberley   Paardeberg   South Africa 1899–1902   Mons   Le Cateau   Retreat from Mons   Marne 1914   Aisne 1914   Messines 1914   Ypres 1914, '15   Neuve Chapelle   St Julien   Bellewaarde   Arras 1917   Scarpe 1917   Cambrai 1917, '18   Somme 1918   St Quentin   Lys   Hazebrouck   Amiens   Albert 1918   Hindenburg Line   St Quentin Canal   Beaurevoir   Sambre   France and Flanders 1914–18   Dyle   Defence of Arras   Arras Counter-Attack   Dunkirk 1940   North-West Europe 1940   Chor es Sufan   Gazala   Alam el Halfa   El Alamein   Advance on Tripoli   Tebaga Gap   El Hamma   Akarit   El Kourzia   Djebel Kournine   Tunis   Creteville Pass   North Africa 1941–43   Citerna   Gothic Line   Capture of Forli   Conventello-Comacchio   Bologna   Sillaro Crossing   Idice Bridgehead   Italy 1944–45

The motto of the regiment was 'Ich Dien' (I Serve), and the regimental marches were 'Cobourg March' (anonymous, slow) and 'God Bless the Prince of Wales' (Richards, quick). The uniform was blue with scarlet facings, and the nickname associated with the 12th Royal Lancers was 'The Supple Twelfth'. Imperial regiments affiliated to the 12th Royal Lancers were the 12th Manitoba Dragoons (Canada) and the Canterbury Yeomanry (New Zealand).

ROYAL ARMOURED CORPS REGIMENTS 8

The Royal Hussars (Prince of Wales's Own)

Colonel-in-Chief
HRH The Princess Alice Duchess of Gloucester

Colonel
Lieutenant-Colonel Sir Piers Bengough

Battle honours
Warburg Beaumont Willems Egypt (with the Sphinx) Salamanca Peninsula Waterloo Bhurtpore Alma Balaklava Inkerman Sevastopol Ali Masjid Afghanistan 1878–80 Egypt 1884 Relief of Kimberley Paardeberg South Africa 1899–1902 Mons Le Cateau Retreat from Mons Marne 1914 Aisne 1914 Messines 1914 Armentieres 1914 Ypres 1914, '15 Langemarck 1914 Gheluvelt Nonne Bosschen Frezenberg Bellewaarde Loos Somme 1916, '18 Flers-Courcelette Arras 1917, '18 Scarpe 1917 Cambrai 1917, '18 St Quentin Rosieres Avre Amiens Albert 1918 Drocourt-Queant Hindenburg Line St Quentin Canal Beaurevoir Selle Pursuit to Mons France and Flanders 1914–18 Somme 1940 Villers Bocage Bourgebus Ridge Mont Pincon Jurques Dives Crossing La Vie Crossing Lisieux Le Touques Crossing Risle Crossing Roer Rhine Ibbenburen Aller North-West Europe 1940, '44–45

Egyptian Frontier 1940   Withdrawal to Matruh   Bir Enba   Sidi Barrani   Buq Buq   Bardia 1941   Capture of Tobruk   Beda Fomm   Halfaya 1941   Sidi Suleiman   Tobruk 1941   Gubi I, II   Gabr Saleh   Sidi Rezegh 1941   Taieb el Essem   Relief of Tobruk   Saunnu   Msus   Gazala   Bir el Aslagh   Defence of Alamein Line   Alam el Halfa   El Alamein   Advance on Tripoli   El Hamma   Enfidaville   El Kourzia   Djebel Kournine   Tunis   North Africa 1940–43   Capture of Naples   Volturno Crossing   Coriano   Santarcangelo   Cosina Canal Crossing   Senio Pocket   Cesena   Valli di Comacchio   Argenta Gap   Italy 1943–45

Regimental headquarters

Lower Barracks, Winchester, Hampshire.

Regimental museum

Southgate Street, Winchester, Hampshire.

Regimental marches

(slow) Cobourg March (anonymous)
(quick) The Merry Month of May (traditional)

Regimental motto

Ich Dien (I Serve)

Nicknames

see below

Uniform

Blue with crimson facings, and crimson trousers

Allied regiments

1st Hussars (Canada)
10th Light Horse (Australia)
The Guides Cavalry (Pakistan)

Regimental history

The Royal Hussars (Prince of Wales's) came into being in October 1969 with the amalgamation of the 10th Royal Hussars (Prince of Wales's Own) and the 11th Hussars (Prince Albert's Own).

The Royal Hussars (Prince of Wales's) had been raised by Brigadier-General Humphrey Gore in 1715 as Gore's Regiment of Dragoons, and the regiment subsequently changed its name with its colonels until 1751, when it was restyled the 10th Dragoons. Royal patronage was received in 1783, when the regiment became the 10th (or The Prince of Wales's Own) Regiment of (Light) Dragoons, the same basic theme being continued when the regiment became the 10th (or The Prince of Wales's Own) Regiment of Light Dragoons (Hussars) in 1806, the 10th (Prince of Wales's Own Royal) Regiment of Light Dragoons (Hussars) in 1811, the 10th (Prince of Wales's Own) Hussars in 1860, and the 10th Royal Hussars (Prince of Wales's Own) in 1921. The battle honours of the regiment were the following:

Warburg   Peninsula   Waterloo   Sevastopol   Ali Masjid   Afghanistan 1878–80   Egypt 1884   Relief of Kimberley   Paardeberg   South Africa 1889–1902   Ypres 1914, '15   Langemarck 1914   Gheluvelt   Nonne Bosschen   Frezenberg   Loos   Arras 1917, '18   Scarpe 1917   Somme 1918   St Quentin   Avre   Amiens   Drocourt-Queant   Hindenburg Line   Beaurevoir   Cambrai 1918   Pursuit to Mons   France and Flanders 1914–18   Somme 1940   North-West Europe 1940   Saunnu   Gazala   Bir el Aslagh   Alam el Halfa   El Alamein   El Hamma   El Kourzia   Djebel Kournine   Tunis   North Africa 1942–43   Coriano   Santarcangelo   Cosina Canal Crossing   Senio Pocket   Cesena   Valli di Comacchio   Argenta Gap   Italy 1944–45

The motto of the regiment was 'Ich Dien' (I Serve), and the regimental marches were 'God Bless the Prince of Wales' (Richards, slow) and 'The Merry Month of May' (traditional, quick). The uniform was blue with a scarlet busby bag, and the nicknames associated with the 10th Royal Hussars were 'The Shiny Tenth', 'The Chainy Tenth', 'China Tenth' and 'Baker's Light Bobs'. Imperial regiments affiliated to the 10th Royal Hussars were the Princess Louise Dragoon Guards (Canada), the 10th Light Horse (Australia), and the Nelson-Marlborough Mounted Rifles (New Zealand).

The 11th Hussars (Prince Albert's Own) had been raised in 1715 by Brigadier-General Philip Honywood as Honywood's Regiment of Dragoons. Thereafter the regiment adopted the name of its current colonel, until in 1751 it became the 11th Regiment of Dragoons. In 1783 it became the 11th Regiment of (Light) Dragoons, and in 1840 became a late addition to the ranks of hussars when it was redesignated the 11th (Prince Albert's Own) Hussars. In 1920 this style changed to the 11th Hussars (Prince Albert's Own), which remained the regiment's title until its amalgamation with the 10th Royal Hussars. The battle honours of the regiment were the following:

Warburg   Beaumont   Willems   Egypt (with the Sphinx)   Salamanca   Peninsula   Waterloo   Bhurtpore   Alma   Balaklava   Inkerman

Sevastopol   Mons   Le Cateau   Retreat from Mons   Marne 1914   Aisne 1914   Messines 1914   Armentieres 1914   Ypres 1914, '15   Frezenberg   Bellewaarde   Somme 1916, '18   Flers-Courcelette   Arras 1917   Scarpe 1917   Cambrai 1917, '18   St Quentin   Rosieres   Amiens   Albert 1918   Hindenburg Line   St Quentin Canal   Beaurevoir   Selle   France and Flanders 1914–18   Villers Bocage   Bourgebus Ridge   Mont Pincon   Jurques   Dives Crossing   La Vie Crossing   Lisieux   Le Touques Crossing   Risle Crossing   Roer   Rhine   Ibbenburen   Aller   North-West Europe 1944–45   Egyptian Frontier 1940   Withdrawal to Matruh   Bir Enba   Sidi Barrani   Buq Buq   Bardia 1941   Capture of Tobruk   Beda Fomm   Halfaya 1941   Sidi Suleiman   Tobruk 1941   Gubi I, II   Gabr Saleh   Sidi Rezegh 1941   Taieb el Essem   Relief of Tobruk   Saunnu   Msus   Gazala   Bir el Aslagh   Defence of Alamein Line   Alam el Halfa   El Alamein   Advance on Tripoli   Enfidaville   Tunis   North Africa 1940–43   Capture of Naples   Volturno Crossing   Italy 1943

The motto of the regiment was 'Treu und Fest' (Staunch and Steadfast), and the regimental marches were 'Cobourg March' (anonymous, slow) and 'Moses in Egypt' (Rossini, quick). The uniform was blue with a crimson busby bag and crimson overalls, and the nicknames associated with the 11th Hussars were 'The Cherrypickers', 'The Cherubims' and 'Lord Cardigan's Bloodhounds'. The sole imperial regiment affiliated to the 11th Hussars was the 1st Hussars (Canada).

13th/18th Royal Hussars (Queen Mary's Own)

Colonel-in-Chief

none

Colonel

Major-General H. S. R. Watson

Battle honours

Albuhera   Vittoria   Orthes   Toulouse   Peninsula   Waterloo   Alma   Balaklava   Inkerman   Sevastopol   Defence of Ladysmith   Relief of Ladysmith   South Africa 1899–1902   Mons   Le Cateau   Retreat from Mons   Marne 1914   Aisne 1914   La Bassee 1914   Messines 1914   Armentieres 1914   Ypres 1914, '15   Gravenstafel   St Julien   Frezenberg   Bellewaarde   Somme 1916, '18   Flers-Courcelette   Arras 1917   Scarpe 1917   Cambrai 1917, '18   St Quentin   Rosieres   Amiens   Albert 1918   Hindenburg Line   Pursuit to Mons   France and Flanders 1914–18   Kut al Amara 1917   Baghdad   Sharqat   Mesopotamia 1916–18   Dyle   Withdrawal to Escaut   Ypres-Comines Canal   Normandy Landing   Bretteville   Caen   Bourgebus Ridge   Mont Pincon   St Pierre la Vielle   Geilenkirchen   Roer   Rhineland   Waal Flats   Goch   Rhine   Bremen   North-West Europe 1940, '44–45

13TH/18TH ROYAL HUSSARS

Regimental headquarters
3/3A Tower Street, York, Yorkshire.

Regimental museum
Cannon Hall Museum, Cawthorne, Barnsley, Yorkshire.

Regimental marches
(slow) 13th and 18th Hussars
(quick) Balaklava

Regimental motto
Viret in Aeternum. Pro Rege, Pro Lege, Pro Patria Conamur
(It Flourishes for Ever. For King, for Law, for Country we Strive)

Nicknames
see below

Uniform
Blue with white facings

Allied regiments
Royal Canadian Hussars (Montreal)
Skinner's Horse (1st Duke of York's Own Cavalry) (India)
6th Lancers (Pakistan)
2nd Royal Reconnaissance Regiment (Malaysia)

Regimental history

The 13th/18th Royal Hussars (Queen Mary's Own) was formed in November 1922 by the amalgamation of the 13th Hussars and the 18th Royal Hussars (Queen Mary's Own). Imperial regiments affiliated to the 13th/18th Royal Hussars were the 17th Duke of York's Royal Canadian Hussars and the 18th Light Horse (Australia).

The 13th had been raised in 1715 by Brigadier-General Richard Munden as Munden's Dragoons, and the regiment was subsequently one of the many that changed its title in accordance with the name of the current colonel. This situation ended in 1751, when the regiment became the 13th

Regiment of Dragoons. Thereafter the title of the regiment changed only infrequently, in 1783 to the 13th Regiment of (Light) Dragoons, and in 1862 to the 13th Hussars. The battle honours of the regiment were the following:

Albuhera   Vittoria   Orthes   Toulouse   Peninsula   Waterloo   Alma   Balaklava   Inkerman   Sevastopol   Relief of Ladysmith   South Africa 1899–1902   France and Flanders 1914–16   Kut al Amara 1917   Baghdad   Sharqat   Mesopotamia 1916–18

The motto of the regiment was 'Viret in Aeternum' (It Flourishes for Ever), and the regimental march was 'The 13th Hussars Slow March' (slow). The uniform was blue with a buff collar, and the nicknames associated with the 13th Hussars were 'The Green Dragoons', 'The Evergreens', 'The Ragged Brigade', 'The Geraniums' and 'The Lillywhites'.

The 18th Royal Hussars (Queen Mary's Own) was a comparative latecomer to the strength of the British army, being raised in its definitive form only in 1858. The origins of such a regiment can be traced further back into history, however, for in 1759 the Marquess of Drogheda raised the 19th Light Dragoons, more popularly known as the Drogheda Light Horse. In 1766 this regiment became the 18th Light Dragoons, and after conversion to a hussar unit in 1807 as the 19th Light Dragoons (Hussars) was disbanded in 1,821. The number remained vacant until 1858 until the regiment was re-formed in Yorkshire as the 18th Hussars. In 1903 royal patronage led to the revised title the 18th (Queen Mary's Own) Hussars. The final version of the title, adopted in 1919 after the end of World War I, was the 18th Royal Hussars (Queen Mary's Own). The battle honours of the regiment were the following:

Peninsula   Waterloo   Defence of Ladysmith   South Africa 1899–1902   Mons   Le Cateau   Retreat from Mons   Marne 1914   Aisne 1914   La Bassee 1914   Messines 1914   Armentieres 1914   Ypres 1914, '15   Gravenstafel   St Julien   Frezenberg   Bellewaarde   Somme 1916, '18   Flers-Courcelette   Arras 1917   Scarpe 1917   Cambrai 1917, '18   St Quentin   Rosieres   Amiens   Albert 1918   Hindenburg Line   Pursuit to Mons   France and Flanders 1914–18

The motto of the regiment was 'Pro Rege, Pro Lege, Pro Patria Conamur' (For King, for Law, for Country we Strive), and the regimental march was '18th Hussars Slow March' (slow). The uniform was blue with a blue busby bag, and the only nickname associated with the 18th Royal Hussars was 'The Drogheda Light Horse'. Imperial regiments affiliated to the 18th Royal Hussars were the Manitoba Mounted Rifles (Canada), and the 18th Light Horse (Australia).

ROYAL ARMOURED CORPS REGIMENTS 10

14th/20th King's Hussars

Colonel-in-Chief
HRH The Princess Royal Mrs Mark Phillips

Colonel
Major-General Sir Michael Parker

Battle honours

Vimiera Douro Talavera Fuentes d'Onor Salamanca Vittoria Pyrenees Orthes Peninsula Chillianwallah Goojerat Punjaub Persia Central India Suakin 1885 Relief of Ladysmith South Africa 1900–02 Mons Retreat from Mons Marne 1914 Aisne 1914 Messines 1914 Ypres 1914, '15 Neuve Chapelle St Julien Bellewaarde Arras 1917 Scarpe 1917 Cambrai 1917, '18 Somme 1918 St Quentin Lys Hazebrouck Amiens Albert 1918 Bapaume 1918 Hindenburg Line St Quentin Canal Beaurevoir Sambre France and Flanders 1914–18 Tigris 1916 Kut al Amara 1917 Baghdad Mesopotamia 1915–18 Persia 1918 Bologna Medicini Italy 1945

Regimental headquarters
Fulwood Barracks, Fulwood, Preston, Lancashire.

Regimental museum

Queen's Park Museum and Art Gallery, Queen's Park, Rochdale Road, Manchester, Lancashire.

Regimental marches

(slow) The Eagle
(quick) Royal Sussex

Regimental motto

Honi Soit Qui Mal y Pense (Evil be to Him who Evil Thinks)

Nickname

The Emperor's Chambermaids

Uniform

Scarlet with yellow facings

Allied regiments

2nd/14th Queensland Mounted Infantry (Australia)
8th/14th Victorian Mounted Rifles (Australia)
Queen Alexandra's Squadron, RNZAC
Zambia Armoured Car Regiment

Regimental history

The 14th/20th King's Hussars came into existence in April 1922 through the amalgamation of the 14th King's Hussars and the 20th Hussars.

The 14th King's Hussars had been raised in 1715 by Brigadier-General James Dormer as Dormer's Dragoons, and the regiment's title was subsequently changed in accordance with its colonels' names until 1751, when it became the 14th Regiment of Dragoons. In 1776 it became the 14th Regiment of (Light) Dragoons, and in 1798 the 14th (or The Duchess of York's Own) Regiment of (Light) Dragoons. The origins of the definitive style can be found in 1830, when the regiment became the 14th (The King's) Regiment of Light Dragoons, modified in 1861 to the 14th (King's) Hussars and in 1921 to the 14th King's Hussars. The battle honours of the regiment were the following:

Douro   Talavera   Fuentes d'Onor   Salamanca   Vittoria   Pyrenees

Orthes   Peninsula   Chillianwallah   Goojerat   Punjaub   Persia
Central India   Relief of Ladysmith   South Africa   1900–02
Tigris 1916   Kut al Amara 1917   Baghdad   Mesopotamia 1915–18
Persia 1918

The motto of the regiment was 'Honi Soit Qui Mal y Pense' (Evil be to Him who Evil Thinks), and the regimental march was 'King of Prussia' (slow). The uniform was blue with a yellow busby bag, and the nicknames associated with the 14th King's Hussars were 'The Chambermaids' and 'The Ramnuggur Boys', the first in reference to the occasion in the Peninsula War (1812–14) when the regiment captured the silver chamberpot of King Joseph, and the second in reference to the regiment's distinguished service in India. Imperial regiments affiliated to the 14th King's Hussars were the 14th Canadian Light Horse and the 14th Light Horse (Australia).

The 20th Hussars was like the 14th King's Hussars a comparatively new regiment, having been formed in 1857 as the 2nd Bengal European Light Cavalry within the army of the Honourable East India Company but transferred to the British army as the 20th Light Dragoons when the HEIC's army was absorbed into the British army as part of the wide-ranging reforms instituted after the Indian Mutiny. Yet even before this the regiment had undergone three incarnations. The first of these started in Ireland during 1759, when the Light Troop of the 6th Inniskilling Dragoons was expanded to regimental size as the 20th Light Inniskilling Dragoons. This first regiment was disbanded in 1763, but a second incarnation began in 1779 with the re-formation of the 20th Light Dragoons, followed by its disbandment in 1783. The third incarnation resulted from the need for a light dragoon regiment in Jamaica, and the 20th Jamaica Light Dragoons was raised in 1791. In 1802 this became the 20th Light Dragoons, which was disbanded in 1819, leaving the designation for eventual use by the Indian establishment and the definitive regiment. Only one year after its arrival within the ranks of the British army, the 20th Light Dragoons became the 20th Hussars, and this title was retained until the amalgamation of the regiment with the 14th King's Hussars. The battle honours of the regiment were the following:

Vimiera   Peninsula   Suakin 1885   South Africa 1901–02   Mons
Retreat from Mons   Marne 1914   Aisne 1914   Messines 1914
Ypres 1914, '15   Neuve Chapelle   St Julien   Bellewaarde
Arras 1917   Scarpe 1917   Cambrai 1917, '18   Somme 1918
St Quentin   Lys   Hazebrouck   Amiens   Albert 1918   Bapaume 1918
Hindenburg Line   St Quentin Canal   Beaurevoir   Sambre
France and Flanders 1914–18

The uniform was blue with a scarlet busby bag, and the nicknames associated with the 20th Hussars were 'The Xs' and 'Nobody's Own'. Imperial regiments affiliated to the 20th Hussars were the 20th Light Horse (Australia), and Queen Alexandra's (Wellington West Coast) Mounted Rifles (New Zealand).

ROYAL ARMOURED CORPS REGIMENTS 11

15th/19th The King's Royal Hussars

Colonel-in-Chief

HRH The Princess Margaret Countess of Snowdon

Colonel

Brigadier J. R. D. Sharpe

Battle honours

Emsdorff   Mysore   Villers-en-Cauchies   Willems   Seringapatam   Egmont-op-Zee   Assaye (with the Elephant)   Sahagun   Vittoria   Niagara   Peninsula   Waterloo   Afghanistan 1878–80   Tel-el-Kebir   Egypt 1882–84   Nile 1884–85   Abu Klea   Defence of Ladysmith   South Africa 1899–1902   Mons   Le Cateau   Retreat from Mons   Marne 1914   Aisne 1914   Armentieres 1914   Ypres 1914, '15   Langemarck 1914   Gheluvelt   Nonne Bosschen   Frezenberg   Bellewaarde   Somme 1916, '18   Flers-Courcelette   Cambrai 1917, '18   St Quentin   Rosieres   Amiens   Albert 1918   Bapaume 1918   Hindenburg Line   St Quentin Canal   Beaurevoir   Pursuit to Mons   France and Flanders 1914–18   Withdrawal to Escaut   Seine 1944   Hechtel   Nederrijn   Venraij   Rhineland   Hochwald   Rhine   Ibbenburen   Aller   North-West Europe 1940, '44–45

Regimental headquarters

Fenham Barracks, Barrack Road, Newcastle-upon-Tyne, Northumberland.

Regimental museum

John George Joicey Museum, City Road, Newcastle-upon-Tyne, Northumberland.

Regimental marches

(slow) Arrangement of Eliott's Light Horse and Denmark
(quick) Arrangement of The Bold King's Hussar and Haste to the Wedding

Regimental motto

Merebimur (We shall be Worthy)

Nicknames

see below

Uniform

Blue with scarlet facings

Allied regiments

The South Alberta Light Horse (Canada)
1st/15th Royal New South Wales Lancers (Australia)
19th Lancers (Pakistan)

Regimental history

The 15th/19th The King's Royal Hussars was formed in April 1922 by the amalgamation of the 15th The King's Hussars and the 19th Royal Hussars (Queen Alexandra's Own).

The 15th The King's Hussars could trace its ancestry back to 1759, when Colonel George Eliott raised the 15th Light Dragoons, also known as Eliott's Light Horse. Shortly after this the army decided to redesignate the new light cavalry regiments in a sequence parallel to that used for heavy cavalry regiments, and in 1766 the 15th Light Dragoons became the 1st (or The King's Royal) Light Dragoons, in 1769 being redesignated the 15th (or The King's) Light Dragoons. Further revision of the title came at the beginning of the 19th century when the nature of the regiment was revised, which produced the title the 15th (or The King's) Light Dragoons (Hussars) in 1807. In 1861 the regiment became the 15th (King's) Hussars, slight revisions modifying this to the 15th (The King's) Hussars in 1901 and to the 15th The King's Hussars in 1921. The battle honours of the regiment were the following:

Emsdorff Villers-en-Cauchies Willems Egmont-op-Zee Sahagun Vittoria Peninsula Waterloo Afghanistan 1870–80 Mons Retreat from Mons Marne 1914 Aisne 1914 Ypres 1914, '15 Langemarck 1914 Gheluvelt Nonne Bosschen Frezenberg Bellewaarde Somme 1916, '18 Flers-Courcelette Cambrai 1917, '18 St Quentin Rosieres Amiens Albert 1918 Bapaume 1918 Hindenburg Line St Quentin Canal Beaurevoir Pursuit to Mons France and Flanders 1914–18

The motto of the regiment was 'Merebimur' (We Shall be Worthy), and the regimental marches were 'Eliott's Light Horse' (slow) and 'The Bold King's Hussar' (quick). The uniform was blue with a scarlet busby bag, and the nicknames associated with the 15th The King's Hussars were 'Eliott's Tailors' and 'The Fighting Fifteenth', the former because the initial recruitment of the regiment included many London tailors then on strike. Imperial regiments affiliated to the 15th The King's Hussars were the 15th Alberta Light Horse (Canada) and the 15th Light Horse (Australia).

The 19th Royal Hussars (Queen Alexandra's Own) parallels the 20th Hussars in having enjoyed three separate incarnations before appearing on the establishment of the army of the Honourable East India Company in the 1850s. The regiment's first life started in 1759, when the 19th Light Horse or Drogheda Light Horse was raised in Ireland. This regiment was renumbered the 18th Light Horse in 1766 but disbanded in 1821, and is more properly the ancestor of the 18th Royal Hussars (now part of the 13th/18th Royal Hussars). The regiment's second existence began in 1779 when the 19th Light Dragoons were raised, enjoying only a four-year life before being disbanded in 1783. The regiment's third turn on the wheel came in 1786, when the 23rd Light Dragoons (raised in 1781) was renumbered the 19th Light Dragoons: in 1817 this became the 19th Lancers and was disbanded in 1821. Finally, the 1st Bengal European Light Cavalry was raised on the HEIC's establishment in India. When the HEIC's army was absorbed into the British army in 1861, this became the 19th Hussars, and royal patronage was secured in 1881 to turn the regiment into the 19th (Princess of Wales's Own) Hussars. In 1902 the regiment became the 19th (Alexandra Princess of Wales's Own) Hussars, and in 1908 the 19th (Queen Alexandra's Own Royal) Hussars. For one year before the amalgamation with the 15th The King's Hussars the regiment was the 19th Royal Hussars (Queen Alexandra's Own). The battle honours of the regiment were the following:

> Seringapatam   Mysore   Assaye (with the Elephant)   Niagara
> Tel-el-Kebir   Egypt 1882–84   Nile 1884–85   Abu Klea   Defence of Ladysmith   South Africa 1899–1902   Le Cateau   Retreat from Mons   Marne 1914   Aisne 1914   Armentieres 1914   Ypres 1914, '15   Frezenberg   Bellewaarde   Somme 1916, '18   Flers-Courcelette   Cambrai 1917, '18   St Quentin   Rosieres   Amiens   Albert 1918   Bapaume 1918   Hindenburg Line   St Quentin Canal   Beaurevoir   Pursuit to Mons   France and Flanders 1914–18

The motto of the regiment was 'Honi Soit Qui Mal y Pense' (Evil be to Him who Evil Thinks), and the regimental marches were 'Denmark' (slow) and 'Haste to the Wedding' (quick). The uniform was blue with a white busby bag, and the nicknames associated with the 19th Royal Hussars were 'The Dumpies' and 'The Terrors of the East'. The only imperial regiment affiliated to the 19th Royal Hussars was the 19th Alberta Dragoons (Canada).

ROYAL ARMOURED CORPS REGIMENTS 12

16th/5th The Queen's Royal Lancers

Colonel-in-Chief

HM The Queen

Colonel

Brigadier J. L. Pownall

Battle honours

Blenheim Ramillies Oudenarde Malplaquet Beaumont Willems Talavera Fuentes d'Onor Salamanca Vittoria Nive Peninsula Waterloo Bhurtpore Ghuznee 1839 Affghanistan 1839 Maharajpore Aliwal Sobraon Suakin 1885 Defence of Ladysmith Relief of Kimberley Paardeberg South Africa 1899–1902 Mons Le Cateau Retreat from Mons Marne 1914 Aisne 1914 Messines 1914 Armentieres 1914 Ypres 1914, '15 Gheluvelt St Julien Bellewaarde Arras 1917 Scarpe 1917 Cambrai 1917 Somme 1918 St Quentin Amiens Hindenburg Line Canal du Nord Pursuit to Mons France and Flanders 1914–18 Kasserine Fondouk Kairouan Bordj Djebel Kournine Tunis Gromballa Bou Ficha North Africa 1942–43 Casino II Liri Valley Monte Piccolo Capture of Perugia Arezzo Advance to Florence Argenta Gap Traghetto Italy 1944–45

Regimental headquarters

Kitchener House, Lammascote Road, Stafford, Staffordshire.

Regimental museum

Kitchener House, Lanmascote Road, Stafford, Staffordshire.

Regimental marches

(slow) The Queen Charlotte (arranged Noble)
(quick) Scarlet and Green (arranged Noble)

Regimental motto

Aut Cursu, aut Cominus Armis (Either in the Charge, or Hand to Hand)

Nickname

The Scarlet Lancers

Uniform

Blue with blue facings

Allied regiment

12th/16th Hunter River Lancers (Australia)

Regimental history

The 16th/5th The Queen's Royal Lancers was formed in April 1922 by the amalgamation of the 16th The Queen's Lancers and the 5th Royal Irish Lancers. The reversed order of seniority indicated in the title of the amalgamated regiment results from the continuous existence of the 16th The Queen's Lancers from 1759, whereas the 5th Royal Irish Lancers could trace its real origins only to 1858.

The 16th The Queen's Lancers had been raised in 1759 by Colonel John Burgoyne as the 16th Regiment of (Light) Dragoons, though the regiment was also known as Burgoyne's Light Horse. In the short-lived 1760s' practice of renumbering light cavalry regiments in a separate sequence parallel to that for heavy cavalry, the regiment in 1766 became the 2nd (or The Queen's) Regiment of Light Dragoons, reverting in 1769 to the standard sequence as the 16th (or The Queen's) Regiment of Light

Dragoons and in 1816 becoming the 16th (or The Queen's) Regiment of Light Dragoons (Lancers). Thereafter the regiment underwent a number of minor redesignations, in 1855 to the 16th (Queen's) Lancers, in 1919 to the 16th (The Queen's Lancers) and in 1921 to the 16th The Queen's Lancers. The battle honours of the regiment were the following:

Beaumont Willems Talavera Fuentes d'Onor Salamanca Vittoria Nive Peninsula Waterloo Bhurtpore Ghuznee 1839 Affghanistan 1839 Maharajpore Aliwal Sobraon Relief of Kimberley Paardeberg South Africa 1900–02 Mons Le Cateau Retreat from Mons Marne 1914 Aisne 1914 Messines 1914 Armentieres 1914 Ypres 1914, '15 Gheluvelt St Julien Bellewaarde Arras 1917 Scarpe 1917 Cambrai 1917 Somme 1918 Amiens Hindenburg Line Canal du Nord Pursuit to Mons France and Flanders 1914–18

The motto of the regiment was 'Aut Cursu, aut Cominus Armis' (Either in the Charge, or Hand to Hand), and the regimental marches were 'The 16th Lancers Slow March' (slow) and 'The English Patrol' (quick). The uniform was scarlet with blue facings, and the nickname associated with the 16th The Queen's Lancers was 'The Scarlet Lancers'. Imperial regiments affiliated to the 16th The Queen's Lancers were the 16th Canadian Light Horse and the 16th Light Horse (Australia).

Although for the purposes of seniority the 5th Royal Irish Lancers dates only from 1858, the antecedents of such a regiment date back to 1689, when Colonel Wynne raised Wynne's Regiment of Enniskillen Dragoons, a title that subsequently changed in accordance with the names of its colonels until 1704, when the regiment became The Royal Dragoons of Ireland. In 1751 this title was revised to the 5th (or Royal Irish) Regiment of Dragoons, which remained unaltered to the time that the regiment was disbanded in 1799. In 1858 a new regiment was raised as the 5th (Royal Irish) Dragoons, and though this assumed the number and honours of the previous regiment, it did not receive its seniority. The new regiment's sole change of title came in 1921, when it became the 5th Royal Irish Lancers. The battle honours of the regiment were the following:

Blenheim Ramillies Oudenarde Malplaquet Suakin 1885 Defence of Ladysmith South Africa 1899–1902 Mons Le Cateau Retreat from Mons Marne 1914 Aisne 1914 Messines 1914 Armentieres 1914 Ypres 1914, '15 Gheluvelt St Julien Bellewaarde Arras 1917 Scarpe 1917 Cambrai 1917 Somme 1918 St Quentin Amiens Hindenburg Line Canal du Nord Pursuit to Mons France and Flanders 1914–18

The motto of the regiment was 'Quis Separabit?' (Who Shall Separate?), and the regimental marches were 'Let Erin Remember' and 'The Harp that Once through Tara's Halls' (slow), and 'St Patrick's Day' (quick). The uniform was blue with scarlet facings, and the nicknames associated with the 5th Royal Irish Lancers were 'The Irish Lancers' and 'The Redbreasts'. The only imperial regiment affiliated to the 5th Royal Irish Lancers was the Otago Mounted Rifles, previously the 5th New Zealand Mounted Rifles (The Otago Hussars).

ROYAL ARMOURED CORPS REGIMENTS 13

17th/21st Lancers

Colonel-in-Chief
HRH The Princess Alexandra the Hon. Mrs Angus Ogilvy

Colonel
Brigadier J. W. Turner

Battle honours
Alma   Balaklava   Inkerman   Sevastopol   Central India   South Africa 1879   Khartoum   South Africa 1900–02   Festubert 1914   Somme 1916, '18   Morval   Cambrai 1917, '18   St Quentin   Avre   Lys   Hazebrouck   Amiens   Hindenburg Line   St Quentin Canal   Beaurevoir   Pursuit to Mons   France and Flanders 1914–18   NW Frontier India 1915, '16   Tebourba Gap   Bou Arada   Kasserine   Thala   Fondouk   El Kourzia   Tunis   Hammam Lif   North Africa 1942–43   Cassino II   Monte Piccolo   Capture of Perugia   Advance to Florence   Argenta Gap   Fossa Cembalina   Italy 1944–45

Regimental headquarters
Prince William of Gloucester Barracks, Grantham, Lincolnshire.

Regimental museum
Belvoir Castle, near Grantham, Rutland.

Regimental marches

(slow) Rienzi (Wagner)
(quick) The White Lancer (Richardson)

Regimental motto

Or Glory

Nicknames

see below

Uniform

Dark blue with white facings

Allied regiment

Lord Strathcona's Horse (Royal Canadians)

Regimental history

The 17th/21st Lancers came into existence in April 1922 through the amalgamation of the 17th Lancers (Duke of Cambridge's Own) and the 21st Lancers (Empress of India's). Imperial regiments affiliated to the 17th/21st Lancers were Lord Strathcona's Horse (Royal Canadians), and the Ceylon Mounted Rifles.

The 17th Lancers (Duke of Cambridge's Own) can be traced back to 1759, when Colonel John Hale brought to England news of General Wolfe's victory at Quebec, and was given permission by George III to raise a cavalry regiment. This was the 18th Regiment of (Light) Dragoons, also known as Hale's Dragoons. In 1763 the 17th (Edinburgh) Regiment of (Light) Dragoons was disbanded after a life of only four years, and the 18th Regiment of (Light) Dragoons was renumbered as the 17th Regiment of (Light) Dragoons. In 1766 the regiment became the 2nd Regiment of (Light) Dragoons, reverting in 1769 to the 17th Regiment of (Light) Dragoons. In 1823 it became the 17th Regiment of (Light) Dragoons (Lancers), and in 1853 the 17th (Light) Dragoons (Lancers). Then in 1876 the regiment received the title 17th (Duke of Cambridge's Own) Lancers, which was modified in 1921 to the 17th Lancers (Duke of Cambridge's Own). The battle honours of the regiment were the following:

Alma   Balaklava   Inkerman   Sevastopol   Central India   South Africa 1879   South Africa 1900–02   Festubert 1914   Somme 1916, '18

Morval   Cambrai 1917, '18   St Quentin   Avre   Lys   Hazebrouck
Amiens   Hindenburg Line   St Quentin Canal   Beaurevoir
Pursuit to Mons   France and Flanders 1914–18

The motto of the regiment was 'Or Glory', and the regimental marches were 'Occasional Overture' (Handel, slow) and 'The White Lancer' (Richardson, quick). The uniform was dark blue with white facings, and the nicknames associated with the 17th Lancers were 'The Death or Glory Boys', 'Bingham's Dandies', 'The Horse Marines' and 'The Tots'.

The 21st Lancers (Empress of India's) appeared in its definitive form in 1857, though the number 21 had undergone three earlier incarnations. The first of these was between 1760 and 1763 as the 21st (Granby's) Light Dragoons, otherwise known as the Royal Foresters. The second life again lasted only a short time, between 1779 and 1783, as the 21st Regiment of (Light) Dragoons. The third incarnation was slightly longer, lasting from 1794 to 1819 for the 21st Regiment of (Light) Dragoons. Then in 1857 the army of the Honourable East India Company raised the 3rd Bengal European Light Cavalry, which was absorbed into the British establishment in 1858 as the 21st Light Dragoons, retitled the 21st Hussars in 1863. The regiment became a lancer unit only in 1897, when it was restyled the 21st Lancers, two years later becoming the 21st (Empress of India's) Lancers. In 1921 this became the 21st Lancers (Empress of India's). The battle honours of the regiment were the following:

Khartoum   NW Frontier India 1915, '16

The motto of the regiment was 'Honi Soit Qui Mal y Pense' (Evil be to Him who Evil Thinks), and the regimental marches were 'Cobourg March' (anonymous, slow) and 'The Merry Month of May' (traditional, quick). The uniform was dark blue with French grey facings, and the nicknames associated with the 21st Lancers were 'The Grey Lancers' and 'The Dumpies'.

ROYAL ARMOURED CORPS REGIMENTS 14

Royal Tank Regiment

Colonel-in-Chief

HM The Queen

Colonel-Commandant

Major-General A. K. F. Walker (1986, out of three)

Battle honours

Somme 1916, '18 Arras 1917, '18 Messines 1917 Ypres 1917 Cambrai 1917 St Quentin 1918 Villers Bretonneux Amiens Bapaume 1918 Hindenburg Line Epehy Selle France and Flanders 1916–18 Gaza Arras Counter Attack Calais 1940 St Omer-La Bassee Somme 1940 Odon Caen Bourgebus Ridge Mont Pincon Falaise Nederrijn Scheldt Venlo Pocket Rhineland Rhine Bremen North-West Europe 1940, '44–45 Abyssinia 1940 Sidi Barrani Beda Fomm Sidi Suleiman Tobruk 1941 Sidi Rezegh 1941 Belhamed Gazala Cauldron Knightsbridge Defence of Alamein Line Alam el Halfa El Alamein Mareth Akarit Fondouk El Kourzia Medjez Plain Tunis North Africa 1940–43 Primosole Bridge Gerbini Adrano Sicily 1943 Sangro Salerno Volturno Crossing Garigliano Crossing Anzio Advance to Florence Gothic Line Coriano Lamone Crossing Rimini Line Argenta Gap Italy 1943–45 Greece 1941 Burma 1942 Korea 1951–53

ROYAL TANK REGIMENT

Regimental headquarters

1 Elverton Street, Horseferry Road, London.

Regimental museum

The Tank Museum, Bovington Camp, Wareham, Dorset.

Regimental marches

(quick) My Boy Willie (traditional)
(slow) Royal Tank Regiment

Regimental motto

Fear Naught

Nicknames

none

Uniform

Blue with black facings

Allied regiments

12e Régiment Blindé de Canada
1st Armoured Regiment Royal Australian Armoured Corps
Royal New Zealand Armoured Corps
2nd Lancers (India)
13th Lancers (Pakistan)

Regimental history

The origins of the Royal Tank Regiment lie with the Machine Gun Corps, which first used tanks in 1916. The original designation of the tank arm was the Heavy Section, Machine Gun Corps which was formed in February 1916, though this was modified to the Heavy Branch, Machine Gun Corps in November 1916. After the tank had been used in service there was little point in attempting to disguise the branch of the army operating the new weapon, and in 1917 the Heavy Branch, Machine Gun Corps became The Tank Corps. This in turn received royal patronage in 1923 as the Royal Tank Corps. However, when the Royal Armoured Corps came into existence during 1939 to embrace the army's dedicated tank arm and the mechanized cavalry regiments, the Royal Tank Corps became the Royal Tank Regiment.

Royal Regiment of Artillery

Captain-General

HM The Queen

Master Gunner, St James's Park

General Sir Thomas Morony

Colonel Commandant

Major-General W. D. Mangham (1986, out of 13)

Battle honours

none (although in 1833 the motto 'Ubique' was recognized as one all-embracing battle honour to indicate that the regiment served 'Everywhere' with the British army)

Regimental headquarters

Government House, New Road, Woolwich, London.

Regimental museums

Old Royal Military Academy, Woolwich, London.
Museum of Artillery (The Rotunda), Repository Road, Woolwich, London.

Regimental marches

(slow) Royal Artillery Slow March, or Duchess of Kent's Slow March
(quick) The British Grenadiers (traditional), and Voice of the Guns (Alford)

Regimental motto

Ubique (Everywhere)

Nicknames

(Royal Horse Artillery) Right of the Line, Four-Wheeled Hussars, Galloping Gunners
(Royal Artillery) The Gunners

Uniform

Blue with scarlet facings

Affiliated regiments

All artillery regiments of Canada, Australia, New Zealand and South Africa

Regimental history

It was only in 1716 that the British army acquired a permanent force of artillery. Up to that time artillery had been raised for any particular campaign by the signature of a royal warrant authorizing the establishment of a train of artillery. This was a time-consuming and ultimately impractical system, as proved by the Jacobite rebellion of 1715, when the train of artillery was not ready for service until after the suppression of the rebellion. In May 1716, therefore, it was authorized by royal warrant that a permanent artillery regiment should be raised, and two companies of field artillery were established at Woolwich. In 1722 these two companies were unified with the independent trains in Gibraltar and Minorca to form the Royal Regiment of Artillery. During the last three-quarters of the eighteenth century the regiment was expanded greatly, and from February 1793 was complemented by the Royal Horse Artillery, which was formed (initially as two troops, later batteries) in response to the increasingly mobile nature of that period's warfare, and the need to provide cavalry with heavy fire support. In 1801 the Royal Regiment of Artillery brought under its aegis the Royal Irish Artillery, which had been raised in 1755 as an independent branch. By the middle of the nineteenth century the Royal Regiment of Artillery had grown to an establishment of 29 batteries of horse artillery, 73 batteries of field artillery, and 88 batteries of garrison artillery. A major modification of the period (more specifically May 1855) was the establishment of the Royal Regiment of Artillery as an intrinsic part of the British army under the control of the War Office: up to that date the regiment had been a separate branch controlled by the Board of Ordnance. In 1899 the regiment was reorganized as two separate branches, namely the Royal Horse and Royal Field Artillery, and the Royal Garrison Artillery, the RGA being responsible for fixed coastal defence batteries, heavy and siege batteries, and mountain batteries. In 1924 the titles Royal Field Artillery and Royal Garrison Artillery were deleted, and the Royal Regiment of Artillery thus became a unitary corps, though the Royal Horse Artillery retained its identity within the corps. A mounted battery of the Royal Horse Artillery was re-formed in 1945 at the express demand of George VI, and this was raised as The Riding Troop, RHA, which in 1947 became The King's Troop, RHA. The Royal Horse Artillery ranks second in precedence to the Household Cavalry, but when on parade with its guns takes the right of the line and has precedence over all other regiments and corps, including the Household Cavalry.

Corps of Royal Engineers

Colonel-in-Chief

HM The Queen

Chief Royal Engineer

General Sir Hugh Beach

Colonel Commandant

Major-General J. P. Groom (1986, out of 12)

Battle honours

none

Corps headquarters

Brompton Barracks, Chatham, Kent.

Corps museum

Brompton Barracks, Chatham, Kent.

Corps march

(quick) Wings

Corps mottoes

Ubique (Everywhere), and
Quo Fas et Gloria Ducunt (Whither Right and Glory Lead)

Nicknames

The Sappers, The Mudlarks

Affiliated corps

The engineer corps of the Canadian, Australian, New Zealand, Indian, Pakistan, Sri Lankan, Malaysian, Zambian and Fijian armies

Corps history

The Corps of Royal Engineers parallels the Royal Regiment of Artillery for much of its history, tracing its origins back to the sixteenth century when the Ordnance Office (later the Board of Ordnance) used engineers for the building and maintenance of fortifications, arsenals and supply depots. When such skilled personnel were required on campaigns they were forcibly conscripted for the duration. As with the artillery branch, it was the events of the Jacobite rebellion of 1715 that brought home the unwelcome truth that the system was inherently inadequate and in any event too tardy, and in 1716 the Board of Ordnance raised a dedicated Corps of Engineers, in this instance of officers only. This became the Corps of Royal Engineers in 1787, the year that also witnessed the formation of the Corps of Military Artificers, a body of non-commissioned men with officers seconded from the Corps of Royal Engineers. In 1813 the Corps of Military Artificers became the Corps of Royal Sappers and Miners in reflection of the altered nature of warfare resulting from the Napoleonic Wars. The Board of Ordnance was removed in 1855, and the two engineer corps now came under the authority of the War Office, which soon appreciated the futility of maintaining separate officer and other-rank engineer corps. In 1856, therefore, the two were amalgamated, the Corps of Royal Sappers and Miners being absorbed into the Corps of Royal Engineers, which has since become one of the most important corps in the British army. Like the Royal Regiment of Artillery, the Corps of Royal Engineers is permitted to treat its motto 'Ubique' as a battle honour in recognition of the fact that the corps serves in every campaign undertaken by the British army.

Royal Corps of Signals

Colonel-in-Chief
HRH The Princess Royal Mrs Mark Phillips

Master of Signals
Major-General J. M. W. Badcock

Colonel Commandant
Major-General A. C. Birtwistle (1986, out of six)

Battle honours
none

Corps headquarters
Cheltenham Terrace, Chelsea, London.

Corps museum
Royal Signals Museum, Blandford Camp, Dorset.

Corps marches

(quick) The Royal Signals March (traditional themes)
(slow) The Royal Signals Slow March, Her Royal Highness The Princess Anne (Ricketts)

Corps motto

Certa Cito (Swift and Sure)

Nicknames

none

Uniform

Blue with scarlet piping and black facings

Affiliated corps

The signals corps of the Canadian, Australian and New Zealand armies

Corps history

The Corps of Signals came into existence in June 1920 and became the Royal Corps of Signals in August 1920. It was successor to the Royal Engineers Signal Service, and was organized as a separate corps in recognition of the growing importance and capability of signalling in modern warfare.

REGIMENTS OF FOOT GUARDS:
ORDER OF PRECEDENCE

1. Grenadier Guards
2. Coldstream Guards
3. Scots Guards
4. Irish Guards
5. Welsh Guards

REGIMENTS OF FOOT GUARDS 1

Grenadier Guards

Colonel-in-Chief

HM The Queen

Colonel

Field-Marshal HRH The Prince Philip Duke of Edinburgh

Battle honours

Tangier 1680   Namur 1695   Gibraltar 1704–05   Blenheim   Ramillies   Oudenarde   Malplaquet   Dettingen   Lincelles   Egmont-op-Zee   Corunna   Barrosa   Nive   Peninsula   Waterloo   Alma   Inkerman   Sevastopol   Tel-el-Kebir   Egypt 1882   Suakin 1885′   Khartoum   Modder River   South Africa 1899–1902   Mons   Retreat from Mons   Marne 1914   Aisne 1914   Ypres 1914, '17   Langemarck 1914   Gheluvelt   Nonne Bosschen   Neuve Chapelle   Aubers   Festubert 1915   Loos   Somme 1916, '18   Ginchy   Flers-Courcelette   Morval   Pilckem   Menin Road   Poelcappelle   Passchendaele   Cambrai 1917, '18   St Quentin   Bapaume 1918   Arras 1918   Lys   Hazebrouck   Albert 1918   Scarpe 1918   Hindenburg Line   Havrincourt   Canal du Nord   Selle   Sambre   France and Flanders 1914–18   Dyle   Dunkirk 1940   Cagny   Mont Pincon   Nijmegen   Reichswald   Rhine   North-West Europe 1940, '44–45   Mareth   Medjez Plain   North Africa 1942–43   Salerno   Volturno Crossing   Monte Camino   Anzio   Gothic Line   Battaglia   Italy 1943–45

Regimental headquarters

Wellington Barracks, Birdcage Walk, London.

Regimental museum

The Guards Museum, Wellington Barracks, Birdcage Walk, London.

Regimental marches

(quick) The British Grenadiers (traditional), and
The Grenadiers March (traditional)
(slow) Scipio (Handel), and The Duke of York (traditional)

Regimental motto

Honi Soit Qui Mal y Pense (Evil be to Him who Evil Thinks)

Nicknames

The Sandbags, The Coalheavers, The Old Eyes, The Bermuda Exiles, (3rd Battalion only) The Bill Brown's (none recognized by the regiment)

Uniform

Scarlet with blue facings, the full dress uniform having evenly spaced buttons, and the bearskin cap having a white plume on the left

Allied regiments

none

Regimental history

The Grenadier Guards is the senior regiment of the Foot Guards, which are the personal attendants of the reigning sovereign, and as such the infantry equivalent of the Household Cavalry. The regiment originated in 1656 as The Royal Regiment of Guards, raised by the exiled Charles II and commanded by Colonel The Lord Wentworth. At the time of Charles II's restoration in 1660 another regiment was raised under Colonel John Russel, and this was styled The King's Own Regiment of Foot Guards. On the death of Lord Wentworth in 1665 the two regiments were amalgamated as The Royal Regiment of Foot Guards, in 1685 redesignated the First Regiment of Foot Guards. After the distinguished part it played in the

Battle of Waterloo, in which it defeated the Imperial Guard of the Emperor Napoleon, the regiment was in 1815 redesignated the First or Grenadier Regiment of Foot Guards. The final modification to the regiment's title came in 1877, when it became the Grenadier Guards. The only imperial regiment affiliated to the Grenadier Guards was the Canadian Grenadier Guards.

REGIMENTS OF FOOT GUARDS 2

Coldstream Guards

Colonel-in-Chief

HM The Queen

Colonel

Major-General Sir George Burns

Battle honours

Tangier 1680   Namur 1695   Gibraltar 1704–05   Blenheim   Oudenarde   Malplaquet   Dettingen   Lincelles   Talavera   Barrosa   Fuentes d'Onor   Salamanca   Nive   Peninsula   Waterloo   Alma   Inkerman   Sevastopol   Tel-el-Kebir   Egypt 1882   Suakin 1885   Modder River   South Africa 1899–1902   Mons   Retreat from Mons   Marne 1914   Aisne 1914   Ypres 1914, '17   Langemarck 1914   Gheluvelt   Nonne Bosschen   Neuve Chapelle   Aubers   Festubert 1915   Loos   Mount Sorrel   Somme 1916, '18   Flers-Courcelette   Morval   Pilckem   Menin Road   Poelcappelle   Passchendaele   Cambrai 1917, '18   St Quentin   Bapaume 1918   Arras 1918   Lys   Hazebrouck   Albert 1918   Scarpe 1918   Drocourt-Queant   Hindenburg Line   Havrincourt   Canal du Nord   Selle   Sambre   France and Flanders 1914–18   Dyle   Defence of Escaut   Dunkirk 1940   Cagny   Mont Pincon   Quarry Hill   Estry   Hepper   Nederrijn   Venraij   Meijel   Hochwald   Rhine   Lingen   Uelzen   North-West Europe 1940, '44–45   Egyptian Frontier 1940   Sidi Barrani

Halfaya 1941   Tobruk 1941, '42   Msus   Knightsbridge   Defence of Alamein Line   Medenine   Mareth   Longstop Hill 1942   Sbiba   Steamroller Farm   Tunis   Hammam Lif   North Africa 1940–43   Salerno   Battipaglia   Cappezano   Volturno Crossing   Monte Camino   Calabritto   Garigliano Crossing   Monte Ornito   Monte Piccolo   Capture of Perugia   Arezzo   Advance to Florence   Monte Domini   Catarelto Ridge   Argenta Gap   Italy 1943–45

Regimental headquarters

Wellington Barracks, Birdcage Walk, London.

Regimental museum

The Guards Museum, Wellington Barracks, Birdcage Walk, London.

Regimental marches

(quick) Milanollo (Van Hamm)
(slow) Figaro (Mozart)

Regimental motto

Nulli Secundus (Second to none)

Nicknames

The Coldstreamers, Nulli Secundus Club

Uniform

Scarlet with blue facings, the full dress uniform having buttons in pairs, and the bearskin cap having a scarlet plume on the right

Allied regiments

The Governor General's Foot Guards (Canada)
2nd/14th Battalion The Royal Australian Regiment

Regimental history

The Coldstream Guards is the second-ranking regiment of Foot Guards, but has in fact a longer record of continuous service than the Grenadier Guards. The regiment also possesses the distinction of being the only current regiment of the British army with a lineal descent from the Parliamentary Army of the Protectorate. The regiment was raised by Colonel George Monck in 1650 from Northumberland troops (five companies of Hesilbridge's Regiment and five companies of Fenwick's Regiment, both at Newcastle) as Colonel Monck's Regiment of Foot. After the elevation of Monck to the peerage as the Duke of Albemarle, the regiment was in 1660 restyled the Duke of Albemarle's Regiment of Foot, which was also known as The Lord General's Regiment of Foot. In 1661 the title was modified slightly to the Duke of Albemarle's Regiment of Foot Guards. Albemarle died in 1670, and his regiment was then retitled the Coldstream Regiment of Foot Guards in recognition of the regiment's march from Coldstream to London to secure the success of Charles II's restoration in 1660. Since 1670 the name of the regiment has changed but once, in 1855 to the Colstream Guards. The only imperial regiment affiliated to the Coldstream Guards was the Governor General's Foot Guards (Canada).

REGIMENTS OF FOOT GUARDS 3

Scots Guards

Colonel-in-Chief

HM The Queen

Colonel

Major-General HRH The Duke of Kent

Battle honours

Namur 1695 Dettingen Lincelles Egypt (with the Sphinx) Talavera Barrosa Fuentes d'Onor Salamanca Nive Peninsula Waterloo Alma Inkerman Sevastopol Tel-el-Kebir Egypt 1882 Suakin 1885 Modder River South Africa 1899–1902 Retreat from Mons Marne 1914 Aisne 1914 Ypres 1914, '17 Langemarck 1914 Gheluvelt Nonne Bosschen Givenchy 1914 Neuve Chapelle Aubers Festubert 1915 Loos Somme 1916, '18 Flers-Courcelette Morval Pilckem Poelcappelle Passchendaele Cambrai 1917, '18 St Quentin Albert 1918 Bapaume 1918 Arras 1918 Drocourt-Queant Hindenburg Line Havrincourt Canal du Nord Selle Sambre France and Flanders 1914–18 Stien Norway 1940 Mont Pincon Quarry Hill Estry Venlo Pocket Rhineland Reichswald Cleve Moyland Hochwald Rhine Lingen Uelzen North-West Europe 1944–45 Halfaya 1941 Sidi Suleiman Tobruk 1941 Gazala Knightsbridge Defence of Alamein Line Medenine Tadjera Khir Medjez Plain Grich el Oued Djebel Bou Aoukaz 1943, I

North Africa 1941–43 Salerno Battipaglia Volturno Crossing
Rocchetta e Croce Monte Camino Anzio Campoleone Carroceto
Trasimene Line Advance to Florence Monte San Michele
Catarelto Ridge Argenta Gap Italy 1944–45 Tumbledown Mountain
Falkland Islands 1982

Regimental headquarters

Wellington Barracks, Birdcage Walk, London.

Regimental museum

The Guards Museum, Wellington Barracks, Birdcage Walk, London.

Regimental marches

(quick) Highland Laddie (traditional)
(slow) In the Garb of Old Gaul (Reid)

Regimental motto

Nemo Me Impune Lacessit (No one Provokes me with Impunity)

Nicknames

The Jocks, The Kiddies

Uniform

Scarlet with blue facings, the full dress uniform having the buttons in triplets, and the bearskin cap having no plume; the tartan is Royal Stuart

Allied regiment

3rd Battalion The Royal Australian Regiment

Regimental history

The Scots Guards is the third regiment of Foot Guards, and was raised in 1662 at the express instruction of Charles II. Adherents of the regiments point out, however, that in 1642 Charles I raised in Scotland a Royal Regiment commanded by the Marquess of Argyll for service in quelling the Irish rebellion of the period. The remnants of this prototype regiment returned to Scotland in 1649, and in 1650 became the Footte Regiment of

His Majesties Lyffe Guardes under the command of Lord Lorne, the son of the Marquess of Argyll. The regiment was splintered in the aftermath of the Battle of Worcester in 1651. On his restoration in 1660, Charles II ordained that the English garrisons in Scottish cities be replaced by Scots units, and two companies were raised for this role, the first in Edinburgh and the second in Dumbarton. In May 1662 Charles II ordered that these two companies should be supplemented by four new companies to make a New Regiment of Foot Guards under the command of the Earl of Linlithgow. This regiment had many links with the erstwhile Footte Regiment of His Majesties Lyffe Guardes, and was known by a number of titles in the period between 1662 and 1686: Our Regiment of Guards, His Majesties Regiment of Guards, The King's Regiment, The King's Foot Guards, The King's Lyfe Guards of Foot, The Regiment of Guard of Foot, and Linlithgow's Regiment. In 1686 the regiment was redesignated the Scotch Guards (or Scotts Guards), and subsequent changes were to the Third Regiment of Foot Guards in 1712, to the Scots Fusilier Guards in 1831 and to the Scots Guards in 1877. The only imperial regiment affiliated to the Scots Guards was the Winnipeg Grenadiers (Canada).

REGIMENTS OF FOOT GUARDS 4

Irish Guards

Colonel-in-Chief

HM The Queen

Colonel

HRH The Grand Duke of Luxembourg

Battle honours

Mons   Retreat from Mons   Marne 1914   Aisne 1914   Ypres 1914, '17   Langemarck 1914   Gheluvelt   Nonne Bosschen   Festubert 1915   Loos   Somme 1916, '18   Flers-Courcelette   Morval   Pilckem   Poelcappelle   Passchendaele   Cambrai 1917, '18   St Quentin   Lys   Hazebrouck   Albert 1918   Bapaume 1918   Arras 1918   Scarpe 1918   Drocourt-Queant   Hindenburg Line   Canal du Nord   Selle   Sambre   France and Flanders 1914–18   Pothus   Norway 1940   Boulogne 1940   Cagny   Mont Pincon   Neerpelt   Nijmegen   Aam   Rhineland   Hochwald   Rhine   Bentheim   North-West Europe 1944–45   Nedjez Plain   Djebel Bou Aoukaz 1943   North Africa 1943   Anzio   Aprilia   Carroceto   Italy 1943–44

Regimental headquarters

Wellington Barracks, Birdcage Walk, London.

Regimental museum

The Guards Museum, Wellington Barracks, Birdcage Walk, London.

Regimental marches

(quick) St Patrick's Day (traditional)
(slow) Let Erin Remember (traditional)

Regimental motto

Quis Separabit? (Who Shall Separate?)

Nicknames

Bob's Own, The Micks

Uniform

Scarlet with blue facings, the full dress uniform having its buttons grouped in fours and the bearskin cap having a blue plume on the right

Allied regiment

2nd/4th Battalion The Royal Australian Regiment

Regimental history

The Irish Guards was raised as recently as April 1900 at the instigation of Queen Victoria, who wished to show her appreciation of the part played by Irish soldiers in the 2nd Boer War. The official mascot of the regiment is an Irish wolfhound.

REGIMENTS OF FOOT GUARDS 5

Welsh Guards

Colonel-in-Chief

HM The Queen

Colonel

HRH The Prince of Wales

Battle honours

Loos   Somme 1916, '18   Ginchy   Flers-Courcelette   Morval   Ypres 1917   Pilckem   Poelcappelle   Passchendaele   Cambrai 1917, '18   Bapaume 1918   Arras 1918   Albert 1918   Drocourt-Queant   Hindenburg Line   Havrincourt   Canal du Nord   Selle   Sambre   France and Flanders 1915–18   Defence of Arras   Boulogne 1940   St Omer-La-Bassee   Bourgebus Ridge   Cagny   Mont Pincon   Brussels   Hechtel   Nederrijn   Rhineland   Lingen   North-West Europe 1940, '44–45   Fondouk   Djebel Rhorab   Tunis   Hammam Lif   North Africa 1943   Monte Ornito   Liri Valley   Monte Piccolo   Capture of Perugia   Arezzo   Advance to Florence   Gothic Line   Battaglia   Italy 1944–45   Falkland Islands 1982

Regimental headquarters

Wellington Barracks, Birdcage Walk, London.

Regimental museum

The Guards Museum, Wellington Barracks, Birdcage Walk, London.

Regimental marches

(quick) The Rising of the Lark (traditional)
(slow) Men of Harlech (traditional)

Regimental motto

Cymru am Byth (Wales for Ever)

Nicknames

The Taffs

Uniform

Scarlet with blue facings, the full dress uniform having its buttons grouped in fives, and the bearskin cap having a green and white plume on its left

Allied regiment

5th/7th Battalion The Royal Australian Regiment

Regimental history

The Welsh Guards was raised in February 1915 by George V, its nucleus being formed by Welshmen from other regiments of the Foot Guards.

REGIMENTS OF INFANTRY: ORDER OF PRECEDENCE

1. The Royal Scots (The Royal Regiment)
2. The Queen's Regiment
3. The King's Own Royal Border Regiment
4. The Royal Regiment of Fusiliers
5. The King's Regiment
6. The Royal Anglian Regiment
7. The Devonshire and Dorset Regiment
8. The Light Infantry
9. The Prince of Wales's Own Regiment of Yorkshire
10. The Green Howards (Alexandra, Princess of Wales's Own Yorkshire Regiment)
11. The Royal Highland Fusiliers (Princess Margaret's Own Glasgow and Ayrshire Regiment)
12. The Cheshire Regiment
13. The Royal Welch Fusiliers
14. The Royal Regiment of Wales (24th/41st Foot)
15. The King's Own Scottish Borderers
16. The Cameronians (Scottish Rifles) (disbanded in 1968 but still shown in the Army List)
17. The Royal Irish Rangers (27th [Inniskilling], 83rd and 87th)
18. The Gloucestershire Regiment
19. The Worcestershire and Sherwood Foresters Regiment (29th/45th Foot)
20. The Queen's Lancashire Regiment
21. The Duke of Wellington's Regiment (West Riding)
22. The Royal Hampshire Regiment
23. The Staffordshire Regiment (The Prince of Wales's)
24. The Black Watch (Royal Highland Regiment)
25. The Duke of Edinburgh's Royal Regiment (Berkshire and Wiltshire)
26. The York and Lancaster Regiment (disbanded in 1968 but still shown in the Army List)
27. The Queen's Own Highlanders (Seaforth and Camerons)
28. The Gordon Highlanders

29. The Argyll and Sutherland Highlanders (Princess Louise's)
30. The Parachute Regiment
31. The Brigade of Gurkhas
32. The Royal Green Jackets

For administrative purposes the regiments of Foot Guards and Infantry (excluding the Brigade of Gurkhas and the three battalions of The Parachute Regiment) are divided into six divisions, organized as follows:

The Guards Division

(Divisional Headquarters at Wellington Barracks, Birdcage Walk, London)

1st Battalion Grenadier Guards
2nd Battalion Grenadier Guards
1st Battalion Coldstream Guards
2nd Battalion Coldstream Guards
1st Battalion Scots Guards
2nd Battalion Scots Guards
1st Battalion Irish Guards
1st Battalion Welsh Guards

The Scottish Division

(Divisional Headquarters at The Castle, Edinburgh, Scotland)

1st Battalion The Royal Scots (The Royal Regiment)
1st Battalion The Royal Highlanders (Princess Margaret's Own Glasgow and Ayrshire Regiment)
1st Battalion The King's Own Scottish Borderers
1st Battalion The Black Watch (Royal Highland Regiment)
1st Battalion The Queen's Own Highlanders (Seaforth and Camerons)
1st Battalion The Gordon Highlanders
1st Battalion The Argyll and Sutherland Highlanders (Princess Louise's)

The Queen's Division

(Divisional Headquarters at Bassingbourn Barracks, Royston, Hertfordshire)

1st Battalion The Queen's Regiment
2nd Battalion The Queen's Regiment
3rd Battalion The Queen's Regiment
4th Battalion The Queen's Regiment (Albuhera Company)
1st Battalion The Royal Regiment of Fusiliers
2nd Battalion The Royal Regiment of Fusiliers
3rd Battalion The Royal Regiment of Fusiliers
1st Battalion The Royal Anglian Regiment
2nd Battalion The Royal Anglian Regiment
3rd Battalion The Royal Anglian Regiment
4th Battalion The Royal Anglian Regiment

The King's Division

(Divisional Headquarters at Imphal Barracks, York, Yorkshire)

1st Battalion The King's Own Border Regiment
1st Battalion The King's Regiment
1st Battalion The Prince of Wales's Own Regiment of Yorkshire
1st Battalion The Green Howards (Alexandra, Princess of Wales's Own Yorkshire Regiment)
1st Battalion The Royal Irish Rangers (27th [Inniskilling], 83rd and 87th)
2nd Battalion The Royal Irish Rangers (27th [Inniskilling], 83rd and 87th)
1st Battalion The Queen's Lancashire Regiment
1st Battalion The Duke of Wellington's Regiment (West Riding)

The Prince of Wales's Division

(Divisional Headquarters at Whittington Barracks, Lichfield, Staffordshire)

1st Battalion The Devonshire and Dorset Regiment
1st Battalion The Cheshire Regiment
1st Battalion The Royal Welch Fusiliers
1st Battalion The Gloucestershire Regiment
1st Battalion The Worcestershire and Sherwood Foresters Regiment (29th/45th Foot)
1st Battalion The Royal Hampshire Regiment
1st Battalion The Staffordshire Regiment (The Prince of Wales's)
1st Battalion The Duke of Edinburgh's Royal Regiment (Berkshire and Wiltshire)

The Light Division

(Divisional Headquarters at Peninsula Barracks, Winchester, Hampshire)

1st Battalion The Light Infantry
2nd Battalion The Light Infantry
3rd Battalion The Light Infantry
1st Battalion The Royal Green Jackets
2nd Battalion The Royal Green Jackets
3rd Battalion The Royal Green Jackets

REGIMENTS OF INFANTRY 1

The Royal Scots (The Royal Regiment) (1st)

Colonel-in-Chief

HRH The Princess Royal Mrs Mark Phillips

Colonel

Lieutenant-General Sir Robert Richardson

Battle honours

Tangier 1680   Namur 1695   Blenheim   Ramillies   Oudenarde   Malplaquet   Louisburg   Havannah   Egmont-op-Zee   Egypt (with the Sphinx)   St Lucia 1803   Corunna   Busaco   Salamanca   Vittoria   St Sebastian   Nive   Peninsula   Niagara   Waterloo   Nagpore   Maheidpoor   Ava   Alma   Inkerman   Sevastopol   Taku Forts   Pekin 1860   South Africa 1899–1902   Mons   Le Cateau   Retreat from Mons   Marne 1914, '18   Aisne 1914   La Bassee 1914   Neuve Chapelle   Ypres 1915, '17, '18   Gravenstafel   St Julien   Frezenberg   Bellewaarde   Aubers   Festubert 1914   Loos   Somme 1916, '18   Albert 1916, '18   Bazentin   Pozieres   Flers-Courcelette   Le Transloy   Ancre Heights   Ancre 1916, '18   Arras 1917, '18   Scarpe 1917, '18   Arleux   Pilckem   Langemarck 1917   Menin Road   Polygon Wood   Poelcappelle   Passchendaele   Cambrai 1917   St Quentin   Rosieres   Lys   Estaires   Messines 1918   Hazebrouck   Bailleul   Kemmel   Bethune   Soissonais-

Ourcq   Tardenois   Amiens   Bapaume 1918   Drocourt-Queant
Hindenburg Line   Canal du Nord   St Quentin Canal   Beaurevoir
Courtrai   Selle   Sambre   France and Flanders 1914–18   Struma
Macedonia 1915–18   Helles   Landing at Helles   Krithia   Suvla
Scimitar Hill   Gallipoli 1915–16   Rumani   Egypt 1915–16   Gaza
El Mughar   Nebi Samwil   Jaffa   Palestine 1917–18   Archangel
1918–19   Dyle   Defence of Escaut   St Omer-La Bassee   Odon
Cheux   Defence of Rauray   Caen   Esquay   Mont Pincon   Aart
Nederrijn   Best   Scheldt   Flushing   Meijel   Venlo Pocket   Roer
Rhineland   Reichwald   Cleve   Goch   Rhine   Uelzen   Bremen
Artlenberg   North-West Europe 1940, '44–45   Gothic Line   Maradi
Monte Gamberaldi   Italy 1944–45   South East Asia 1941   Donbaik
Kohima   Relief of Kohima   Aradura   Shwebo   Mandalay
Burma 1943–45

Regimental headquarters

The Castle, Edinburgh, Scotland.

Regimental museum

The Castle, Edinburgh, Scotland.

Regimental marches

(quick) Dumbarton's Drums (traditional),
and The Daughter of the Regiment (Donizetti)
(slow) In the Garb of Old Gaul (Reid)

Regimental motto

Nemo Me Impune Lacessit (No one Provokes me with Impunity)

Nickname

Pontius Pilate's Bodyguard

Uniform

Archer green doublet with blue facings, and Hunting Stuart trews

Allied regiments

The Canadian Scottish Regiment (Princess Mary's)
The Newfoundland Regiment (Canada)
10th Princess Mary's Own Gurkha Rifles (affiliated regiment)

Regimental history

The Royal Scots (The Royal Regiment) is undoubtedly the regiment of the British army with the longest record of continuous service, as indicated by the regiment's nickname. The regiment originated in 1633, when Sir John Hepburn was authorized by Charles I to raise a Scots regiment for French service under Louis XIII's flag. The regiment was later bolstered by the survivors of a Scots force under Earl Gray. This had been despatched by James I to the aid of Bohemia in the Thirty Years War, had itself been augmented by Mackay's Scots force in Denmark to create the Green Brigade of some 13 regiments. Moreover, Le Régiment d'Hébron (French rendition of Hepburn) raised in 1633 was officered by descendants of the Garde Ecossaise raised by Charles III of France, 'The Simple' (893–923), and later transformed into the Scottish Archer Corps by Henri IV of France (1589–1610), a fact which sometimes leads to spurious claims for an even greater antiquity on behalf of The Royal Scots. In 1637 Le Régiment d'Hébron became Le Régiment de Douglas, and twice crossed to England to secure the restoration of Charles II. In 1661 the regiment became part of the British establishment, but it was not until 1678 that the regiment returned to Britain and became the Earl of Dumbarton's Regiment (1st Foot). The regiment was then shipped to Tangier, and for its services as part of the garrison in that enclave was renamed The Royal Regiment of Foot during 1684. In 1751 it was restyled the 1st (or the Royal) Regiment of Foot, and restoration of the Scottish connection followed in 1812, when the regiment was retitled the 1st (or the Royal Scots) Regiment of Foot. Further development along the same lines resulted in the titles the 1st (or the Royal) Regiment of Foot in 1821, the 1st (The Royal Scots) Regiment in 1871, the Lothian Regiment (The Royal Scots) in 1881, The Royal Scots (Lothian Regiment) in 1882 and the definitive The Royal Scots (The Royal Regiment) in 1920. The exceptional service of the regiment over some 350 years is well illustrated by the impressive list of battle honours. The only imperial regiment affiliated to The Royal Scots (The Royal Regiment) was the Canadian Scottish Regiment (Highlanders).

REGIMENTS OF INFANTRY 2

The Queen's Regiment (2nd, 3rd, 31st, 35th, 50th, 57th, 70th, 77th, 97th and 107th)

Colonels-in-Chief

HRH Princess Juliana of the Netherlands, and HM Queen Margarethe II of Denmark

Colonel

Brigadier H. C. Millman

Battle honours

Tangier 1662–80 Namur 1695 Gibraltar 1704–05 Blenheim Ramillies Oudenarde Malplaquet Dettingen Louisburg Guadaloupe 1759 Quebec 1759 Belleisle Martinique 1762 Havannah St Lucia 1778 Mysore Martinique 1794 Seringapatam Egypt (with the Sphinx) Maida Vimiera Corunna Douro Talavera Guadaloupe 1810 Albuhera Almarez Ciudad Rodrigo Badajoz Salamanca Vittoria Pyrenees Nivelle Nive Orthes Toulouse Peninsula Ghuznee 1839 Khelat Affghanistan 1839 Cabool 1842 Punniar Mookdee Ferozeshah Aliwal Sobraon South Africa 1851–53 Alma Inkerman Sevastopol Lucknow Taku Forts Pekin 1860 New Zealand Afghanistan 1878–79 South Africa

1870 Egypt 1882 Abu Klea Nile 1884–85 Suakin 1885 Burmah 1885–87 Chitral Tirah Relief of Ladysmith Relief of Kimberley Paardeberg South Africa 1899–1902 Mons Le Cateau Retreat from Mons Marne 1914, '18 Aisne 1914 La Bassee 1914 Messines 1914, '17, '18 Armentieres 1914 Ypres 1914, '15, '17, '18 Langemarck 1914, '17 Gheluvelt Nonne Bosschen Givenchy 1914 Neuve Chapelle Hill 60 Gravenstafel St Julien Frezenberg Bellewaarde Aubers Festubert 1915 Hooge 1915 Loos Somme 1916, '18 Albert 1916, '18 Bazentin Delville Wood Pozieres Guillemont Ginchy Flers-Courcelette Morval Thiepval Le Transloy Ancre Heights Ancre 1916, '18 Bapaume 1917, '18 Arras 1917, '18 Vimy 1917 Scarpe 1917, '18 Arleux Oppy Bullecourt Pilckem Menin Road Polygon Wood Broodseinde Poelcappelle Passchendaele Cambrai 1917, '18 St Quentin Rosieres Avre Villers Bretonneux Lys Estaires Hazebrouck Bailleul Kemmel Scherpenberg Soisonnais-Ourcq Amiens Drocourt-Queant Hindenburg Line Epehy Canal du Nord St Quentin Canal Beaurevoir Courtrai Selle Valenciennes Sambre France and Flanders 1914–18 Piave Vittorio Veneto Italy 1917–18 Struma Doiran 1917, '18 Macedonia 1917–18 Suvla Landing at Suvla Scimitar Hill Gallipoli 1915 Rumani Egypt 1915–17 Gaza El Mughar Nebi Samwil Jerusalem Jericho Jordan Tell' Asur Megiddo Sharon Palestine 1917–18 Aden Defence of Kut al Amara Tigris 1916 Kut al Amara 1917 Baghdad Khan Baghdadi Sharqat Mesopotamia 1915–18 NW Frontier India 1915, '16–17 Murman 1918–19 Dukhovskaya Siberia 1918–19 Dyle Defence of Escaut Amiens 1940 St Omer-La Bassee Foret de Nieppe Ypres-Comines Canal Dunkirk 1940 Withdrawal to Seine Normandy Landing Cambes Breville Villers Bocage Odon Caen Orne Hill 112 Bourgebus Ridge Troarn Mont Pincon Falaise Seine 1944 Nederrijn Le Havre Lower Maas Venraij Meijel Geilenkirchen Venlo Pocket Roer Rhineland Reichswald Goch Rhine Lingen Brinkum Bremen North-West Europe 1940, '44–45 Karora-Marsa Taclai Cub Cub Mescelit Pass Keren Mt Englahat Massawa Abyssinia 1941 Syria 1941 Sidi Barrani Sidi Suleiman Tobruk 1941 Tobruk Sortie Omars Alem Hamza Benghazi Alam el Halfa Deir el Munassib El Alamein El Agheila Advance on Tripoli Medenine Mareth Tebaga Gap El Hamma Akarit Djebel el Meida Djebel Roumana Djebel Abiod Tebourba Djebel Azzag 1942, '43 Robaa Valley Fort McGregor Oued Zarga Djebel Bech Chekaoui Djebel Ang Heidous Djebel Djaffa Pass Medjez Plain Longstop Hill 1943 Si Abdallah Tunis Montarnaud North Africa 1940–43 Francofonte Sferro Adrano Sferro Hills Centuripe Monte Rivoglia Sicily 1943 Termoli Trigno San Salvo

Sangro Romagnoli Impossible Bridge Villa Grande Salerno Monte Stella Scafati Bridge Volturno Crossing Monte Camino Garigliano Crossing Damiano Anzio Carroceto Cassino Monastery Hill Castle Hill Liri Valley Aquino Piedimonte Hill Rome Trasimene Line Arezzo Advance to Florence Monte Scalari Gothic Line Coriano Pian di Castello Gemmano Ridge Monte Reggiano Capture of Forli Casa Fortis Senio Pocket Senio Floodbank Rimini Line Casa Fabbri Ridge Savio Bridgehead Monte Pianoereno Monte Spaduro Monte Grande Senio Menate Filo Argenta Gap Italy 1943–45 Greece 1944–45 Leros Middle East 1943 Malta 1940–42 Kampar Malaya 1941–42 Hong Kong South-East Asia 1941 North Arakan Razabil Mayu Tunnels Kohima Defence of Kohima Pinwe Shweli Myitson Taungtha Yenangyaung 1945 Sittang 1945 Chindits 1944 Burma 1943–45 Naktong Bridgehead Chongju Chongchon II Chaum-i Kapyong-chon Kapyong Korea 1950–51

Regimental headquarters

Howe Barracks, Canterbury, Kent.

Regimental museum

Howe Barracks, Canterbury, Kent.

Regimental marches

(quick) The Soldiers of the Queen (Stuart)
(slow) The Caledonian (traditional)

Regimental motto

Unconquered I Serve

Nicknames

see below

Uniform

Scarlet with blue facings

Allied regiments

The Queen's York Rangers (1st American Regiment) (Canada)
The South Alberta Light Horse (Canada)

The Queen's Own Rifles of Canada
The Hastings and Prince Edward Regiment (Canada)
1st Battalion The Royal New Brunswick Regiment (Carleton and York) (Canada)
The Essex and Kent Scottish Regiment (Canada)
The Royal New South Wales Regiment (Australia)
The Royal Western Australia Regiment
The University of New South Wales Regiment
2nd Battalion (Canterbury, Nelson, Marlborough and West Coast) The Royal New Zealand Infantry Regiment
5th Battalion (Wellington, West Coast and Taranaki) The Royal New Zealand Infantry Regiment
12th, 14th, 15th and 17th Battalions The Punjab Regiment (Pakistan)
The Royal Hong Kong Regiment (The Volunteers)

Regimental history

The Queen's Regiment was formed in December 1966 by the amalgamation of four existing regiments, namely The Queen's Royal Surrey Regiment; The Queen's Own Buffs, The Royal Kent Regiment; The Royal Sussex Regiment; and The Middlesex Regiment (Duke of Cambridge's Own). Each of these regiments was itself the result of a previous amalgamation in the period from 1959 to 1966, so The Queen's Regiment in fact combines 10 infantry regiments existing in the period before the Cardwell army reforms of 1881.

The Queen's Royal Surrey Regiment (2nd, 31st and 70th) was brought into existence in October 1959 by the amalgamation of The Queen's Royal Regiment (West Surrey) and The East Surrey Regiment.

The Queen's Own Buffs, The Kent Regiment (3rd, 50th and 97th) was formed in March 1961 by the amalgamation of The Buffs (Royal East Kent Regiment) and The Queen's Own Royal West Kent Regiment.

The Royal Sussex Regiment (35th and 107th) came into being in 1881 through the amalgamation of the 35th (Royal Sussex) Regiment and the 107th (Bengal Infantry) Regiment.

The Middlesex Regiment (Duke of Cambridge's Own) (57th and 77th) was produced in 1881 by the amalgamation of the 57th (West Middlesex) Regiment and the 77th (East Middlesex) Regiment (Duke of Cambridge's Own).

The senior component of The Queen's Royal Surrey Regiment was The Queen's Royal Regiment (West Surrey) (2nd), which could trace its origins back to 1661, when the Earl of Peterborough raised The Tangier Regiment of Foot as part of the garrison of Tangier. In 1684 this regiment became The Queen's Regiment of Foot, in 1686 The Queen Dowager's Regiment of Foot, in 1703 The Queen's Royal Regiment, in 1714 HRH The Princess of Wales's Own Regiment of Foot, in 1727 The Queen's Own Regiment of Foot, in 1751 The Queen's (Second) Royal Regiment of Foot, in 1855 the 2nd (Queen's Royal) Regiment, in 1881 The Queen's (Royal West Surrey Regiment) and in 1921 The Queen's Royal Regiment (West Surrey). The battle honours of the regiment were the following:

Tangier 1662–80   Namur 1695   Egypt (with the Sphinx)   Vimiera   Corunna   Salamanca   Vittoria   Pyrenees   Nivelle   Toulouse   Peninsula   Ghuznee 1839   Khelat   Affghanistan 1839   South Africa 1851–53   Taku Forts   Pekin 1860   Burmah 1885–87   Tirah   Relief of Ladysmith   South Africa 1899–1902   Mons   Retreat from Mons   Marne 1914, '18   Aisne 1914   Ypres 1914, '17, '18   Langemarck 1914   Gheluvelt   Aubers   Festubert 1915   Loos   Somme 1916, '18   Albert 1916   Bazentin   Delville Wood   Pozieres   Guillemont   Flers-Courcelette   Morval   Thiepval   Le Transloy   Ancre Heights   Ancre 1916, '18   Arras 1917, '18   Scarpe 1917   Bullecourt   Messines 1917   Pilckem   Menin Road   Polygon Wood   Broodseinde   Passchendaele   Cambrai 1917, '18   St Quentin   Bapaume 1918   Rosieres   Avre   Villers Bretonneux   Lys   Hazebrouck   Bailleul   Kemmel   Soisonnais-Ourcq   Amiens   Hindenburg Line   Epehy   St Quentin Canal   Courtrai   Selle   Sambre   France and Flanders 1914–18   Piave   Vittorio Veneto   Italy 1917–18   Struma   Doiran 1917   Macedonia 1916–17   Suvla   Landing at Suvla   Scimitar Hill   Gallipoli 1915   Rumani   Egypt 1915–17   Gaza   El Mughar   Nebi Samwil   Jerusalem   Jericho   Jordan   Tell' Asur   Megiddo   Sharon   Palestine 1917–18   Khan Baghdadi   Mesopotamia 1915–18   NW Frontier   India 1916–17   Afghanistan 1919   Defence of Escaut   Villers Bocage   Mont Pincon   Lower Maas   Roer   North-West Europe 1940, '44–45   Syria 1941   Sidi Barrani   Tobruk 1941   Tobruk Sortie   Deir el Munassib   El Alamein   Advance on Tripoli   Medenine   Tunis   North Africa 1940–43   Salerno   Monte Stella   Scafati Bridge   Volturno Crossing   Monte Camino   Garigliano Crossing   Damiano   Anzio   Gothic Line   Gemmano Ridge   Senio Pocket   Senio Floodbank   Casa Fabbri Ridge   Menate   Filo   Argenta Gap   Italy 1943–45   North Arakan   Kohima   Yenangyaung 1945   Sittang 1945   Chindits 1944   Burma 1943–45

The mottoes of the regiment were 'Pristinae Virtutis Memor' (Mindful of Former Virtue) and 'Vel Exuviae Triumphant' (Even in Defeat Triumphant), and the regimental marches were 'Old Queens', 'Braganza' and 'We'll gang nae mair to Yon Town' (quick) and 'Scipio' (slow). The uniform was scarlet with blue facings, and the nicknames associated with The Queen's Royal Regiment were 'The Queens', 'The Tangerines', 'Kirke's Lambs', 'The Lambs' and 'The Mutton Lancers', the reference to Tangiers celebrating the regiment's garrison period there, that to Kirke commemorating the regiment's association with Kirke of the 'Bloody Assizes', and that to sheep indicating the regiment's badge. Imperial regiments affiliated to The Queen's Royal Regiment (West Surrey) were The Queen's Rangers and the 1st American Regiment (Canada), and the 2nd Battalion, Australian Infantry.

The second component of The Queen's Royal Surrey Regiment was The East Surrey Regiment (31st and 70th), formed in 1881 by the amalgamation of the 31st (Huntingdonshire) Regiment and the 70th (Surrey) Regiment. The battle honours of the regiment were the following:

Gibraltar 1704–05   Dettingen   Martinique 1794   Talavera   Guadaloupe 1810   Albuhera   Vittoria   Pyrenees   Nivelle   Nive   Orthes   Peninsula   Cabool 1842   Mookdee   Ferozeshah   Aliwal   Sobraon   Sevastopol   Taku Forts   New Zealand   Afghanistan 1878–79   Suakin 1885   Relief of Ladysmith   South Africa 1899–1902   Mons   Le Cateau   Retreat from Mons   Marne 1914   Aisne 1914   La Bassee 1914   Armentieres 1914   Hill 60   Ypres 1915, '17, '18   Gravenstafel   St Julien   Frezenberg   Bellewaarde   Loos   Somme 1916, '18   Albert 1916, '18   Bazentin   Delville Wood   Pozieres   Guillemont   Flers-Courcelette   Morval   Thiepval   Le Transloy   Ancre Heights   Ancre 1916   Arras 1917, '18   Vimy 1917   Scarpe 1917   Messines 1917   Pilckem   Langemarck 1917   Menin Road   Polygon Wood   Broodseinde   Poelcappelle   Passchendaele   Cambrai 1917, '18   St Quentin   Bapaume 1918   Rosieres   Avre   Lys   Estaires   Hazebrouck   Amiens   Hindenburg Line   Epehy   Canal du Nord   St Quentin Canal   Courtrai   Selle   Sambre   France and Flanders 1914–18   Italy 1917–18   Struma   Doiran 1918   Macedonia 1915–18   Egypt 1915   Aden   Mesopotamia 1917–18   Murman 1919   Defence of Escaut   Dunkirk 1940   North-West Europe 1940   Tebourba   Fort McGregor   Oued Zarga   Djebel Ang   Djebel Djaffa Pass   Medjez Plain   Longstop Hill 1943   Tunis   Montarnaud   North Africa 1942–43   Adrano   Centuripe   Sicily 1943   Trigno   Sangro   Cassino   Capture of Forli   Argenta Gap   Italy 1943–45   Greece 1944–45   Kampar   Malaya 1941–42

The motto of the regiment was 'Honi Soit Qui Mal y Pense' (Evil be to Him who Evil Thinks), and the regimental marches were 'A Southerly Wind and a Cloudy Sky', 'The Lass o' Gowrie' and (from 1942) 'A Life on the Ocean Wave' (quick), and 'Lord Charles Montague's Huntingdonshire March' (slow). The uniform was scarlet with white facings, and the nicknames associated with The East Surrey Regiment were 'The Young Buffs' (1st Battalion) and 'The Glasgow Greys' (2nd Battalion). Imperial regiments affiliated to The East Surrey Regiment were the South Alberta Regiment (Canada), the 17th Battalion, Australian Infantry, and the Otago Regiment (New Zealand).

The senior of the components of The East Surrey Regiment was the 31st

(Huntingdonshire) Regiment, initially raised in 1702 by Colonel George Villiers and named Colonel Villiers' Regiment of Marines. The name changed in accordance with the names of the regiment's colonels until 1713, when the title 31st Regiment of Foot was adopted. In 1782 this was changed to the 31st (or Huntingdonshire) Regiment of Foot, and in 1855 that was further modified to the 31st (Huntingdonshire) Regiment. The battle honours of the regiment were the following:

Gibraltar 1704–05   Dettingen   Martinique 1794   Talavera   Albuhera   Vittoria   Pyrenees   Nivelle   Nive   Orthes   Peninsula   Cabool 1842   Mookdee   Ferozeshah   Aliwal   Sobraon   Sevastopol   Taku Forts

The uniform of the regiment was scarlet with buff facings, and the nickname associated with the 31st (Huntingdonshire) Regiment was 'The Young Buffs'.

The junior partner in The East Surrey Regiment was the 70th (Surrey) Regiment, which had been raised in 1756 in Glasgow as the 2nd Battalion of the 31st Regiment of Foot, but two years later separated as an independent regiment, the 70th Regiment of Foot. In 1782 this became the 70th (or The Surrey) Regiment of Foot before reverting to its Scots association in 1813 with the designation 70th (or Glasgow Lowland) Regiment of Foot. In 1825, however, the title changed to the 70th (or Surrey) Regiment of Foot, and finally in 1855 to the 70th (Surrey) Regiment. The battle honours of the regiment were the following:

Guadaloupe 1810   New Zealand   Afghanistan 1879–80

The uniform was scarlet with black facings, and the nickname associated with the 70th (Surrey) Regiment was 'The Glasgow Greys'.

The second component element of The Queen's Regiment was The Queen's Own Buffs, The Royal Kent Regiment (3rd, 50th and 97th). The regiment was formed in March 1961 by the amalgamation of The Buffs (Royal East Kent Regiment) (3rd) and The Queen's Own Royal West Kent Regiment (50th and 97th).

The senior of the two regiments was The Buffs, which had been raised in 1665 by Colonel Robert Sydney as The Holland Regiment in recognition of the fact that many of the officers and men had previously served with the London 'Train-Bands' which had served the Protestant cause in Holland between 1572 and 1665. In 1689 the regiment became Prince George of Denmark's Regiment of Foot (3rd Foot), but was properly known as The Buffs. This latter was recognized officially in 1751, when the regiment became the 3rd (or The Buffs) Regiment of Foot. Further changes followed, and the regiment became the 3rd (or the East Kent) Regiment of Foot, or The Buffs in 1782, the 3rd (East Kent, The Buffs) Regiment in 1855, The Buffs (East Kent Regiment) in 1881 and finally The Buffs (Royal East Kent Regiment) in 1935. The battle honours of the regiment were the following:

Blenheim Ramillies Oudenarde Malplaquet Dettingen Guadaloupe 1759 Belleisle Douro Talavera Albuhera Vittoria Pyrenees Nivelle Nive Orthes Toulouse Peninsula Punniar Sevastopol Taku Forts South Africa 1879 Chitral Relief of Kimberley Paardeberg South Africa 1900–02 Aisne 1914 Armentieres 1914 Ypres 1915, '17 Gravenstafel St Julien Frezenberg Bellewaarde Hooge 1915 Loos Somme 1916, '18 Albert 1916, '18 Bazentin Delville Wood Pozieres Flers-Courcelette Morval Thiepval Le Transloy Ancre Heights Ancre 1916 '18 Arras 1917 Scarpe 1917 Messines 1917 Pilckem Passchendaele Cambrai 1917, '18 St Quentin Avre Amiens Bapaume 1918 Hindenburg Line Epehy St Quentin Canal Selle Sambre France and Flanders 1914–18 Struma Doiran 1918 Macedonia 1915–18 Gaza Jerusalem Tell' Asur Palestine 1917–18 Aden Tigris 1916 Kut al Amara 1917 Baghdad Mesopotamia 1915–18 Defence of Escaut St Omer-La Bassee Withdrawal to Seine North-West Europe 1940 Sidi Suleiman Alem Hamza Alam el Halfa El Alamein El Agheila Advance on Tripoli Tebaga Gap Djebel Bech Chekaoui Heidous Medjez Plain Longstop Hill 1943 North Africa 1941–43 Centuripe Monte Rivoglia Sicily 1943 Termoli Trigno Sangro Anzio Carroceto Cassino I Liri Valley Aquino Rome Trasimene Line Coriano Monte Spaduro Senio Argenta Gap Italy 1943–45 Leros Middle East 1943 Malta 1940–42 Shweli Myitson Burma 1945

The mottoes of the regiment were 'Veteri Frondescit Honore' (Ever Green with Ancient Honour) and 'Invicta' (Unconquered), and the regimental marches were 'The Buffs' (quick) and 'The Men of Kent' (slow). The uniform was scarlet with buff facings, and the nicknames associated with The Buffs were 'The Old Buffs', 'The Nutcrackers' and 'The Resurrectionists', the last in reference to the regiment's claim to a lineage at least as long as that of The Royal Scots. Imperial regiments affiliated to The Buffs were the Queen's Own Rifles (Canada), the Irish Fusiliers (Vancouver Regiment) (Canada), and the 3rd Battalion, Australian Infantry.

The junior partner in The Queen's Own Buffs, The Royal Kent Regiment was The Queen's Own Royal West Kent Regiment, the result of the 1881 amalgamation of the 50th (Queen's Own) Regiment and the 97th (Earl of Ulster's) Regiment of Foot. The initial name of the new regiment was The Queen's Own (Royal West Kent Regiment), which was changed to The Royal West Kent Regiment (Queen's Own) in 1921 and to The Queen's Own Royal West Kent Regiment during 1922. The battle honours of the combined regiment were the following:

Egypt (with the Sphinx) Vimiera Corunna Almarez Vittoria Pyrenees Nive Orthes Peninsula Punniar Mookdee

Ferozeshah Aliwal Sobraon Alma Inkerman Sevastopol Lucknow New Zealand Egypt 1882 Nile 1884–85 South Africa 1900–02 Mons Le Cateau Retreat from Mons Marne 1914 Aisne 1914 La Bassee 1914 Messines 1914, '17 Ypres 1914, '15, '17, '18 Hill 60 Gravenstafel St Julien Frezenberg Loos Somme 1916, '18 Albert 1916, '18 Bazentin Delville Wood Pozieres Guillemont Flers-Courcelette Morval Thiepval Le Transloy Ancre Heights Ancre 1916, '18 Arras 1917, '18 Vimy 1917 Scarpe 1917 Oppy Pilckem Langemarck 1917 Menin Road Polygon Wood Broodseinde Passchendaele Cambrai 1917, '18 St Quentin Rosieres Avre Villers Bretonneux Lys Estaires Hazebrouck Kemmel Amiens Bapaume 1918 Hindenburg Line Epehy Canal du Nord St Quentin Canal Courtrai Selle Sambre France and Flanders 1914–18 Italy 1917–18 Suvla Landing at Suvla Scimitar Hill Gallipoli 1915 Rumani Egypt 1915–16 Gaz El Mughar Jerusalem Jericho Tell' Asur Palestine 1917–18 Defence of Kut al Amara Sharqat Mesopotamia 1915–18 Afghanistan 1919 Defence of Escaut Foret de Nieppe North-West Europe 1940 Alam el Halfa El Alamein Djebel Abiod Djebel Azzag 1942 Oued Zarga Djebel Ang Medjez Plain Longstop Hill 1943 Si Abdallah North Africa 1942–43 Centuripe Monte Rivoglia Sicily 1943 Termoli San Salvo Sangro Romagnoli Impossible Bridge Villa Grande Cassino Castle Hill Liri Valley Piedimonte Hill Trasimene Line Arezzo Advance to Florence Monte Scalari Casa Fortis Rimini Line Savio Bridgehead Monte Pianoereno Monte Spaduro Senio Argenta Gap Italy 1943–45 Greece 1944–45 Leros Malta 1940–42 North Arakan Razabil Mayu Tunnels Defence of Kohima Myitson Taungtha Sittang 1945 Burma 1943–45

The mottoes of the regiment were 'Quo Fas et Gloria Ducunt' (Whither Right and Glory Lead) and 'Invicta' (Unconquered), and the regimental marches were 'A Hundred Pipers' (quick) and 'The Men of Kent' (slow). The uniform was scarlet with blue facings, and the nicknames associated with The Queen's Own Royal West Kent Regiment were 'The Gallant 50th', 'The Dirty Half Hundred', 'The Black Half Hundred' and 'The Blind Half Hundred' (1st Battalion), 'The Celestials' (2nd Battalion), 'The Devil's Royals' and 'Old Black Cuffs'. Imperial regiments affiliated with The Queen's Own Royal West Kent Regiment were the Carleton Light Infantry (Canada), the Kent Regiment (Canada), and the Canterbury Regiment (New Zealand).

Within the Queen's Own Royal West Kent Regiment the senior of the components was the 50th (Queen's Own) Regiment, which had been raised in January 1756 by Colonel James Abercromby as the 52nd Regiment of Foot but redesignated in December 1756 as the 50th Regiment of Foot. In

1782 the regiment became the 50th or West Kent Regiment of Foot, in 1827 the 50th (or the Duke of Clarence's) Regiment of Foot, in 1831 the 50th or The Queen's Own Regiment of Foot, and finally in 1855 the 50th (Queen's Own) Regiment. The battle honours of the regiment were the following:

> Egypt (with the Sphinx)   Vimiera   Corunna   Almaraz   Vittoria
> Pyrenees   Nive   Orthes   Peninsula   Punniar   Mookdee
> Ferozeshah   Aliwal   Sobraon   Alma   Inkerman   Sevastopol
> New Zealand

The motto of the regiment was 'Invicta' (Unconquered), and the regimental march was 'A Hundred Pipers' (quick). The uniform was scarlet with blue facings, and the nicknames associated with the 50th (Queen's Own) Regiment were 'The Dirty Half Hundred' and 'The Blind Half Hundred'.

The junior component of The Queen's Own Royal West Kent Regiment was the 97th (Earl of Ulster's) Regiment of Foot, which was raised in 1824 and remained unchanged in name until its amalgamation with the 50th (Queen's Own) Regiment in 1881. The two battle honours of the regiment were the following:

> Sevastopol   Lucknow

The motto of the regiment was 'Quo Fas et Gloria Ducunt' (Whither Right and Glory Lead), and the regimental march was 'Paddy's Resource' (quick). The uniform was scarlet with sky blue facings, and the nickname associated with the 97th (Earl of Ulster's) Regiment of Foot was 'The Celestials' for the colour of the regiment's facings.

The third major component of The Queen's Regiment was The Royal Sussex Regiment (35th and 107th), itself formed in 1881 by the amalgamation of the 35th (Royal Sussex) Regiment and the 107th (Bengal Infantry) Regiment. The battle honours of the regiment were the following:

> Gibraltar 1704–05   Louisburg   Quebec 1759   Martinique 1762
> Havannah   St Lucia 1778   Maida   Egypt 1882   Abu Klea   Nile
> 1884–85   South Africa 1900–02   Mons   Retreat from Mons   Marne
> 1914   Aisne 1914   Ypres 1914, '17, '18   Gheluvelt   Nonne Boschen
> Givenchy 1914   Aubers   Loos   Somme 1916, '18   Albert 1916, '18
> Bazentin   Delville Wood   Pozieres   Flers-Courcelette   Morval
> Thiepval   Le Transloy   Ancre Heights   Ancre 1916, '18   Arras
> 1917, '18   Vimy 1917   Scarpe 1917   Arleux   Messines 1917   Pilckem
> Langemarck 1917   Menin Road   Polygon Wood   Broodseinde
> Poelcappelle   Passchendaele   Cambrai 1917, '18   St Quentin
> Bapaume 1918   Rosieres   Avre   Lys   Kemmel   Scherpenberg
> Soisonnais-Ourcq   Amiens   Drocourt-Queant   Hindenburg Line
> Epehy   St Quentin Canal   Beaurevoir   Courtrai   Selle   Sambre

France and Flanders 1914–18   Piave   Vittorio Veneto   Italy 1917–18
   Suvla   Landing at Suvla   Scimitar Hill   Gallipoli 1915   Rumani
Egypt 1915–17   Gaza   El Mughar   Jerusalem   Jericho   Tell' Asur
Palestine 1917–18   NW Frontier India 1915, '16–17   Murman 1918–19
   Defence of Escaut   Amiens 1940   St Omer-La Bassee   Foret de
Nieppe   North-West Europe 1940   Karora-Marsi Taclai   Cub Cub
   Mescelit Pass   Keren   Mt Englahat   Massawa   Abyssinia 1941
       Omars   Benghazi   Alam el Halfa   El Alamein   Akarit
Djebel el Meida   Tunis   North Africa 1940–43   Cassino   Monastery Hill
   Gothic Line   Pian di Castello   Monte Reggiano   Italy 1944–45
       North Arakan   Pinwe   Shweli   Burma 1943–45

The motto of the regiment was 'Honi Soit Qui Mal y Pense' (Evil be to Him who Evil Thinks), and the regimental marches were 'The Royal Sussex' (quick) and 'Roussillon' (slow). The uniform was scarlet with blue facings, and the nickname associated with The Royal Sussex Regiment was 'The Orange Lilies' in commemoration of the regiment's capture of the Roussillon Grenadiers' standard (with golden fleur-de-lys motif) at Quebec in 1759, and of its adherence to William of Orange. Imperial regiments affiliated to The Royal Sussex Regiment were the Hastings and Prince Edward Regiment (Canada) and the 11th Battalion, Australian Infantry.

Senior of the two regiments that went to form The Royal Sussex Regiment was the 35th (Royal Sussex) Regiment, which had been raised during 1701 in Belfast by the Earl of Donegal as The Earl of Donegal's Regiment of Foot, but was also known as The Belfast Regiment. Up to 1751 the regiment changed names with its colonels, but then became the 35th Regiment of Foot. In 1782 the regiment became the 35th (or the Dorsetshire) Regiment of Foot, and in 1805 the 35th (or the Sussex) Regiment of Foot, a trend continued in 1832 when the regiment became the 35th (Royal Sussex) Regiment. The battle honours of the regiment were the following:

   Quebec 1759   Louisburg   Maida

The regimental marches were 'The Royal Sussex' (quick) and 'Roussillon' (slow), and the uniform was scarlet with blue facings. The nickname associated with the 35th was 'The Orange Lilies'.

Junior of The Royal Sussex Regiment's components was the 107th (Bengal Infantry) Regiment, which had been raised in 1854 as the 3rd Bengal European Infantry in the army of the Honourable East India Company. The regiment was reallocated to the British establishment in 1861 as the 107th (Bengal Infantry) Regiment. The regimental march was 'The Lass of Richmond Hill' (quick), and the uniform was scarlet with white facings. The 107th had no battle honours.

The last major component of The Queen's Regiment was The Middlesex Regiment (Duke of Cambridge's Own) (57th and 77th), which had been formed in 1881 as The Duke of Cambridge's Own (Middlesex Regiment) by the amalgamation of the 57th (West Middlesex) Regiment with the 77th (East Middlesex) Regiment (Duke of Cambridge's Own). In 1922 the combined regiment was redesignated The Middlesex Regiment (Duke of Cambridge's Own). The battle honours of the combined regiment were the following:

Mysore   Seringapatam   Albuhera   Ciudad Rodrigo   Badajoz   Salamanca   Vittoria   Pyrenees   Nivelle   Nive   Peninsula   Alma   Inkerman   Sevastopol   New Zealand   South Africa 1870   Relief of Ladysmith   South Africa 1900–02   Mons   Le Cateau   Retreat from Mons   Marne 1914   Aisne 1914   La Bassee 1914   Messines 1914, '17, '18   Neuve Chapelle   Ypres 1914, '17, '18   Gravenstafel   St Julien   Frezenberg   Bellewaarde   Aubers   Hooge 1915   Loos   Somme 1916, '18   Albert 1916, '18   Bazentin   Delville Wood   Pozieres   Ginchy   Flers-Courcelette   Morval   Thiepval   Le Transloy   Ancre Heights   Ancre 1916, '18   Bapaume 1917, '18   Arras 1917   Vimy 1917   Scarpe 1917, '18   Arleux   Pilckem   Langemarck 1917   Menin Road   Polygon Wood   Broodseinde   Poelcappelle   Passchendaele   Cambrai 1917, '18   St Quentin   Rosieres   Avre   Villers Bretonneux   Lys   Estaires   Hazebrouck   Bailleul   Kemmel   Scherpenberg   Hindenburg Line   Canal du Nord   St Quentin Canal   Courtrai   Selle   Valenciennes   Sambre   France and Flanders 1914–18   Italy 1917–18   Struma   Doiran 1918   Macedonia 1915–18   Suvla   Landing at Suvla   Scimitar Hill   Gallipoli 1915   Rumani   Egypt 1915–17   Gaza   El Mughar   Jerusalem   Jericho   Jordan   Tell' Asur   Megiddo   Palestine 1917–18   Mesopotamia 1917–18   Murman 1918–19   Dukhovskaya   Siberia 1918–19   Dyle   Defence of Escaut   Ypres-Comines Canal   Dunkirk 1940   Normandy Landing   Cambes   Breville   Odon   Caen   Orne   Hill 112   Bourgebus Ridge   Troarn   Mont Pincon   Falaise   Seine 1944   Nederrijn   Le Havre   Lower Maas   Venraij   Meijel   Geilenkirchen   Venlo Pocket   Rhineland   Reichswald   Goch   Rhine   Lingen   Brinkum   Bremen   North-West Europe 1940, '44–45   El Alamein   Advance on Tripoli   Mareth   Akarit   Francofonte   Sferro   Sferro Hills   Sicily 1943   Anzio   Carroceto   Gothic Line   Monte Grande   Italy 1944–45   Hong Kong   South-East Asia 1941   Naktong Bridgehead   Chongju   Chongchon II   Chaum-Ni   Kapyong-chon   Kapyong   Korea 1950–51

The motto of the regiment was 'Ich Dien' (I Serve), and the regimental marches were 'Sir Manley Power' and 'Paddy's Resource' (quick), and 'Caledonian' and 'In the Garb of Old Gaul' (slow). The uniform was scarlet with lemon yellow facings, and the nicknames associated with The Middlesex Regiment were 'The Die Hards' (1st Battalion), 'The Pot Hooks' (2nd Battalion), and 'The Steel Backs'. Imperial regiments affiliated to

The Middlesex Regiment were the Peterborough Rangers (Canada), the Wentworth Regiment (Canada), the Middlesex Light Infantry (Canada), the 57th Battalion, Australian Infantry, and the Taranki Regiment (New Zealand).

Senior of The Middlesex Regiment's components was the 57th (West Middlesex) Regiment, which had been raised in 1755 as the 59th Regiment of Foot, being renumbered the 57th Regiment of Foot in 1957. In 1782 the regiment became the 57th (or the West Middlesex) Regiment of Foot, and this title remained unaltered until the regiment's amalgamation with the 77th (East Middlesex) Regiment in 1881. The battle honours of the regiment were the following:

Albuhera   Vittoria   Pyrenees   Nivelle   Nive   Peninsula   Inkerman
Sevastopol   New Zealand   South Africa 1879

The motto of the regiment was 'Honi Soit Qui Mal y Pense' (Evil be to Him who Evil Thinks), and the regimental marches were 'Sir Manley Power' (quick) and 'Caledonian' (slow). The uniform was scarlet with yellow facings, and the nicknames associated with the 57th (West Middlesex) Regiment were 'The Die Hards' and 'The Steel Backs', the former in recognition of the 57th's stand at Albuhera in 1811, when the regiment lost 422 out of 570 all ranks, all hit in the front.

Junior of The Middlesex Regiment's components was the 77th (East Middlesex) Regiment, raised in 1787 as the 77th Regiment of Foot. In 1807 the regiment became the 77th (The East Middlesex) Regiment of Foot, and in 1876 the 77th (East Middlesex) Regiment (Duke of Cambridge's Own). The battle honours of the regiment were the following:

Mysore   Seringapatam   Ciudad Rodrigo   Badajoz   Peninsula   Alma
Inkerman   Sevastopol

The motto of the regiment was 'Honi Soit Qui Mal y Pense' (Evil be to Him who Evil Thinks), and the regimental march was 'Paddy's Resource' (quick). The uniform was scarlet with yellow facings, and the nickname associated with the 77th (East Middlesex) Regiment was 'The Pot Hooks' in reference to the regiment's numerical designation.

REGIMENTS OF INFANTRY 3

The King's Own Royal Border Regiment (4th, 34th and 55th)

Colonel-in-Chief

HRH The Princess Alexandra the Hon. Mrs Angus Ogilvy

Colonel

Major-General D. E. Miller

Battle honours

Namur 1695 Gibraltar 1704-05 Guadaloupe 1759 Havannah St Lucia 1778 Corunna Albuhera Arroyo dos Molinos Badajoz Salamanca Vittoria St Sebastian Pyrenees Nivelle Nive Orthes Peninsula Bladensburg Waterloo China (with the Dragon) Alma Inkerman Sevastopol Lucknow Abyssinia South Africa 1879 Relief of Ladysmith South Africa 1899-1902 Le Cateau Retreat from Mons Marne 1914 Aisne 1914 Armentieres 1914 Ypres 1914, '15, '17, '18 Langemarck 1914, '17 Gheluvelt Neuve Chapelle Gravenstafel St Julien Frezenberg Bellewaarde Aubers Festubert 1915 Lox Somme 1916, '18 Albert 1916, '18 Bazentin Delville Wood Pozieres Guillemont Ginchy Flers-Courcelette Morval Thiepval Le Transloy Ancre Heights Ancre 1916 Arras 1917, '18 Scarpe 1917, '18 Arleux Bullecourt Messines 1917, '18 Pilckem Menin Road Polygon Wood Broodseinde Poelcappelle

Passchendaele   Cambrai 1917, '18   St Quentin   Rosieres   Lys Estaires   Hazebrouck   Bailleul   Kemmel   Bethune   Scherpenberg   Aisne 1918   Amiens   Bapaume 1918   Drocourt-Queant   Hindenburg Line   Epehy   Canal du Nord   St Quentin Canal   Beaurevoir   Courtrai   Selle   Valenciennes   Sambre   France and Flanders 1914-18   Piave   Vittorio Veneto   Italy 1917-18   Struma   Doiran 1917, '18   Macedonia 1915-18   Helles   Landing at Helles   Krithia   Suvla   Sari Bair   Landing at Suvla   Scimitar Hill   Gallipoli 1915-16   Egypt 1916   Tigris 1916   Kut al Amara 1917   Baghdad   Mesopotamia 1916-18   NW Frontier India 1916-17   Afghanistan 1919   Defence of Escaut   St Omer-La Bassee   Dunkirk 1940   Somme 1940   Arnhem 1944   North-West Europe 1940, '44   Defence of Habbaniya   Falluja   Iraq 1941   Merjayun   Jebel Mazar   Syria 1941   Tobruk 1941   Tobruk Sortie   North Africa 1940-42   Landing in Sicily   Montone   Citta di Castello   San Martino Sogliano   Lamone Bridgehead   Italy 1944-45   Malta 1941-42   Imphal   Sakawng   Tamu Road   Shenam Pass   Kohima   Ukhrul   Mandalay   Myinmu Bridgehead   Meiktila   Rangoon Road   Pyawbwe   Sittang 1945   Chindits 1944   Burma 1943-45

Regimental headquarters

The Castle, Carlisle, Cumbria.

Regimental museums

(The King's Own Royal Regiment) City Museum, Market Square, Lancaster, Lancashire.
(The Border Regiment and The King's Own Royal Border Regiment) The Castle, Carlisle, Cumbria.

Regimental marches

(quick) Arrangement of D'Ye Ken John Peel, Lass O'Gowrie and Corn Rigs are Bonnie
(slow) And Shall Trelawny Die

Regimental motto

Honi Soit Qui Mal y Pense (Evil be to Him who Evil Thinks)

Nicknames

see below

Uniform

Blue with scarlet piping and blue facings

Allied regiments

The King's Own Calgary Regiment (Canada)
The Queensland Regiment (Australia)
15th Battalion The Frontier Force Regiment (Pakistan)

Regimental history

The King's Own Royal Border Regiment was formed in April 1959 by the amalgamation of The King's Own Royal Regiment (Lancaster) and The Border Regiment.

The senior of these two components was The King's Own Royal Regiment (Lancaster) (4th), whose history went back to 1680 and the raising of a Tangier garrison regiment by the Earl of Plymouth. This was ranked as the 4th Foot, and was named The Earl of Plymouth's Regiment of Foot for Tangier. The regiment then underwent the usual series of title changes, first to The Duchess of York and Albany's Regiment in 1684, then to The Queen's Own Regiment of Foot in 1685, then to the Royal Regiment of Marines in 1703, then to designations based on its colonels' names between 1710 and 1715, and to The King's Own Regiment of Foot in 1715. This association with the king was retained thereafter, the regiment becoming the 4th (or The King's Own) Regiment of Foot in 1747, the 4th (The King's Own) Regiment of Foot) in 1759, The King's Own (Royal Lancaster Regiment) in 1881 and The King's Own Regiment (Lancaster) in 1921. The regiment's battle honours were the following:

Namur 1695   Gibraltar 1704–05   Guadaloupe 1759   St Lucia 1778   Corunna   Badajoz   Salamanca   Vittoria   St Sebastian   Pyrenees   Nive   Peninsula   Bladensburg   Waterloo   Alma   Inkerman   Sevastopol   Abyssinia   South Africa 1879   Relief of Ladysmith   South Africa 1899–1902   Le Cateau   Retreat from Mons   Marne 1914   Aisne 1914   Armentieres 1914   Ypres 1915, '17   Gravenstafel   St Julien   Frezenberg   Bellewaarde   Festubert 1915   Loos   Somme 1916, '18   Albert 1916, '18   Bazentin   Delville Wood   Pozieres   Guillemont   Ginchy   Flers-Courcelette   Morval   Le Transloy   Ancre Heights   Ancre 1916   Arras 1917, '18   Scarpe 1917, '18   Arleux   Messines 1917   Pilckem   Menin Road   Polygon Wood   Broodseinde   Poelcappelle   Passchendaele   Cambrai 1917, '18   St Quentin   Lys   Estaires   Hazebrouck   Bethune   Bapaume 1918   Drocourt-Queant   Hindenburg Line   Epehy   Canal du Nord   Selle   Valenciennes   Sambre   France and Flanders 1914–18   Struma   Doiran 1917, '18

Macedonia 1915–18   Suvla   Sari Bair   Gallipoli 1915   Egypt 1916
Tigris 1916   Kut al Amara 1917   Baghdad   Mesopotamia 1916–18
St Omer-La Bassee   Dunkirk 1940   North-West Europe 1940   Defence
of Habbaniya   Falluja   Iraq 1941   Merjayun   Jebel Mazar   Syria 1941
Tobruk 1941   Tobruk Sortie   North Africa 1940–42   Montone
Citta di Castello   San Martino Sogliano   Lamone Bridgehead
Italy 1944–45   Malta 1941–42   Chindits 1944   Burma 1944

The motto of the regiment was 'Honi Soit Qui Mal y Pense' (Evil be to Him who Evil Thinks), and the regimental marches were 'Corn Rigs are Bonnie' (quick) and 'And Shall Trelawny Die' (slow). The uniform was blue with scarlet pipings and blue facings, and the nicknames associated with The King's Own Royal Regiment were 'The Lions' and 'Barrell's Blues'. The only imperial regiment affiliated to The King's Own Royal Regiment was the Calgary Regiment (Canada).

The junior partner to The King's Own Royal Regiment in The King's Own Royal Regiment (Lancaster) was The Border Regiment (34th and 55th), formed in 1881 by the amalgamation of the 34th (Cumberland) Regiment and the 55th (Westmorland) Regiment. The battle honours of this combined regiment were the following:

Havannah   St Lucia 1778   Albuhera   Arroyo dos Molinos   Badajoz
Vittoria   Pyrenees   Nivelle   Nive   Orthes   Peninsula   Alma
Inkerman   Sevastopol   Lucknow   Relief of Ladysmith   South Africa
1899–1902   Ypres 1914, '15, '17, '18   Langemarck 1914, '17   Gheluvelt
Neuve Chapelle   Frezenberg   Bellewaarde   Aubers   Festubert
1915   Loos   Somme 1916, '18   Albert 1916, '18   Bazentin   Delville
Wood   Pozieres   Guillemont   Flers-Courcelette   Morval   Thiepval
Le Transloy   Ancre Heights   Ancre 1916   Arras 1917, '18   Scarpe 1917
Bullecourt   Messines 1917, '18   Pilckem   Polygon Wood
Broodseinde   Poelcappelle   Passchendaele   Cambrai 1917, '18
St Quentin   Rosieres   Lys   Estaires   Hazebrouck   Bailleul   Kemmel
Scherpenberg   Aisne 1918   Amiens   Bapaume 1918   Hindenburg
Line   Epehy   St Quentin Canal   Beaurevoir   Courtrai   Selle
Sambre   France and Flanders 1914–18   Piave   Vittorio Veneto   Italy
1917–18   Struma   Doiran 1917, '18   Macedonia 1915–18   Helles
Landing at Helles   Krithia   Suvla   Landing at Suvla   Scimitar Hill
Gallipoli 1915–16   Egypt 1916   NW Frontier India 1916–17   Afghanistan
1919   Defence of Escaut   Dunkirk 1940   Somme 1940   Arnhem 1944
North-West Europe 1940, '44   Tobruk 1941   Landing in Sicily   Imphal
Sakawng   Tamu Road   Shenam Pass   Kohima   Ukhrul   Mandalay
Myinmu Bridgehead   Meiktila   Rangoon Road   Pyawbwe
Sittang 1945   Chindits 1944   Burma 1943–45

The motto of the regiment was 'Honi Soit Qui Mal y Pense' (Evil be to Him who Evil Thinks), and the regimental march was an arrangement of 'D'Ye Ken John Peel', '34me Regiment March' and 'Lass O'Gowrie'. The uniform was scarlet with yellow piping and facings, and nicknames associated with The Border Regiment were 'The Cattle Reeves' and 'The Two Fives'. Imperial regiments affiliated to The Border Regiment were the Saskatchewan Border Regiment (Canada) and the 31st Battalion, Australian Infantry.

Of the two regiments that joined in 1881 to form The Border Regiment, the senior was the 34th (Cumberland) Regiment, originally raised in 1702 as Lord Lucas's Regiment of Foot, and known in the period up to 1747 by the names of its colonels. In 1747 the regiment became the 34th Regiment of Foot, and in 1782 the 34th (or Cumberland) Regiment of Foot. The battle honours of the regiment were the following:

    Albuhera   Arroyo dos Molinos   Vittoria   Pyrenees   Nivelle   Nive   Orthes   Peninsula   Sevastopol   Lucknow

The motto of the regiment was 'Honi Soit Qui Mal y Pense' (Evil be to Him who Evil Thinks), and the regimental march was 'D'Ye Ken John Peel' (quick). The uniform was scarlet with yellow facings, and the nickname associated with the 34th was 'The Cattle Reeves'. At the battle of Arroyo dos Molinos (1811), the regiment captured the French 34me Regiment complete with band equipment, and on the anniversary the drums are trooped by the regimental drummer boys in French uniform.

Junior partner to the 34th (Cumberland) Regiment was the 55th (Westmorland) Regiment, which had been raised in 1755 as the 57th Regiment of Foot. In 1757 this was restyled the 55th Regiment of Foot, and in 1782 became the 55th (or the Westmorland) Regiment of Foot. The regiment's battle honours were the following:

    China (with the Dragon)   Alma   Inkerman   Sevastopol

The motto of the regiment was 'Honi Soit Qui Mal y Pense' (Evil be to Him who Evil Thinks), and the regimental march was 'The Lass o'Gowrie' (quick). The uniform was scarlet with facings of Kendal green, and the nickname associated with the 55th was 'The Two Fives'.

REGIMENTS OF INFANTRY 4

The Royal Regiment of Fusiliers (5th, 6th, 7th and 20th)

Colonel-in-Chief

Major-General HRH The Duke of Kent

Colonel

Major-General J. C. Reilly

Battle honours

Namur 1695   Dettingen   Minden   Wilhelmstahl   St Lucia 1778   Martinique 1794, 1809   Egmont-op-Zee   Egypt (with the Sphinx)   Maida   Rolica   Vimiera   Corunna   Talavera   Busaco   Ciudad Rodrigo   Badajoz   Albuhera   Salamanca   Vittoria   Pyrenees   Nivelle   Orthes   Toulouse   Peninsula   Niagara   South Africa 1846–47, 1851–53   Alma   Inkerman   Sevastopol   Lucknow   Kandahar 1880   Afghanistan 1878–80   Atbara   Khartoum   Modder River   Relief of Ladysmith   South Africa 1899–1902   Mons   Le Cateau   Retreat from Mons   Marne 1914, '18   Aisne 1914, '18   La Bassee 1914   Messines 1914, '17, '18   Armentieres 1914   Ypres 1914, '15, '17, '18   Langemarck 1914, '17   Gheluvelt   Nonne Bosschen   Neuve Chapelle   Gravenstafel   St Julien   Frezenberg   Bellewaarde   Hooge 1915   Aubers   Festubert 1915   Loos   Somme 1916, '18   Albert 1916, '18   Bazentin   Delville Wood   Pozieres   Guillemont

Ginchy Flers-Courcelette Morval Thiepval Le Transloy Ancre Heights Ancre 1916, '18 Arras 1917, '18 Vimy 1917 Scarpe 1917, '18 Arleux Bullecourt Oppy Pilckem Menin Road Polygon Wood Broodseinde Poelcappelle Passchendaele Cambrai 1917, '18 St Quentin Bapaume 1918 Rosieres Avres Villers Bretonneux Lys Estaires Hazebrouck Bailleul Kemmel Bethune Scherpenberg Amiens Drocourt-Queant Hindenburg Line Havrincourt Epehy Canal du Nord St Quentin Canal Beaurevoir Courtrai Selle Valenciennes Sambre France and Flanders 1914-18 Piave Vittorio Veneto Italy 1917-18 Struma Doiran 1917 Macedonia 1915-18 Helles Landing at Helles Krithia Suvla Sari Bair Landing at Suvla Scimitar Hill Gallipoli 1915-16 Rumani Egypt 1915-17 Megiddo Nablus Palestine 1918 Tigris 1916 Kut al Amara 1917 Baghdad Mesopotamia 1916-18 Baku Persia 1918 Troitsa Archangel 1919 Kilimanjaro Behobeho Nyangao East Africa 1915-17 Defence of Escaut Arras Counter Attack St Omer-La Bassee Wormhoudt Ypres-Comines Canal Dunkirk 1940 Normandy Landing Odon Caen Bourgebus Ridge Cagny Mont Pincon Falaise Nederrijn Venraij Rhineland Lingen Brinkum Bremen North-West Europe 1940, '44-45 Agordat Keren Syria 1941 Sidi Barrani Defence of Tobruk Tobruk 1941 Belhamed Cauldron Ruweisat Ridge El Alamein Advance on Tripoli Medenine Djebel Tebaga Medjez el Bab Oued Zarga Peter's Corner North Africa 1940-43 Adrano Sicily 1943 Termoli Trigno Sangro Mozzagrogna Caldari Salerno St Lucia Battipaglia Teano Volturno Crossing Monte Camino Garigliano Crossing Damiano Anzio Cassino II Ripa Ridge Trasimene Line Gabbiano Advance to Florence Monte Scalari Gothic Line Coriano Croce Monte Ceco Casa Fortis Monte Spaduro Savio Bridgehead Valli di Comacchio Senio Argenta Gap Italy 1943-45 Athens Greece 1944-45 Malta 1941-42 Singapore Island Rathedaung Htizwe Kohima Naga Village Chindits 1944 Burma 1943-45 Seoul Imjin Kowang-San Korea 1950-53

Regimental headquarters

HM Tower of London, London.

Regimental museums

(Royal Northumberland Fusiliers) The Abbot's Tower, Alnwick Castle, Alnwick, Northumberland.
(The Royal Warwickshire Fusiliers) St John's House, Warwick, Warwickshire.

(The Royal Fusiliers) HM Tower of London, London.
(The Lancashire Fusiliers) Wellington Barracks, Bury, Lancashire.

Regimental marches

(quick) The British Grenadiers (traditional)
(slow) Rule Britannia (Arne)

Regimental motto

Honi Soit Qui Mal y Pense (Evil be to Him who Evil Thinks)

Nicknames

see below

Uniform

Scarlet with scarlet piping and blue facings

Allied regiments

The Elgin Regiment (Canada)
The Royal Canadian Regiment
The Lorne Scots (Peel, Dufferin and Halton Regiment) (Canada)
Les Fusiliers de St Laurent (Canada)
The Royal Westminster Regiment (Canada)
5th/6th Battalion The Royal Victoria Regiment (Australia)
6th Battalion (Hauraki) The Royal New Zealand Infantry Regiment

Regimental history

The Royal Regiment of Fusiliers was formed in April 1968 by the amalgamation of four celebrated fusilier regiments, namely The Royal Northumberland Fusiliers, The Royal Warwickshire Fusiliers, The Royal Fusiliers (City of London Regiment), and The Lancashire Fusiliers. The official mascot of the regiment is an Indian black buck.

The senior of the regiments that went into the amalgamation was The Royal Northumberland Fusiliers (5th), which had been raised in 1674 by Colonel Daniel O'Brien, Viscount Clare for service in Holland as part of the forces of Prince William of Orange. The regiment was thus known at first as Lord O'Brien's Regiment (or The Irish Regiment), and though recalled to Britain by James II in 1685, it returned to Holland in the following year and only came onto the British permanent establishment with the accession of William of Orange in 1688. The regiment was then ranked as the 5th Foot, and was known as Colonel Tollemache's Regiment of Foot. Up to 1751 the regiment changed its name with its colonels, but in that year became the 5th (or the Northumberland) Regiment of Foot. In 1836 it became the 5th Regiment of Foot (Northumberland Fusiliers), the regiment's two last changes of name following in 1881 to The Northumberland Fusiliers, and in 1935 to The Royal Northumberland Fusiliers. The regiment's battle honours were the following:

Wilhelmstahl   St Lucia 1778   Rolica   Vimiera   Corunna   Busaco   Ciudad Rodrigo   Badajoz   Salamanca   Vittoria   Nivelle   Orthes   Toulouse   Peninsula   Lucknow   Afghanistan 1878–80   Khartoum   Modder River   South Africa 1899–1902   Mons   Le Cateau   Retreat from Mons   Marne 1914   Aisne 1914   La Bassee 1914   Messines 1914, '17, '18   Armentieres 1914   Ypres 1914, '15, '17, '18   Nonne Bosschen   Gravenstafel   St Julien   Frezenberg   Bellewaarde   Loos   Somme 1916, '18   Albert 1916, '18   Bazentin   Delville Wood   Pozieres   Flers-Courcelette   Morval   Thiepval   Le Transloy   Ancre Heights   Ancre 1916   Arras 1917, '18   Scarpe 1917, '18   Arleux   Pilckem   Langemarck 1917   Menin Road   Polygon Wood   Broodseinde   Passchendaele   Cambrai 1917, '18   St Quentin   Bapaume 1918   Rosieres   Lys   Estaires   Hazebrouck   Bailleul   Kemmel   Bethune   Scherpenberg   Drocourt-Queant   Hindenburg Line   Epehy   Canal du Nord   St Quentin Canal   Beaurevoir   Courtrai   Selle   Valenciennes   Sambre   France and Flanders 1914–18   Piave   Vittorio Veneto   Italy 1917–18   Struma   Macedonia 1915–18   Suvla   Landing at Suvla   Scimitar Hill   Gallipoli 1915   Egypt 1916–17   Defence of Escaut   Arras Counter Attack   St Omer-La Bassee   Dunkirk 1940   Odon   Caen   Cagny   Falaise   Nederrijn   Rhineland   North-West Europe 1940, '44–45   Sidi Barrani   Defence of Tobruk   Tobruk 1941   Belhamed   Cauldron   Ruweisat Ridge   El Alamein   Advance on Tripoli   Medenine   North Africa 1940–43   Salerno   Volturno Crossing   Monte Camino   Garigliano Crossing   Cassino II   Italy 1943–45   Singapore Island   Seoul   Imjin   Kowang-San   Korea 1950–51

The motto of the regiment was 'Quo Fata Vocant' (Whither the Fates Summon), and the regimental marches were 'Blaydon Races' and 'The British Grenadiers' (quick), and 'St George' (slow). The uniform was scarlet with gosling green piping and facings, and the nicknames associated with The Royal Northumberland Fusiliers were 'The Fighting Fifth', 'The Old and Bold', 'The Shiners' and 'Wellesley's Bodyguard'. Imperial regiments affiliated to The Royal Northumberland Fusiliers were the Northumberland Regiment (Canada), the Elgin Regiment (Canada) and the 35th Battalion, Australian Infantry.

Next in seniority was The Royal Warwickshire Fusiliers (6th), raised in

1674 through the amalgamation of several companies fighting under the command of Sir Walter Vane in Holland for Prince William of Orange. This new regiment was commanded by Colonel Luke Lillingston, and was thus known as Colonel Lillingston's Regiment of Foot. The regiment moved to Britain with William of Orange in 1688, and came onto the British regular establishment as Colonel Babbington's Regiment of Foot, thereafter changing its name with its colonels in the period up to 1751, when it became the 6th Regiment of Foot. In 1782 the regiment became the 6th (or the 1st Warwickshire) Regiment of Foot, and in 1832 royal patronage was received to turn the regiment into the 6th (The Royal 1st Warwickshire) Regiment of Foot. Further changes came in 1881, when the regiment became The Royal Warwickshire Regiment, and in 1963, when the regiment became The Royal Warwickshire Fusiliers. The regiment's battle honours were the following:

Namur 1695   Martinique 1794   Rolica   Vimiera   Corunna   Vittoria   Pyrenees   Nivelle   Orthes   Peninsula   Niagara   South Africa 1846–47, '51–53   Alma   Inkerman   Sevastopol   Lucknow   Kandahar 1880   Afghanistan 1878–80   Atbara   Khartoum   South Africa 1899–1902   Le Cateau   Retreat from Mons   Marne 1914   Aisne 1914, '18   Armentieres 1914   Ypres 1914, '15, '17, '18   Langemarck 1914, '17   Gheluvelt   Neuve Chapelle   St Julien   Frezenberg   Bellewaarde   Aubers   Festubert 1915   Loos   Somme 1916, '18   Albert 1916, '18   Bazentin   Delville Wood   Pozieres   Guillemont   Flers-Courcelette   Morval   Le Transloy   Ancre Heights   Ancre 1916   Arras 1917, '18   Vimy 1917   Scarpe 1917, '18   Arleux   Oppy   Bullecourt   Messines 1917, '18   Pilckem   Menin Road   Polygon Wood   Broodseinde   Poelcappelle   Passchendaele   Cambrai 1917, '18   St Quentin   Bapaume 1918   Rosieres   Lys   Estaires   Hazebrouck   Bailleul   Kemmel   Bethune   Drocourt-Queant   Hindenburg Line   Epehy   Canal du Nord   Beaurevoir   Selle   Valenciennes   Sambre   France and Flanders 1914–18   Piave   Vittorio Veneto   Italy 1917–18   Suvla   Sari Bair   Gallipoli 1916–16   Tigris 1916   Kut al Amara 1917   Baghdad   Mesopotamia 1916–18   Baku   Persia 1918   Defence of Escaut   Wormhoudt   Ypres-Comines Canal   Normandy Landing   Caen   Bourgebus Ridge   Mont Pincon   Falaise   Venraij   Rhineland   Lingen   Brinkum   Bremen   North-West Europe 1940, '44–45   Burma 1945

The motto of the regiment was 'Honi Soit Qui Mal y Pense' (Evil be to Him who Evil Thinks), and the regimental marches were 'Warwickshire Lads' and 'The British Grenadiers' (quick), and 'MacBean's Slow March' (slow). The uniform was scarlet with scarlet piping and blue facings, and the nicknames associated with The Royal Warwickshire Fusiliers were 'The Dutch Guards', 'Guise's Geese' and 'The Saucy Sixth'. Imperial regiments affiliated to The Royal Warwickshire Fusiliers were the Weyburn Regiment (Canada), the Westminster Regiment (Canada) and the Hauraki Regiment (New Zealand).

Third in seniority of the regiments that disappeared to form The Royal Regiment of Fusiliers was The Royal Fusiliers (City of London Regiment) (7th), which had been raised originally in 1685 and based at the Tower of London as escort to the immensely important Train of Artillery, which was also located in the Tower. This association with the artillery was confirmed by the appointment of Lord Dartmouth, the Master-General of the Ordnance, as colonel of the new Royal Regiment of Fuzilieers, which was otherwise known as the Ordnance Regiment. In 1688 the regiment was redesignated the 7th Regiment of Foot (or the Royal Fuzileers). During the eighteenth century the spelling 'fusiliers' came into vogue, and in 1881 the Royal Fusiliers was restyled The Royal Fusiliers (City of London Regiment), a name that lasted until the amalgamation of 1968. The regiment's battle honours were the following:

Namur 1695   Martinique 1809   Talavera   Busaco   Albuhera   Badajoz   Salamanca   Vittoria   Pyrenees   Orthes   Toulouse   Peninsula   Alma   Inkerman   Sevastopol   Kandahar 1880   Afghanistan 1879–80   Relief of Ladysmith   South Africa 1899–1902   Mons   Le Cateau   Retreat from Mons   Marne 1914   Aisne 1914   La Bassee 1914   Messines 1914, '17   Armentieres 1914   Ypres 1914, '15, '17, '18   Nonne Bosschen   Gravenstafel   St Julien   Frezenberg   Bellewaarde   Hooge 1915   Somme 1916, '18   Albert 1916, '18   Bazentin   Delville Wood   Pozieres   Flers-Courcelette   Thiepval   Le Transloy   Ancre Heights   Ancre 1916, '18   Arras 1917, '18   Vimy 1917   Scarpe 1917   Arleux   Pilckem   Langemarck 1917   Bullecourt   Menin Road   Polygon Wood   Broodseinde   Poelcappelle   Passchendaele   Cambrai 1917, '18   St Quentin   Bapaume 1918   Rosieres   Avres   Villers Bretonneux   Lys   Estaires   Hazebrouck   Bethune   Amiens   Drocourt-Queant   Hindenburg Line   Havrincourt   Epehy   Canal du Nord   Sambre   France and Flanders 1914–18   Italy 1917–18   Struma   Macedonia 1915–18   Helles   Landing at Helles   Krithia   Suvla   Scimitar Hill   Gallipoli 1915–16   Egypt 1916   Megiddo   Nablus   Palestine 1918   Troitsa   Archangel 1919   Kilimanjaro   Behobeho   Nyangao   East Africa 1915–17   Dunkirk 1940   North-West Europe 1940   Agordat   Keren   Syria 1941   Sidi Barrani   Djebel Tebaga   Peter's Corner   North Africa 1940, '43   Sangro   Mozzagrogna   Caldari   Salerno   St Lucia   Battipaglia   Teano   Monte Camino   Garigliano Crossing   Damiano   Anzio   Cassino II   Ripa Ridge   Gabbiano   Advance to Florence   Monte Scalari   Gothic Line   Coriano   Croce   Casa Fortis   Savio Bridgehead

Valli di Comacchio   Senio   Argenta Gap   Italy 1943–45
Athens   Greece 1944–45

The motto of the regiment was 'Honi Soit Qui Mal y Pense' (Evil be to Him who Evil Thinks), and the regimental marches were 'The British Grenadiers' (quick) and 'De Normandie' (slow). The uniform was scarlet with scarlet piping and blue facings, and the nicknames associated with The Royal Fusiliers were 'The Elegant Extracts', 'The Royals' and 'The Hanoverian White Horse', the first in celebration of the fact that up to 1854 the regiment had no ensigns, who had to be posted into The Royal Fusiliers from other regiments. Imperial regiments affiliated to The Royal Fusiliers were the Canadian Fusiliers (City of London Regiment) and the 6th Battalion, Australian Infantry.

The most junior of the components of The Royal Regiment of Fusiliers was The Lancashire Fusiliers (20th), which began life as Colonel Sir Robert Peyton's Companies of Foot, raised from a number of independent companies for service with William III and expanded to regimental size in 1689 as Colonel Sir Robert Peyton's Regiment of Foot. Thereafter the name of the regiment changed with its colonels until 1751, when it became the 20th Regiment of Foot. In 1782 it became the 20th (or the East Devonshire) Regiment of Foot, and in 1881 The Lancashire Fusiliers, a title it retained until its amalgamation into The Royal Regiment of Fusiliers. The regiment's battle honours were the following:

Dettingen   Minden   Egmont-op-Zee   Egypt (with the Sphinx)   Maida   Vimiera   Corunna   Vittoria   Pyrenees   Orthes   Toulouse   Peninsula   Alma   Inkerman   Sevastopol   Lucknow   Khartoum   Relief of Ladysmith   South Africa 1899–1902   Le Cateau   Retreat from Mons   Marne 1914   Aisne 1914, '18   Armentieres 1914   Ypres 1915, '17, '18   St Julien   Bellewaarde   Somme 1916, '18   Albert 1916, '18   Bazentin   Delville Wood   Pozieres   Ginchy   Flers-Courcelette   Morval   Thiepval   Le Transloy   Ancre Heights   Ancre 1916, '18   Arras 1917, '18   Scarpe 1917, '18   Arleux   Messines 1917   Pilckem   Langemarck 1917   Menin Road   Polygon Wood   Broodseinde   Poelcappelle   Passchendaele   Cambrai 1917, '18   St Quentin   Bapaume 1918   Rosieres   Lys   Estaires   Hazebrouck   Bailleul   Kemmel   Bethune   Scherpenberg   Amiens   Drocourt-Queant   Hindenburg Line   Havrincourt   Epehy   Canal du Nord   St Quentin Canal   Courtrai   Selle   Sambre   France and Flanders 1914–18   Doiran 1917   Macedonia 1915–18   Helles   Landing at Helles   Krithia   Suvla   Landing at Suvla   Scimitar Hill   Gallipoli 1915   Rumani   Egypt 1915–17   Defence of Escaut   St Omer-La Bassee   Caen   North-West Europe 1940   Medjez el Bab   Oued Zarga   North Africa 1942–43   Adrano   Sicily 1943   Termoli   Trigno   Sangro   Cassino II   Trasimene Line   Monte Ceco   Monte Spaduro   Senio   Argenta Gap

Malta 1941–42   Rathedaung   Htizwe   Kohima   Naga Village
Chindits 1944   Burma 1943–45

The motto of the regiment was 'Omnia Audax' (In all things Daring), and the regimental marches were 'The Minden March' and 'The British Grenadiers' (quick), and 'The Lancashire Fusiliers Slow March' (slow). The uniform was scarlet with scarlet piping and white facings, and the nicknames associated with The Lancashire Fusiliers were 'The Double X's', 'The Two Tens', 'The Minden Boys' and 'Kingsley's Stand', the last two in celebration of the regiment's stand at the Battle of Minden (1759) under Colonel Kingsley. The only imperial regiment affiliated to The Lancashire Fusiliers was the Peel and Dufferin Regiment (Canada).

REGIMENTS OF INFANTRY 5

The King's Regiment (8th, 63rd and 96th)

Colonel-in-Chief

HM Queen Elizabeth The Queen Mother

Colonel

Colonel Sir Geoffrey Errington

Battle honours

Blenheim Ramillies Oudenarde Malplaquet Dettingen Guadaloupe 1759 Egmont-op-Zee Egypt (with the Sphinx) Peninsula Martinique 1809 Gaudaloupe 1810 Niagara New Zealand Alma Inkerman Sevastopol Delhi 1857 Lucknow Peiwar Kotal Afghanistan 1878–80 Egypt 1882 Burmah 1885–87 Defence of Ladysmith South Africa 1899–1902 Mons Le Cateau Retreat from Mons Marne 1914 Aisne 1914 La Bassee 1914 Armentieres 1914 Ypres 1914, '15, '17, '18 Langemarck 1914, '17 Gheluvelt Nonne Bosschen Givenchy 1914 Neuve Chapelle Gravenstafel St Julien Frezenberg Bellewaarde Aubers Festubert 1915 Loos Somme 1916, '18 Albert 1916, '18 Bazentin Delville Wood Guillemont Ginchy Flers-Courcelette Morval Thiepval Le Transloy Ancre Heights Ancre 1916, '18 Bapaume 1917, '18 Arras 1917, '18 Scarpe 1917, '18 Arleux Bullecourt

THE KING'S REGIMENT

Messines 1917, '18   Pilckem   Menin Road   Polygon Wood
Broodseinde   Poelcappelle   Passchendaele   Cambrai 1917, '18
St Quentin   Rosieres   Avre   Lys   Estaires   Bailleul   Kemmel
Bethune   Amiens   Scherpenberg   Drocourt-Queant   Hindenburg
Line   Epehy   Canal du Nord   St Quentin Canal   Beaurevoir
Courtrai   Selle   Sambre   France and Flanders 1914-18   Piave
Vittorio Veneto   Italy 1917-18   Doiran 1917   Macedonia 1915-18
Helles   Krithia   Suvla   Landing at Suvla   Scimitar Hill   Gallipoli 1915
Rumani   Egypt 1915-17   Megiddo   Sharon   Palestine 1918
Tigris 1916   Kut el Amara 1917   Baghdad   Mesopotamia 1916-18
NW Frontier India 1915   Archangel 1918-19   Afghanistan 1919
Dyle   Withdrawal to Escaut   Defence of Escaut   Defence of Arras
St Omer-La Bassee   Ypres-Comines Canal   Normandy Landing   Caen
Esquay   Falaise   Nederrijn   Scheldt   Walcheren Causeway
Flushing   Lower Maas   Venlo Pocket   Roer   Ourthe   Rhineland
Reichswald   Goch   Weeze   Rhine   Ibbenburen   Dreierwalde
Aller   Bremen   North-West Europe 1940, '44-45   Cassino II
Trasimene Line   Tuori   Gothic Line   Monte Gridolfo   Coriano
San Clemente   Gemmano Ridge   Montilgallo   Capture of Forli
Lamone Crossing   Defence of Lamone Bridgehead   Rimini Line
Montescudo   Cesena   Italy 1944-45   Malta 1940   Athens
Greece 1944-45   Singapore Island   Malaya 1941-42   North Arakan
Kohima   Pinwe   Shwebo   Myinmu Bridgehead   Irrawaddy
Chindits 1943   Chindits 1944   Burma 1943-45   The Hook 1953
Korea 1952-53

Regimental headquarters

TA Centre, Townsend Avenue, Liverpool, Lancashire.

Regimental museum

(The King's Regiment [Liverpool])
Merseyside County Museums, William Brown Street, Liverpool, Lancashire.
(The Manchester Regiment) Queen's Park Museum and Art Gallery, Queen's Park, Rochdale Road, Manchester, Lancashire.

Regimental marches

(quick) The Kingsman
(slow) Lord Ferrars March

Regimental motto

Nec Aspera Terrent (Nor do Difficulties Deter)

Nicknames

see below

Uniform

Scarlet with deep green piping and facings

Allied regiments

The Royal Regiment of Canada
The Royal South Australia Regiment
4th Battalion (Otago and Southland) The Royal New Zealand Infantry Regiment
1st Battalions (Scinde) The Frontier Force Regiment (Pakistan)

Regimental history

The King's Regiment came into existence in December 1968 with the redesignation of The King's Regiment (Manchester and Liverpool), itself the product of the September 1958 amalgamation of The King's Regiment (Liverpool) and The Manchester Regiment.

Of these two components the senior was The King's Regiment (Liverpool) (8th), which had originally been raised in 1685 by the Earl Ferrers as The Princess Anne of Denmark's Regiment of Foot. In 1702 this became The Queen's Regiment of Foot, and in 1716 The King's Regiment of Foot. In 1751 it was redesignated the 8th (or the King's) Regiment of Foot, and the beginning of the definitive title was adopted in 1881, when the regiment became The King's (Liverpool Regiment), modified in 1921 to The King's Regiment (Liverpool). The battle honours of the regiment were the following:

Blenheim   Ramillies   Oudenarde   Malplaquet   Dettingen   Egypt (with the Sphinx)   Martinique 1809   Niagara   Delhi 1857   Lucknow   Peiwar Kotal   Afghanistan 1878–80   Burmah 1885–87   Defence of Ladysmith   South Africa 1899–1902   Mons   Retreat from Mons   Marne 1914   Aisne 1914   Ypres 1914, '15, '17, '18   Langemarck 1914, '17   Gheluvelt   Nonne Bosschen   Neuve Chapelle   Gravenstafel   St Julien   Frezenberg   Bellewaarde   Aubers   Festubert 1915   Loos   Somme 1916, '18   Albert 1916, '18   Bazentin   Delville Wood   Guillemont   Ginchy   Flers-Courcelette   Morval   Le Transloy

Ancre 1916   Bapaume 1917, '18   Arras 1917, '18   Scarpe 1917, '18   Arleux   Pilckem   Menin Road   Polygon Wood   Poelcappelle   Passchendaele   Cambrai 1917, '18   St Quentin   Rosieres   Avre   Lys   Estaires   Messines 1918   Bailleul   Kemmel   Bethune   Scherpenberg   Drocourt-Queant   Hindenburg Line   Epehy   Canal du Nord   St Quentin Canal   Selle   Sambre   France and Flanders 1914–18   Doiran 1917   Macedonia 1915–18   NW Frontier India 1915   Archangel 1918–19   Afghanistan 1919   Normandy Landing   North-West Europe 1944   Cassino II   Trasimene Line   Tuori   Capture of Forli   Rimini Line   Italy 1944–45   Athens   Greece 1944–45   Chindits 1943   Chindits 1944   Burma 1943–45   The Hook 1953   Korea 1952–53

The motto of the regiment was 'Nec Aspera Terrent' (Nor do Difficulties Deter), and the regimental marches were 'Here's to the Maiden of Bashful Fifteen' (traditional, quick) and 'Zakhmi Dil' (traditional Pathan, quick), and 'Lord Ferrars March' (slow). The uniform was scarlet with blue piping and facings, and the nicknames associated with The King's Regiment (Liverpool) were 'The Leather Hats' and 'The King's Men'. Imperial regiments affiliated to The King's Regiment (Liverpool) were the Toronto Regiment (Canada) and the 8th Battalion, Australian Infantry.

The junior component of The King's Regiment was The Manchester Regiment, itself an 1881 amalgamation of the 63rd (West Suffolk) Regiment of Foot and the 96th Regiment of Foot. The combined regiment's battle honours were the following:

Guadaloupe 1759   Egmont-op-Zee   Egypt (with the Sphinx)   Peninsula   Martinique 1809   Guadaloupe 1810   New Zealand   Alma   Inkerman   Sevastopol   Afghanistan 1879–80   Egypt 1882   Defence of Ladysmith   South Africa 1899–1902   Mons   Le Cateau   Retreat from Mons   Marne 1914   Aisne 1914   La Bassee 1914   Armentieres 1914   Givenchy 1914   Neuve Chapelle   Ypres 1915, '17, '18   Gravenstafel   St Julien   Frezenberg   Bellewaarde   Aubers   Somme 1916, '18   Albert 1916, '18   Bazentin   Delville Wood   Guillemont   Flers-Courcelette   Thiepval   Le Transloy   Ancre Heights   Ancre 1916, '18   Arras 1917, '18   Scarpe 1917   Bullecourt   Messines 1917   Pilckem   Langemarck 1917   Menin Road   Polygon Wood   Broodseinde   Poelcappelle   Passchendaele   St Quentin   Bapaume 1918   Rosieres   Lys   Kemmel   Bethune   Amiens   Hindenburg Line   Epehy   Canal du Nord   St Quentin Canal   Beaurevoir   Cambrai 1918   Courtrai   Selle   Sambre   France and Flanders 1914–18   Piave   Vittorio Veneto   Italy 1917–18   Doiran 1917   Macedonia 1915–18   Helles   Krithia   Suvla   Landing at Suvla   Scimitar Hill   Gallipoli 1915   Rumani   Egypt 1915–17   Megiddo   Sharon   Palestine 1918   Tigris 1916   Kut al Amara 1917   Baghdad   Mesopotamia 1916–18

Dyle   Withdrawal to Escaut   Defence of Escaut   Defence of Arras   St Omer-La Bassee   Ypres-Comines Canal   Caen   Esquay   Falaise   Nederrijn   Scheldt   Walcheren Causeway   Flushing   Lower Maas   Venlo Pocket   Roer   Ourthe   Rhineland   Reichswald   Goch   Weeze   Rhine   Ibbenburen   Dreierwalde   Aller   Bremen   North-West Europe 1940, '44–45   Gothic Line   Monte Gridolfo   Coriano   San Clemente   Gemmano Ridge   Montilgallo   Capture of Forli   Lamone Crossing   Defence of Lamone Bridgehead   Rimini Line   Montescudo   Cesena   Italy 1944   Malta 1940   Singapore Island   Malaya 1941–42   North Arakan   Kohima   Pinwe   Shwebo   Myinmu Bridgehead   Irrawaddy   Burma 1943–45

The motto of the regiment was 'Honi Soit Qui Mal y Pense' (Evil be to Him who Evil Thinks), and the regimental march was 'The Young May Moon' (traditional, quick and slow versions). The uniform was scarlet with white facings, and the nicknames associated with The Manchester Regiment were 'The Bendovers', 'The Bloodsuckers' and 'The British Musketeers'. The only imperial regiment affiliated to The Manchester Regiment was the Southland Regiment (New Zealand).

Of the two regiments that went to form The Manchester Regiment in 1881, the senior was the 63rd (West Suffolk) Regiment of Foot, originally raised in 1756 as the 2nd Battalion of the 8th (The King's) Regiment of Foot but two years later made independent as the 63rd Regiment of Foot. In 1782 this became the 63rd (or the West Suffolk) Regiment of Foot, which was in 1881 amalgamated with the 96th Regiment of Foot. The battle honours of the regiment were the following:

Egmont-op-Zee   Martinique 1809   Guadaloupe 1810   Alma   Inkerman   Sevastopol   Afghanistan 1878–80

The uniform was scarlet with Lincoln green facings, and the nickname associated with the 63rd was 'The Bloodsuckers'.

The 96th Regiment of Foot had been raised in 1824 as successor to the first 96th (or The Queen's Own) Regiment of Foot raised in 1798 and disbanded in 1818. The battle honours of the regiment were the following:

Egypt (with the Sphinx)   Peninsula   New Zealand

The uniform was scarlet with yellow facings, and the nickname associated with the 96th was 'The Ups and Downs'.

REGIMENTS OF INFANTRY 6

The Royal Anglian Regiment (9th, 10th, 12th, 16th, 17th, 44th, 48th, 56th and 58th)

Colonel-in-Chief

HM Queen Elizabeth The Queen Mother

Colonel

General Sir Timothy Creasey

Battle honours

Namur 1695 Blenheim Ramillies Oudenarde Malplaquet Dettingen Louisburg Minden Quebec 1759 Belleisle Martinique 1762 Moro Havannah Gibraltar 1779–83 Martinique 1794 India Seringapatam Surinam Maida Rolica Vimiera Peninsula Corunna Douro Talavera Busaco Albuhera Badajoz Salamanca Vittoria Pyrenees St Sebastian Nivelle Nive Orthes Toulouse Bladensburg Waterloo Ava Affghanistan 1839 Ghuznee 1839 Khelat Cabool 1842 Mookdee Ferozeshah Sobraon New Zealand Mooltan Goojerat Punjaub South Africa 1851–53 Alma Inkerman Sevastopol Lucknow Taku Forts South Africa 1879 Afghanistan 1878–80 Ali Masjid Kabul 1879 Nile 1884–85 Chitral Tirah Atbara Khartoum South Africa 1899–1902

Modder River   Relief of Kimberley   Paardeberg   Defence of Ladysmith   Mons   Le Cateau   Retreat from Mons   Marne 1914   Aisne 1914   La Bassee 1914   Messines 1914, '17, '18   Armentieres 1914   Givenchy 1914   Ypres 1914, '15, '17, '18   Langemarck 1914, '17   Gheluvelt   Nonne Bosschen   Festubert 1914, '15   Neuve Chapelle   Hill 60   Gravenstafel   St Julien   Frezenberg   Bellewaarde   Aubers   Hooge 1915   Loos   Somme 1916, '18   Albert 1916, '18   Bazentin   Delville Wood   Pozieres   Guillemont   Flers-Courcelette   Morval   Thiepval   Le Transloy   Ancre Heights   Ancre 1916, '18   Bapaume 1917, '18   Arras 1917, '18   Vimy 1917   Scarpe 1917, '18   Arleux   Oppy   Pilckem   Menin Road   Polygon Wood   Broodseinde   Poelcappelle   Passchendaele   Cambrai 1917, '18   St Quentin   Rosieres   Avre   Villers Bretonneux   Lys   Estaires   Hazebrouck   Bailleul   Kemmel   Bethune   Scherpenberg   Amiens   Drocourt-Queant   Hindenburg Line   Havrincourt   Epehy   Canal du Nord   St Quentin Canal   Beaurevoir   Courtrai   Selle   Valenciennes   Sambre   France and Flanders 1914–18   Helles   Landing at Helles   Italy 1917–18   Struma   Doiran 1918   Macedonia 1915–18   Krithia   Suvla   Landing at Suvla   Scimitar Hill   Gallipoli 1915–16   Rumani   Egypt 1915–17   Gaza   El Mughar   Nebi Samwil   Jerusalem   Jaffa   Tell' Asur   Megiddo   Sharon   Damascus   Palestine 1917–18   Tigris 1916   Shaiba   Kut al Amara 1915, '17   Ctesiphon   Defence of Kut al Amara   Baghdad   Mesopotamia 1914–18   Vist   Norway 1940   Defence of Escaut   St Omer-La Bassee   Defence of Arras   Ypres-Comines Canal   Dunkirk 1940   St Valery-en-Caux   Normandy Landing   Cambes   Tilly sur Seulles   Fontenay le Pesnil   Odon   Defence of Rauray   Caen   Orne   Bourgebus Ridge   Troarn   Le Perier Ridge   Brieux Bridgehead   Falaise   Nederrijn   Le Havre   Antwerp-Turnhout Canal   Scheldt   Venraij   Venlo Pocket   Zetten   Rhineland   Hochwald   Lingen   Brinkum   Bremen   Arnhem 1945   North-West Europe 1940, '44–45   Abyssinia 1940   Falluja   Baghdad 1941   Iraq 1941   Palmyra   Jebel Mazar   Syria 1941   Sidi Barrani   Tobruk 1941   Tobruk Sortie   Belhamed   Mersa Matruh   Defence of Alamein Line   Deir el Shein   Ruweisat   Ruweisat Ridge   El Alamein   Matmata Hills   Akarit   Enfidaville   Djebel Garci   Djedeida   Djebel Djaffa   Montagne Farm   Sedjenane I   Mine de Sedjenane   Oued Zarga   Djebel Tanngoucha   Argoub Sellah   Sidi Ahmed   Tunis   Ragoubet Souissi   North Africa 1940–43   Landing in Sicily   Adrano   Sicily 1943   Trigno   Sangro   Villa Grande   Salerno   Vietri Pass   Capture of Naples   Cava di Tirreni   Volturno Crossing   Calabritto   Garigliano Crossing   Monte Tuga   Anzio   Cassino I–II   Castle Hill   Hangman's Hill   Monte Gabbione   Trasimene Line   Gothic Line   Monte Gridolfo   Gemmano Ridge   Lamone Crossing   Monte Colombo   San Marino   Monte La Pieve   Argenta Gap   Italy

1943–45 Athens Greece 1944–45 Crete Heraklion Madagascar Kampar Johore Muar Batu Pahat Singapore Island Malaya 1941–42 Donbaik Point 201 (Arakan) Yu North Arakan Buthidaung Nyakyedauk Pass Imphal Tamu Road Bishenpur Aradura Monywa 1945 Mandalay Myinmu Bridgehead Irrawaddy Ramree Chindits 1944 Burma 1945–45 Maryang-San Korea 1951–52

Regimental headquarters

The Keep, Gibraltar Barracks, Bury St Edmunds, Suffolk.

Regimental museums

(The Royal Norfolk Regiment) Britannia Barracks, Norwich, Norfolk.
(The Suffolk Regiment) The Keep, Gibraltar Barracks, Bury St Edmunds, Suffolk.
(The Royal Lincolnshire Regiment) Museum of Lincolnshire Life, Burton Road, Lincoln, Lincolnshire.
(The Northamptonshire Regiment) Abington Park, Northampton, Northamptonshire.
(The Bedfordshire and Hertfordshire Regiment) Luton Museum, Wardown Park, Old Bedford Road, Luton.
(The Essex Regiment) Oaklands Park, Moulsham Street, Chelmsford, Essex.
(The Royal Leicestershire Regiment) The Magazine, Leicester, Leicestershire.

Regimental marches

(quick) Arrangement of Rule Britannia (Arne) and Speed the Plough (traditional)
(slow) The Northamptonshire (traditional)

Regimental motto

Honi Soit Qui Mal y Pense (Evil be to Him who Evil Thinks)

Nicknames

see below

Uniform

Blue with scarlet piping and blue facings

Allied regiments

The Sherbrooke Hussars (Canada)
The Lincoln and Welland Regiment (Canada)
The Essex and Kent Scottish Regiment (Canada)
The Lake Superior Scottish Regiment (Canada)
The Royal Tasmania Regiment (Australia)
3rd Battalion (Auckland [Countess of Ranfurly's Own] and Northland) The Royal New Zealand Infantry Regiment
5th Battalion The Frontier Force Regiment (Pakistan)
1st Battalion The Royal Malay Regiment
The Barbados Regiment
The Bermuda Regiment
The Gibraltar Regiment

Regimental history

The Royal Anglian Regiment came into being during September 1964 through the amalgamation of four earlier regiments, namely the 1st East Anglian Regiment (Royal Norfolk and Suffolk), the 2nd East Anglian Regiment (Duchess of Gloucester's Own Royal Lincolnshire and Northamptonshire), the 3rd East Anglian Regiment (16th/44th Foot), and The Royal Leicestershire Regiment. The first three of these were themselves the results of previous amalgamations, and The Royal Anglian Regiment is thus a combination of nine older regiments.

The 1st East Anglian Regiment (Royal Norfolk and Suffolk) was created in August 1959 by the amalgamation of The Royal Norfolk Regiment and The Suffolk Regiment. There was little of note about the regiment, which existed as such for a mere five years. The uniform was blue with yellow piping and facings.

The senior of the 1st East Anglian Regiment's components was The Royal Norfolk Regiment (9th), which had been raised in 1685 as Colonel Henry Cornwall's Regiment of Foot. The regiment subsequently changed its title in accordance with the names of its colonels until 1751, when it became the 9th Regiment of Foot. In 1782 it became the 9th (or the East Norfolk) Regiment of Foot, and later changes resulted in the revised titles The Norfolk Regiment in 1881 and The Royal Norfolk Regiment in 1935. The battle honours of the regiment were the following:

Belleisle   Havannah   Martinique 1794   Rolica   Vimiera   Corunna   Busaco   Salamanca   Vittoria   St Sebastian   Nive   Peninsula   Cabool 1842   Mookdee   Ferozeshah   Sobraon   Sevastopol   Kabul 1879   Afghanistan 1879–80   Paardeberg   South Africa 1900–02   Mons   Le Cateau   Retreat from Mons   Marne 1914   Aisne 1914   La Bassee 1914   Ypres 1914, '15, '17, '18   Gravenstafel   St Julien

Frezenberg Bellewaarde Loos Somme 1916, '18 Albert 1916, '18 Delville Wood Pozieres Guillemont Flers-Courcelette Morval Thiepval Le Transloy Ancre Heights Ancre 1916, '18 Arras 1917 Vimy 1917 Scarpe 1917 Arleux Oppy Pilckem Langemarck 1917 Polygon Wood Broodseinde Poelcappelle Passchendaele Cambrai 1917, '18 St Quentin Bapaume 1918 Lys Bailleul Kemmel Scherpenberg Amiens Hindenburg Line Epehy Canal du Nord St Quentin Canal Beaurevoir Selle Sambre France and Flanders 1914–18 Italy 1917–18 Suvla Landing at Suvla Scimitar Hill Gallipoli 1915 Egypt 1915–17 Gaza El Mughar Nebi Samwil Jerusalem Jaffa Tell' Asur Megiddo Sharon Palestine 1917–18 Shaiba Kut al Amara 1915, '17 Ctesiphon Defence of Kut al Amara Mesopotamia 1914–18 Defence of Escaut St Omer-La Bassee St Valery-en-Caux Normandy Landing Caen Le Perier Ridge Brieux Bridgehead Venraij Rhineland Hochwald Lingen Brinkum North-West Europe 1940, '44–45 Johore Muar Batu Pahat Singapore Island Malaya 1942 Kohima Aradura Mandalay Burma 1944–45 Korea 1951–52

The motto of the regiment was 'Honi Soit Qui Mal y Pense' (Evil be to Him who Evil Thinks), and the regimental march was 'Rule Britannia (Arne, quick). The uniform was scarlet with yellow piping and facings, and the nicknames associated with The Royal Norfolk Regiment were 'The Fighting Ninth', 'The Norfolk Howards' and 'The Holy Boys', the last because in the Peninsula campaign the Spaniards mistook the regiment's badge (the figure of Britannia) for the Virgin Mary. Imperial regiments affiliated to The Royal Norfolk Regiment were the Norfolk Regiment of Canada and the 9th Battalion, Australian Infantry.

The Suffolk Regiment (12th) was The Royal Norfolk Regiment's junior partner in the 1st East Anglian Regiment. The Suffolk Regiment had originated in 1660 as a garrison company for Windsor Castle, under the command of Henry Howard, Duke of Norfolk. In 1685 the company was raised to regimental strength and became the Duke of Norfolk's Regiment of Foot, and thereafter the regiment changed names with its colonels until 1751, when it became the 12th Regiment of Foot. In 1782 this was changed to the 12th (or the East Suffolk) Regiment of Foot, and in 1881 to The Suffolk Regiment. The battle honours of the regiment were the following:

Dettingen Minden Gibraltar 1779–83 Seingapatam India South Africa 1851–53 New Zealand Afghanistan 1878–80 South Africa 1899–1902 Mons Le Cateau Retreat from Mons Marne 1914 Aisne 1914 La Bassee 1914 Givenchy 1914 Neuve Chapelle Ypres 1915, '17, '18 Gravenstafel St Julien Frezenberg Bellewaarde Aubers Hooge 1915 Loos Somme 1916, '18 Albert 1916, '18 Bazentin Delville Wood Pozieres Flers-Courcelette Morval Thiepval

Le Transloy   Ancre Heights   Ancre 1916, '18   Arras 1917, '18   Scarpe 1917, '18   Arleux   Pilckem   Langemarck 1917   Menin Road   Polygon Wood   Poelcappelle   Passchendaele   Cambrai 1917, '18   St Quentin   Bapaume 1918   Lys   Estaires   Messines 1918   Hazebrouck   Bailleul   Kemmel   Bethune   Scherpenberg   Amiens   Hindenburg Line   Epehy   Canal du Nord   Courtrai   Selle   Valenciennes   Sambre   France and Flanders 1914–18   Struma   Doiran 1918   Macedonia 1915–18   Suvla   Landing at Suvla   Scimitar Hill   Gallipoli 1915   Egypt 1915–17   Gaza   El Mughar   Nebi Samwil   Jerusalem   Jaffa   Tell' Asur   Megiddo   Sharon   Palestine 1917–18   Dunkirk 1940   Normandy Landing   Odon   Falaise   Venraij   Brinkum   North-West Europe 1940, '44–45   Singapore Island   Malaya 1942   North Arakan   Imphal   Burma 1943–45

The motto of the regiment was 'Montis Insignia Calpe' (from the badge of Gibraltar), and the regimental marches were 'Speed the Plough' (traditional, quick) and 'The Slow March of the Suffolk Regiment' (slow). The uniform was scarlet with yellow piping and facing, and the nickname associated with The Suffolk Regiment was 'The Old Dozen'. Imperial regiments affiliated to The Suffolk Regiment were the 12th Battalion, Australian Infantry, and the Auckland Regiment (Countess of Ranfurly's Own) (New Zealand).

The second of the major components of The Royal Anglian Regiment was the 2nd East Anglian Regiment (Duchess of Gloucestershire's Own Royal Lincolnshire and Northamptonshire), itself formed as recently as June 1960 by the amalgamation of The Royal Lincolnshire Regiment (10th) and The Northamptonshire Regiment (48th and 58th). The uniform was blue with scarlet piping and blue facings.

Senior of the elements that went into the 2nd East Anglian Regiment was The Royal Lincolnshire Regiment (10th), which had been raised in 1685 by Colonel John Granville, Earl of Bath as The Earl of Bath's Regiment of Foot, otherwise known as Granville's Regiment. In common with other regiments of the period this changed names with its colonels until 1751, when it became the 10th Regiment of Foot, a title changed in 1782 to the 10th (or North Lincolnshire) Regiment of Foot. In 1881 this became The Lincolnshire Regiment, and in 1946 The Royal Lincolnshire Regiment. The battle honours of the regiment were the following:

Blenheim   Ramillies   Oudenarde   Malplaquet   Egypt (with the Sphinx)   Peninsula   Sobraon   Mooltan   Goojerat   Punjaub   Lucknow   Atbara   Khartoum   Paardeberg   South Africa 1900–02   Mons   Le Cateau   Retreat from Mons   Marne 1914   Aisne 1914, '18   La Bassee 1914   Messines 1914, '17, '18   Armentieres 1914   Ypres 1914, '15, '17   Nonne Bosschen   Neuve Chapelle   Gravenstafel   St Julien   Frezenberg   Bellewaarde   Aubers   Loos   Somme 1916, '18   Albert

1916, '18   Bazentin   Delville Wood   Pozieres   Flers-Courcelette
Morval   Thiepval   Ancre 1916, '18   Arras 1917, '18   Scarpe 1917, '18
Arleux   Pilckem   Langemarck 1917   Menin Road   Polygon Wood
Broodseinde   Poelcappelle   Passchendaele   Cambrai 1917, '18
St Quentin   Bapaume 1918   Lys   Estaires   Bailleul   Kemmel
Amiens   Drocourt-Queant   Hindenburg Line   Epehy   Canal du Nord
St Quentin Canal   Beaurevoir   Selle   Sambre   France and Flanders
1914–18   Suvla   Landing at Suvla   Scimitar Hill   Gallipoli 1915   Egypt
1916   Vist   Norway 1940   Dunkirk 1940   Normandy Landing   Cambes
Fontenay le Pesnil   Defence of Rauray   Caen   Orne   Bourgebus
Ridge   Troarn   Nederrijn   Le Havre   Antwerp-Turnhout Canal
Venraij   Venlo Pocket   Rhineland   Hochwald   Lingen   Bremen
Arnhem 1945   North-West Europe 1940, '44–45   Sedjenane I
Mine de Sedjenane   Argoub Sellah   North Africa 1943   Salerno
Vietri Pass   Capture of Naples   Cava di Tirreni   Volturno Crossing
Garigliano Crossing   Monte Tuga   Gothic Line   Monte Gridolfo
Gemmano Ridge   Lamone Crossing   San Marino   Italy 1943–45
Donbaik   Point 201 (Arakan)   North Arakan   Buthidaung
Nyakyedauk Pass   Ramree   Burma 1943–45

The motto of the regiment was 'Honi Soit Qui Mal y Pense' (Evil be to Him who Evil Thinks), and the regimental march was 'The Lincolnshire Poacher' (traditional, quick). The uniform was scarlet with white (1881–1946) or blue (1946–1960) facings, and the nickname associated with The Royal Lincolnshire Regiment was 'The Poachers'. Imperial regiments affiliated to The Lincolnshire Regiment were the Lincolnshire Regiment of Canada and the Bermuda Volunteer Rifle Corps.

Partnering the Royal Lincolnshire Regiment in the 2nd East Anglian Regiment was The Northamptonshire Regiment, itself produced by the amalgamation in 1881 of the 48th (Northamptonshire) Regiment of Foot and the 58th (Rutlandshire) Regiment of Foot. The battle honours of the combined regiment were the following:

Louisburg   Quebec 1759   Martinique 1763   Havannah   Gibraltar
1779–83   Martinique 1794   Maida   Douro   Talavera   Albuhera
Badajoz   Salamanca   Vittoria   Pyrenees   Nivelle   Egypt (with the
Sphinx)   Orthes   Toulouse   Peninsula   New Zealand   Sevastopol
South Africa 1879   Tirah   Modder River   South Africa 1899–1902
Mons   Retreat from Mons   Marne 1914   Aisne 1914, '18   Ypres 1914,
'17   Langemarck 1914, '17   Gheluvelt   Nonne Bosschen   Givenchy
1914   Neuve Chapelle   Aubers   Loos   Somme 1916, '18   Albert
1916, '18   Bazentin   Delville Wood   Pozieres   Flers-Courcelette
Morval   Thiepval   Le Transloy   Ancre Heights   Ancre 1916, '18
Bapaume 1917, '18   Arras 1917, '18   Vimy 1917   Scarpe 1917, '18
Arleux   Messines 1917   Pilckem   Passchendaele   Cambrai 1917, '18

St Quentin   Rosieres   Avre   Villers Bretonneux   Amiens   Drocourt-Queant   Hindenburg Line   Epehy   St Quentin Canal   Selle   Sambre   France and Flanders 1914–18   Suvla   Landing at Suvla   Scimitar Hill   Gallipoli 1915   Egypt 1915–17   Gaza   El Mughar   Nebi Samwil   Jerusalem   Jaffa   Tell' Asur   Megiddo   Sharon   Palestine 1917–18   Defence of Escaut   Defence of Arras   Ypres-Comines Canal   North-West Europe 1940, '45   Djedeida   Djebel Djaffa   Oued Zarga   Djebel Tanngoucha   Sidi Ahmed   North Africa 1942–43   Landing in Sicily   Adrano   Sicily 1943   Sangro   Garigliano Crossing   Anzio   Cassino II   Monte Gabbione   Trasimene Line   Monte La Pieve   Argenta Gap   Italy 1943–45   Madagascar   Yu   Imphal   Tamu Road   Bishenpur   Monywa 1945   Myinmu Bridgehead   Irrawaddy   Burma 1943–45

The motto of the regiment was 'Montis Insignia Calpe' (from the badge of Gibraltar), and the regimental marches were 'The Northamptonshire' (quick) and 'The Duchess' (slow). The uniform was scarlet with buff piping and facings, and the nicknames associated with The Northamptonshire Regiment were 'The Heroes of Talavera' (1st Battalion), 'The Steelbacks' (2nd Battalion) and 'The Black Cuffs' (2nd Battalion), the first in celebration of the battalion's part in the Battle of Talavera (1809), the second for the battalion's legendary ability to take floggings, and the third in remembrance of its original facings.

The two components of The Northamptonshire Regiment were the 48th (Northamptonshire) Regiment of Foot and the 58th (Rutlandshire) Regiment of Foot.

The 48th (Northamptonshire) Regiment of Foot had been raised in 1741 as the 59th Regiment of Foot, otherwise known as Colonel Cholmondeley's Regiment of Foot. The second name was changed with the colonel, and in 1748 the regiment was renumbered the 48th Regiment of Foot. In 1751 it was officially styled the 48th Regiment of Foot, in 1782 becoming the 48th (or the Northamptonshire) Regiment of Foot. The battle honours of the regiment were the following:

Louisburg   Quebec   Douro   Talavera   Albuhera   Badajoz   Salamanca   Vittoria   Pyrenees   Nivelle   Orthes   Toulouse   Peninsula   Sevastopol

The uniform was scarlet with buff facings.

The 58th (Rutlandshire) Regiment of Foot had been raised in 1755 as the 60th Regiment of Foot, being renumbered the 58th Regiment of Foot in 1757. The only other change of style came in 1782, when the regiment became the 58th (or Rutlandshire) Regiment of Foot. The battle honours of the regiment were the following:

Louisburg   Quebec   Gibraltar (with Castle and Key)   Egypt (with the

Sphinx) Maida Salamanca Vittoria Pyrenees Nivelle Orthes Peninsula New Zealand South Africa 1879

The motto of the regiment was 'Montis Insignia Calpe' (from the badge of of Gibraltar), and the uniform was scarlet with black facings.

The third element to go into The Royal Anglian Regiment was the 3rd East Anglian Regiment (16th/44th Foot), formed in June 1958 by the amalgamation of The Bedfordshire and Hertfordshire Regiment (16th) and The Essex Regiment (44th and 56th).

The Bedfordshire and Hertfordshire Regiment (16th) had been raised in 1688 as Colonel Douglas's Regiment of Foot, almost immediately afterwards retitled Colonel Hodges's Regiment of Foot when Colonel Douglas's adherence to James II resulted in his replacement on the accession of William III. In 1751 it became the 16th Regiment of Foot, later changes altering this to the 16th (or the Buckinghamshire) Regiment of Foot in 1782, to the 16th (or Bedfordshire) Regiment of Foot in 1809, to The Bedfordshire Regiment in 1881 and to The Bedfordshire and Hertfordshire Regiment in 1919. The battle honours of the regiment were the following:

Namur 1695 Blenheim Ramillies Oudenarde Malplaquet Surinam Chitral South Africa 1900–02 Mons Le Cateau Retreat from Mons Marne 1914 Aisne 1914 La Bassee 1914 Ypres 1914, '15, '17 Langemarck 1914, '17 Gheluvelt Nonne Bosschen Neuve Chapelle Hill 60 Gravenstafel St Julien Frezenberg Bellewaarde Aubers Festubert 1915 Loos Somme 1916, '18 Albert 1916, '18 Bazentin Delville Wood Pozieres Guillemont Flers-Courcelette Morval Thiepval Le Transloy Ancre Heights Ancre 1916, '18 Bapaume 1917, '18 Arras 1917, '18 Vimy 1917 Scarpe 1917 Arleux Oppy Messines 1917 Pilckem Polygon Wood Broodseinde Poelcappelle Passchendaele Cambrai 1917, '18 St Quentin Bapaume 1918 Rosieres Avre Villers Bretonneux Lys Hazebrouck Scherpenberg Amiens Drocourt-Queant Hindenburg Line Epehy Canal du Nord St Quentin Canal Selle Sambre France and Flanders 1914–18 Italy 1917–18 Suvla Landing at Suvla Scimitar Hill Gallipoli 1915 Egypt 1915–17 Gaza El Mughar Nebi Samwil Jerusalem Jaffa Tell' Asur Megiddo Sharon Palestine 1917–18 Dunkirk 1940 North-West Europe 1940 Tobruk 1941 Tobruk Sortie Belhamed Tunis North Africa 1941, '43 Cassino II Trasimene Line Italy 1944–45 Athens Greece 1944–45 Singapore Island Malaya 1942 Chindits 1944 Burma 1944

The motto of the regiment was 'Honi Soit Qui Mal y Pense' (Evil be to Him who Evil Thinks), and the regimental march was 'Mandolinata' (quick). The uniform was scarlet with white piping and facings, and the nicknames associated with The Bedfordshire and Hertfordshire Regiment were 'The Old Bucks', 'The Featherbeds' and 'The Peacemakers', the first because of the regiment's association with Buckinghamshire, and the other two for the regiment's long period of garrison duty after the Battle of Dettingen (1743). Imperial regiments affiliated to The Bedfordshire and Hertfordshire Regiment were the Prince Albert Volunteers (Canada), the 16th Battalion, Australian Infantry, and the 1st City Regiment (South Africa).

The Bedfordshire and Hertfordshire Regiment's junior partner was The Essex Regiment (44th and 56th), itself the result of an 1881 amalgamation of the 44th (East Essex) Regiment of Foot and the 56th (West Essex) Regiment of Foot. The battle honours of the combined regiment were the following:

> Moro   Havannah   Gibraltar 1779–83   Egypt (with the Sphinx)   Badajoz   Salamanca   Peninsula   Bladensburg   Waterloo   Ava   Alma   Inkerman   Sevastopol   Taku Forts   Nile 1884–85   Relief of Kimberley   Paardeberg   South Africa 1899–1902   Le Cateau   Retreat from Mons   Marne 1914   Aisne 1914   Messines 1914   Armentieres 1914   Ypres 1915, '17   St Julien   Frezenberg   Bellewaarde   Loos   Somme 1916, '18   Albert 1916, '18   Bazentin   Delville Wood   Pozieres   Flers-Courcelette   Morval   Thiepval   Le Transloy   Ancre Heights   Ancre 1916, '18   Bapaume 1917, '18   Arras 1917, '18   Scarpe 1917, '18   Arleux   Pilckem   Langemarck 1917   Menin Road   Broodseinde   Poelcappelle   Passchendaele   Cambrai 1917, '18   St Quentin   Avre   Villers Bretonneux   Lys   Hazebrouck   Bethune   Amiens   Drocourt-Queant   Hindenburg Line   Havrincourt   Epehy   St Quentin Canal   Selle   Sambre   France and Flanders 1914–18   Helles   Landing at Helles   Krithia   Suvla   Landing at Suvla   Scimitar Hill   Gallipoli 1915–16   Rumani   Egypt 1915–17   Gaza   Jaffa   Megiddo   Sharon   Palestine 1917–18   St Omer-La Bassee   Tilly sur Seulles   Le Havre   Antwerp-Turnhout Canal   Scheldt   Zetten   Arnhem 1945   North-West Europe 1940, '44–45   Abyssinia 1940   Falluja   Baghdad 1941   Iraq 1941   Palmyra   Syria 1941   Tobruk 1941   Belhamed   Mersa Matruh   Defence of Alamein Line   Deir el Shein   Ruweisat   Ruweisat Ridge   El Alamein   Matmata Hills   Akarit   Enfidaville   Djebel Garci   Tunis   Ragoubet Souissi   North Africa 1941–43   Trigno   Sangro   Villa Grande   Cassino I   Castle Hill   Hangman's Hill   Italy 1943–44   Athens   Greece 1944–45   Kohima   Chindits 1944   Burma 1943–45

The motto of the regiment was 'Montis Insignia Calpe' (from the badge of Gibraltar), and the regimental marches were 'The Hampshire' (quick) and 'The Essex' (slow). The uniform was scarlet with purple piping and facings, and the nicknames associated with The Essex Regiment were 'The Two Fours' and 'The Little Fighting Fours' (1st Battalion), and 'The Pompadours' and 'The Saucy Pompeys' (2nd Battalion), the latter because the colour of the 56th's facings was chosen from the livery of Madame de Pompadour. Imperial regiments affiliated to The Essex Regiment were the Essex Scottish (Highlanders) of Canada and the 44th Battalion, Australian Infantry.

Within The Essex Regiment the senior component was the 44th (East Essex) Regiment of Foot, which had been raised in 1741 as the 55th Foot by Colonel James Long as Colonel Long's Regiment of Foot. The title of the regiment subsequently changed with its colonels until 1748, when it became the 44th Regiment of Foot. The only further change before the amalgamation came in 1782, when the regiment became the 44th (or the East Essex) Regiment of Foot. The regiment's battle honours were the following:

> Egypt (with the Sphinx) Badajoz Salamanca Peninsula
> Bladensburg Waterloo Ava Alma Inkerman Sevastopol
> Taku Forts

The uniform was scarlet with yellow facings, and the regiment's nicknames were those later passed on to the 1st Battalion of The Essex Regiment.

Junior partner in The Essex Regiment was the 56th (West Essex) Regiment of Foot, which had been raised as the 58th Regiment of Foot in 1755 by Lord Manners. In 1757 the regiment was renumbered the 56th Regiment of Foot, and in 1782 it became the 56th (or the West Essex) Regiment of Foot. The battle honours of the regiment were the following:

> Moro Havannah Gibraltar Sevastopol

The uniform was scarlet with purple facings, and the regiment's nicknames were those later passed on to the 2nd Battalion of The Essex Regiment.

The only regiment to come into The Royal Anglian Regiment in much its true form was The Royal Leicestershire Regiment, which had been raised in 1688 as Colonel Solomon Richards's Regiment of Foot. The regiment's name changed with the colonels until 1751, when it became the 17th Regiment of Foot. In 1782 the regiment became the 17th (or the Leicestershire) Regiment of Foot, in 1881 The Leicestershire Regiment, and in 1946 The Royal Leicestershire Regiment. The battle honours of the regiment were the following:

> Namur 1695 Louisburg Martinique 1762 Havannah Hindoostan
> Ghuznee 1839 Khelat Affghanistan 1839 Sevastopol Ali Masjid
> Afghanistan 1878–79 Defence of Ladysmith South Africa 1899–1902
> Aisne 1914 La Bassee 1914 Armentieres 1914 Festubert 1914, '15
> Neuve Chapelle Aubers Hooge 1915 Somme 1916, '18 Bazentin
> Flers-Courcelette Morval Le Transloy Ypres 1917 Polygon
> Wood Cambrai 1917, '18 St Quentin Lys Bailleul Kemmel
> Scherpenberg Albert 1918 Bapaume 1918 Hindenburg Line

Epehy   St Quentin Canal   Beaurevoir   Selle   Sambre   France and Flanders 1914–18   Megiddo   Sharon   Damascus   Palestine 1918   Tigris 1916   Kut al Amara 1917   Baghdad   Mesopotamia 1915–18   Norway 1940   Antwerp-Turnhout Canal   Scheldt   Zetten   North-West Europe 1944–45   Jebel Mazar   Syria 1941   Sidi Barrani   Tobruk 1941   Montagne Farm   North Africa 1940–41, '43   Salerno   Calabritto   Gothic Line   Monte Gridolfo   Monte Colombo   Italy 1943–45   Crete   Heraklion   Kampar   Malaya 1941–42   Chindits 1944   Maryang-San   Korea 1951–52

The motto of the regiment was 'Veni et Vici' (I Came and I Conquered, used only between 1841 and 1845), and the regimental marches were an arrangement of 'A Hunting Call', '1772' and 'Romaika' (quick), and 'General Monckton' (slow). The uniform was blue with pearl grey piping and facings, and the nicknames associated with The Royal Leicestershire Regiment were 'The Tigers', 'The Green Tigers', 'The Bengal Tigers' and 'The Lily Whites', the first three in reference to the regiment's outstanding services in India and the last to the period after 1881 when white facings were used on the uniform. Imperial regiments affiliated to The Royal Leicestershire Regiment were the Sherbrooke Regiment (Canada) and the 32nd Battalion, Australian Infantry.

REGIMENTS OF INFANTRY 7

The Devonshire and Dorset Regiment (11th, 39th and 54th)

Colonel-in-Chief

Major-General HRH The Duke of Kent

Colonel

Major-General C. T. Shortis

Battle honours

Dettingen Plassey Gibraltar 1779–83 Martinique 1794 Egypt (with the Sphinx) Marabout Albuhera Salamanca Vittoria Pyrenees Nivelle Nive Orthes Toulouse Peninsula Ava Maharajpore Sevastopol Afghanistan 1879–80 Tirah Defence of Ladysmith Relief of Ladysmith South Africa 1899–1902 Mons Le Cateau Retreat from Mons Marne 1914 Aisne 1914 La Bassee 1914 Armentieres 1914 Neuve Chapelle Hill 60 Ypres 1915, '17 Gravenstafel St Julien Frezenberg Bellewaarde Aubers Loos Somme 1916, '18 Albert 1916, '18 Bazentin Delville Wood Guillemont Flers-Courcelette Morval Thiepval Ancre 1916, '18 Arras 1917 Vimy 1917 Scarpe 1917 Bullecourt Messines 1917 Pilckem Langemarck 1917 Polygon Wood Broodseinde Poelcappelle Passchendaele St Quentin Rosieres Villers Bretonneux Lys Hazebrouck Bois des Buttes Marne 1918

THE DEVONSHIRE AND DORSET REGIMENT

Tardenois   Amiens   Bapaume 1918   Hindenburg Line   Havrincourt   Epehy   Canal du Nord   St Quentin Canal   Beaurevoir   Cambrai 1918   Selle   Sambre   France and Flanders 1914–18   Piave   Vittorio Veneto   Italy 1917–18   Doiran 1917, '18   Macedonia 1915–18   Suvla   Landing at Suvla   Scimitar Hill   Gallipoli 1915   Egypt 1916–17   Gaza   El Mughar   Nebi Samwil   Jerusalem   Tell' Asur   Megiddo   Sharon   Palestine 1917–18   Basra   Shaiba   Kut al Amara 1915, '17   Ctesiphon   Defence of Kut al Amara   Tigris 1916   Baghdad   Khan Baghdadi   Mesopotamia 1916–18   St Omer-La Bassee   Normandy Landing   Port en Bessin   Villers Bocage   Tilly sur Seulles   Caen   Mont Pincon   St Pierre la Vielle   Nederrijn   Arnhem 1944   Aam   Geilenkirchen   Roer   Goch   Rhine   Ibbenburen   Twente Canal   North-West Europe 1940, '44–45   Landing in Sicily   Agira   Regalbuto   Sicily 1943   Landing at Porto San Venere   Italy 1943   Malta 1940–42   Imphal   Shenam Pass   Tamu Road   Kohima   Ukhrul   Mandalay   Myinmu Bridgehead   Kyaukse 1945   Mt Popa   Burma 1943–45

Regimental headquarters

Wyvern Barracks, Barrack Road, Exeter, Devon.

Regimental museums

(The Devonshire Regiment) Wyvern Barracks, Barrack Road, Exeter, Devon.
(The Devonshire and Dorset Regiment, and The Dorset Regiment) The Keep, Dorchester, Dorset.

Regimental marches

(quick) Arrangement of Widecombe Fair, We've Lived and Loved Together, and Maid of Glenconnel
(slow) The Rose of Devon, and Maid of Glenconnel

Regimental mottoes

Semper Fidelis (Ever Faithful), and Primus in Indis (First in India)

Nicknames

see below

Uniform

Scarlet with grass green pipings and facings

Allied regiments

Les Fusiliers de Sherbrooke (Canada)
The Royal New South Wales Regiment (Australia)
6th Battalion The Royal Malay Regiment

Regimental history

The Devonshire and Dorset Regiment was formed in May 1958 by the amalgamation of The Devonshire Regiment and The Dorset Regiment.

The senior of these was The Devonshire Regiment (11th), which had been raised in June 1685 by the Duke of Beaufort as The Duke of Beaufort's Musketeers, and in October of the same year restyled The Marquess of Worcester's Regiment of Foot when Beaufort handed command to his son. The regiment was subsequently known by the names of its various colonels until 1751, when it became the 11th Regiment of Foot. In 1782 this was redesignated the 11th (or the North Devonshire) Regiment of Foot, and in 1881 The Devonshire Regiment. The battle honours of the regiment were the following:

Dettingen   Salamanca   Pyrenees   Nivelle   Nive   Orthes   Toulouse   Peninsula   Afghanistan 1887–80   Tirah   Defence of Ladysmith   Relief of Ladysmith   South Africa 1899–1902   Aisne 1914, '18   La Bassee 1914   Armentieres 1914   Neuve Chapelle   Hill 60   Ypres 1915, '17   Gravenstafel   St Julien   Frezenberg   Aubers   Loos   Somme 1916, '18   Albert 1916   Bazentin   Delville Wood   Guillemont   Flers-Courcelette   Morval   Arras 1917   Vimy 1917   Scarpe 1917   Bullecourt   Pilckem   Langemarck 1917   Polygon Wood   Broodseinde   Poelcappelle   Passchendaele   Rosieres   Villers Bretonneux   Lys   Hazebrouck   Bois des Buttes   Marne 1918   Tardenois   Bapaume 1918   Hindenburg Line   Havrincourt   Epehy   Canal du Nord   Beaurevoir . Cambrai 1918   Selle   Sambre   France and Flanders 1914–18   Piave   Vittorio Veneto   Italy 1917–18   Doiran 1917, '18   Macedonia 1915–18   Egypt 1916–17   Gaza   Nebi Samwil   Jerusalem   Tell' Asur   Palestine 1917–18   Tigris 1916   Kut al Amara 1917   Mesopotamia 1916–18   Normandy Landing   Port en Bessin   Tilly sur Seulles   Caen   St Pierre la Vielle   Nederrijn   Roer   Rhine   Ibbenburen   North-West Europe 1944–45   Landing in Sicily   Regalbuto   Sicily 1943   Landing at Porto San Venere   Italy 1943   Malta 1940–42   Imphal   Shenam Pass   Tamu Road   Kohima   Ukhrul   Myinmu Bridgehead   Kyaukse 1945   Burma 1943–45

The motto of the regiment was 'Semper Fidelis' (Ever Faithful), and the regimental marches were 'We've Lived and Loved Together' and 'Widecombe Fair' (quick), and 'The Rose of Devon' (slow). The uniform was scarlet with Lincoln green piping and facings, and the nickname associated with The Devonshire Regiment was 'The Bloody Eleventh'. No imperial regiments were affiliated to The Devonshire Regiment.

The junior partner to The Devonshire Regiment in The Devonshire and Dorset Regiment was The Dorset Regiment (39th and 54th), itself the result of the amalgamation in 1881 of the 39th (Dorsetshire) Regiment of Foot and the 54th (West Norfolk) Regiment of Foot. The battle honours of the combined regiment were the following:

Plassey   Gibraltar 1779–83   Martinique 1794   Marabout   Egypt (with the Sphinx)   Albuhera   Vittoria   Pyrenees   Nivelle   Nive   Orthes   Peninsula   Ava   Maharajpore   Sevastopol   Tirah   Relief of Ladysmith   South Africa 1899–1902   Mons   Le Cateau   Retreat from Mons   Marne 1914   Aisne 1914   La Bassee 1914   Armentieres 1914   Ypres 1915, '17   Gravenstafel   St Julien   Bellewaarde   Somme 1916, '18   Albert 1916, '18   Flers-Courcelette   Thiepval   Ancre 1916, '18   Arras 1917   Vimy 1917   Scarpe 1917   Messines 1917   Langemarck 1917   Polygon Wood   Broodseinde   Poelcappelle   Passchendaele   St Quentin   Amiens   Bapaume 1918   Hindenburg Line   Epehy   Canal du Nord   St Quentin Canal   Beaurevoir   Cambrai 1918   Selle   Sambre   France and Flanders 1914–18   Suvla   Landing at Suvla   Scimitar Hill   Gallipoli 1915   Egypt 1916   Gaza   El Mughar   Nebi Samwil   Jerusalem   Tell' Asur   Megiddo   Sharon   Palestine 1917–18   Basra   Shaiba   Kut al Amara 1915, '17   Ctesiphon   Defence of Kut al Amara   Baghdad   Khan Baghdadi   Mesopotamia 1914–18   St Omer-La Bassee   Normandy Landing   Villers Bocage   Tilly sur Seulles   Caen   Mont Pincon   St Pierre la Vielle   Arnhem 1944   Aam   Geilenkirchen   Goch   Rhine   Twente Canal   North-West Europe 1940, '44–45   Landing in Sicily   Agira   Regalbuto   Sicily 1943   Landing at Porto San Venere   Italy 1943   Malta 1940–42   Kohima   Mandalay   Mt Popa   Burma 1944–45

The motto of the regiment was 'Primus in Indis' (First in India), and the regimental marches were quick and slow versions of 'The Maid of Glenconnel'. The uniform was scarlet with grass green piping and facings, and the nicknames associated with The Dorset Regiment were 'Sankey's Horse', 'The Green Linnets' and 'The Flamers', the first because the regiment arrived at the Battle of Almanza (1707) on mules, the second for the regiment's green facings, and the third for an episode in 1857 when the regiment successfully fought a major fire on the troopship in which it was embarked. The only imperial regiment affiliated to The Dorset Regiment was the 39th Battalion, Australian Infantry.

The two components of The Dorset Regiment were the 39th (Dorsetshire) Regiment of Foot and the 54th (West Norfolk) Regiment of Foot.

The senior of these was the 39th (Dorsetshire) Regiment of Foot, which had been raised in 1702 as Colonel Richard Coote's Regiment of Foot. The name of the regiment then changed with its colonels until 1751, when it became the 39th Regiment of Foot, this in turn being modified to the 39th (or East Middlesex) Regiment of Foot in 1782. The Dorset association arrived in 1809, when the regiment became the 39th (or Dorsetshire) Regiment of Foot. The battle honours of the regiment were the following:

> Plassey   Gibraltar (with Castle and Key)   Albuhera   Vittoria
> Pyrenees   Nivelle   Nive   Orthes   Peninsula   Maharajpore
> Sevastopol

The motto of the regiment was 'Primus in Indis' (First in India), in reference to the fact that this was the first British army rather than Honourable East India Company army regiment to serve in India, and the uniform was scarlet with grass green facings. The nicknames associated with the regiment were 'Sankey's Horse' and 'The Green Linnets'.

Junior partner to the 39th (Dorsetshire) Regiment of Foot in The Dorset Regiment was the 54th (West Norfolk) Regiment of Foot, which had been raised in 1755 by Lieutenant-Colonel John Campbell as the 56th Regiment of Foot. In 1757 the regiment was renumbered the 54th Regiment of Foot, and in 1782 this became the 54th (or West Norfolk) Regiment of Foot. The regiment's battle honours were the following:

> Egypt (with the Sphinx)   Marabout   Ava

The uniform was scarlet with grass green facings, and the nickname associated with the regiment was 'The Flamers'.

REGIMENTS OF INFANTRY 8

The Light Infantry (13th, 32nd, 46th, 51st, 53rd, 68th, 85th, 105th and 106th)

Colonel-in-Chief

HM Queen Elizabeth The Queen Mother

Colonel

Major-General B. M. Lane

Battle honours

Gibraltar 1704–05 Dettingen Minden Nieuport St Lucia 1796 Tournay Dominica Egypt (with the Sphinx) Corunna Rolica Vimiera Martinique 1809 Talavera Fuentes d'Onor Salamanca Vittoria Pyrenees Nivelle Nive Orthes Toulouse Peninsula Bladensburg Waterloo Ava Aliwal Sobraon Ghuznee 1839 Affghanistan 1839 Cabool 1842 Jellalabad Mooltan Goojerat Punjaub Alma Inkerman Sevastopol Reshire Bushire Koosh-Ab Persia Lucknow New Zealand Pegu Ali Masjid South Africa 1878–79 Afghanistan 1878–80 Tel-el-Kebir Egypt 1882 Nile 1884–85 Suakin 1885 Burma 1885–87 Modder River Paardeberg Relief of Ladysmith South Africa 1899–1902 Mons Le Cateau Retreat from Mons Marne 1914, '18 Aisne 1914, '18 La Bassee 1914 Messines 1914, '17, '18 Armentieres 1914 Ypres 1914, '15, '17, '18 Hill 60 Gravenstafel St Julien Frezenberg Bellewaarde Hooge 1915 Loos

Mount Sorrel   Somme 1916, '18   Albert 1916, '18   Bazentin   Delville Wood   Pozieres   Guillemont   Flers-Courcelette   Morval   Le Transloy   Ancre Heights   Ancre 1916, '18   Bapaume 1917, '18   Arras 1917, '18   Vimy 1917   Scarpe 1917, '18   Arleux   Hill 70   Pilckem   Langemarck 1917   Menin Road   Polygon Wood   Broodseinde   Poelcappelle   Passchendaele   Cambrai 1917, '18   St Quentin   Rosieres   Avre   Lys   Estaires   Hazebrouck   Bailleul   Kemmel   Bethune   Scherpenberg   Marne 1918   Soissonais-Ourcq   Tardenois   Amiens   Drocourt-Queant   Bligny   Hindenburg Line   Havrincourt   Epehy   Canal du Nord   St Quentin Canal   Beaurevoir   Courtrai   Selle   Valenciennes   Sambre   France and Flanders 1914–18   Piave   Vittorio Veneto   Italy 1917–18   Struma   Doiran 1917, '18   Macedonia 1915–18   Suvla   Landing at Suvla   Scimitar Hill   Gallipoli 1915   Rumani   Egypt 1915–17   Gaza   El Mughar   Nebi Samwil   Jerusalem   Jericho   Tell' Asur   Megiddo   Sharon   Palestine 1917–18   Tigris 1916   Sharqat   Mesopotamia 1916–18   NW Frontier India 1915, '16–17   Aden   Archangel 1918–19   Afghanistan 1919   Kvam   Norway 1940   Dyle   Defence of Escaut   Arras Counter Attack   St Omer-La Bassee   Dunkirk 1940   Normandy Landing   Villers Bocage   Tilly sur Seulles   Odon   Fontenay le Pesnil   Cheux   Defence of Rauray   Caen   Hill 112   Bourgebus Ridge   Cagny   Troarn   Mont Pincon   Souleuvre   Le Perier Ridge   St Pierre la Vielle   Noireau Crossing   Falaise   Seine 1944   Antwerp   Hechel   Gheel   Nederrijn   Le Havre   Antwerp-Turnhout Canal   Lower Maas   Opheusden   Venraij   Geilenkirchen   Venlo Pocket   Roer   Rhineland   Cleve   Goch   Hochwald   Xanten   Rhine   Ibbenburen   Lingen   Aller   Bremen   North-West Europe 1940, '44–45   Syria 1941   Halfaya 1941   Tobruk 1941   Relief of Tobruk   Gazala   Gabr el Fachri   Zt El Mrasses   Mersa Matruh   Point 174   El Alamein   Mareth   Sedjenane I   Mine de Sedjenane   El Kourzia   Argoub Sellah   Medjez Plain   Gueriat el Atach Ridge   Si Abdallah   Tunis   Djebel Bou Aoukaz 1943 I   North Africa 1940–43   Landing in Sicily   Solarino   Primosole Bridge   Sicily 1943   Salerno   Salerno Hill   Cava di Tirreni   Volturno Crossing   Monte Camino   Garigliano Crossing   Minturno   Monte Tuga   Anzio   Campoleone   Carroceto   Cassino II   Trasimene Line   Arezzo   Advance to Florence   Incontro   Gothic Line   Gemmano Ridge   Carpineta   Capture of Forli   Cosina Canal Crossing   Defence of Lamone Bridgehead   Pergola Ridge   Rimini Line   Cesena   Monte Ceco   Monte Grande   Sillaro Crossing   Italy 1943–45   Athens   Greece 1944–45   Cos   Middle East 1942   Sittang 1942   Donbaik   North Arakan   Buthidaung   Nyakyedauk Pass   Kohima   Mandalay   Burma 1942, '43–45   Kowang-San   Hill 227 I   Korea 1951–53

THE LIGHT INFANTRY

Regimental headquarters

Peninsula Barracks, Winchester, Hampshire.

Regimental museums

(The Somerset Light Infantry) Somerset County Museum, Taunton Castle, Taunton, Somerset.
(The Duke of Cornwall's Light Infantry) The Keep, Bodmin, Cornwall.
(The King's Own Yorkshire Light Infantry) Light Infantry Office (Yorkshire), Wakefield Road, Pontefract, Yorkshire.
(The King's Shropshire Light Infantry) Sir John Moore Barracks, Copthorne, Shrewsbury, Shropshire.
(The Durham Light Infantry) Aykley Heads, Durham, Co Durham.

Regimental marches

(quick) Light Infantry
(slow) The Keel Row

Regimental mottoes

Aucto Splendore Resurgo (I Rise Again with Greater Splendour), and Cede Nullis (Yield to None)

Nicknames

see below

Uniform

Dark green jacket and blue trousers with white piping and blue facings

Allied regiments

The Royal Hamilton Light Infantry (Wentworth Regiment) (Canada)
Le Régiment de Maisonneuve (Canada)
The North Saskatchewan Regiment (Canada)
The Monash University Regiment (Australia)
2nd Battalion (Canterbury and Nelson, Marlborough and West Coast)
The Royal New Zealand Infantry Regiment
11th Battalion The Baluch Regiment (Pakistan)
13th Battalion The Baluch Regiment (Pakistan)
1st Battalion The Kenya Rifles
The Mauritius Special Mobile Force

Regimental history

The Light Infantry came into existence in July 1968 through the amalgamation of four light infantry regiments already formed by a process of amalgamation from nine older regiments. The four regiments involved in the 1968 consolidation were The Somerset and Cornwall Light Infantry, The King's Own Yorkshire Light Infantry, The King's Shropshire Light Infantry, and The Durham Light Infantry.

The most senior of the four regiments was The Somerset and Cornwall Light Infantry, which had been formed in October 1959 by the amalgamation of The Somerset Light Infantry (Prince Albert's) (13th) and The Duke of Cornwall's Light Infantry (32nd and 46th).

The Somerset Light Infantry (Prince Albert's) (13th) had been raised in 1685 by the Earl of Huntingdon as The Earl of Huntingdon's Regiment of Foot, and the title of the regiment changed thereafter with its colonels until 1751, when the regiment became the 13th Regiment of Foot. It is worth noting that during the War of the Spanish Succession (1701–1714) the regiment existed in two forms during the campaign in Spain: the Earl of Peterborough was short of cavalry, and so during 1706 converted The Earl of Barrymore's Regiment of Foot (as the regiment was currently designated) into Pearce's Dragoons, a unit that survived to 1713; Barrymore meanwhile raised another regiment of foot. In 1782 the regiment became the 13th (1st Somersetshire) Regiment of Foot, and in 1822 succumbed to the need for light infantry when it became the 13th (or 1st Somersetshire) Regiment of Foot (Light Infantry). In 1842 this became the 13th or Prince Albert's Regiment of Light Infantry. In 1881 there were two changes, firstly to Prince Albert's Light Infantry (Somersetshire Regiment), and secondly to Prince Albert's (Somerset Light Infantry). The two changes of the twentieth century saw the regiment become, in 1912, Prince Albert's (Somerset Light Infantry) and, in 1921, The Somerset Light Infantry (Prince Albert's). The battle honours of the regiment were the following:

Gibraltar 1704–05   Dettingen   Martinique 1809   Ava   Ghuznee 1839   Affghanistan 1839   Cabool 1842   Jellalabad   Sevastopol   South Africa 1878–79   Burmah 1885–87   Relief of Ladysmith   South Africa 1899–1902   Le Cateau   Retreat from Mons   Marne 1914, '18   Aisne 1914   Armentieres 1914   Ypres 1914, '15, '17, '18   St Julien   Frezenberg   Bellewaarde   Hooge 1915   Loos   Mount Sorrel   Somme 1916, '18   Albert 1916, '18   Delville Wood   Guillemont   Flers-Courcelette   Morval   Le Transloy   Ancre 1916, '18   Arras 1917, '18   Vimy 1917   Scarpe 1917, '18   Arleux   Langemarck 1917   Menin Road   Polygon Wood   Broodseinde   Poelcappelle   Passchendaele   Cambrai 1917, '18   St Quentin   Bapaume 1918   Rosieres   Avre   Lys   Hazebrouck   Bethune   Soissonais-Ourcq   Drocourt-Queant   Hindenburg Line   Havrincourt   Epehy   Canal du Nord   Courtrai   Selle   Valenciennes

Sambre   France and Flanders 1914–18   Gaza   El Mughar
Nebi Samwil   Jerusalem   Megiddo   Sharon   Palestine 1917–18
Tigris 1916   Sharqat   Mesopotamia 1916–18   NW Frontier India
1915   Odon   Caen   Hill 112   Mont Pincon   Noireau Crossing
Seine 1944   Nederrijn   Geilenkirchen   Roer   Rhineland
Cleve   Goch   Hochwald   Xanten   Rhine   Bremen
North-West Europe 1944–45   Cassino II   Trasimene Line   Arezzo
Advance to Florence   Capture of Forli   Cosina Canal Crossing
Italy 1944–45   Athens   Greece 1944–45   North Arakan   Buthidaung
Nyakyedauk Pass   Burma 1943–44

The motto of the regiment was 'Honi Soit Qui Mal y Pense' (Evil be to Him who Evil Thinks), and the regimental marches were 'Prince Albert' (Glover, quick) and 'Palace Guard' (James, slow). The uniform was a dark green jacket and blue trousers with white piping and blue facings, and the nicknames associated with The Somerset Light Infantry were 'The Illustrious Garrison', 'The Jellalabad Heroes', 'The Yellow-Banded Robbers' and 'The Bleeders', the first and second in appreciation of the regiment's six-month defence of Jellalabad (1841–42). Imperial regiments affiliated to The Somerset Light Infantry were the Royal Hamilton Light Infantry (Canada) and the 13th Battalion, Australian Infantry.

Junior partner to The Somerset Light Infantry in The Somerset and Cornwall Light Infantry was The Duke of Cornwall's Light Infantry, itself an amalgamation in 1881 of the 32nd (Cornwall) Light Infantry and the 46th (South Devonshire) Regiment of Foot. The combined regiment's battle honours were the following:

Gibraltar 1704–04   Dettingen   St Lucia 1778   Dominica   Rolica
Vimiera   Corunna   Salamanca   Pyrenees   Nivelle   Nive   Orthes
Peninsula   Waterloo   Mooltan   Goojerat   Punjaub   Sevastopol
Lucknow   Tel-el-Kebir   Egypt 1882   Nile 1884–85   Paardeberg
South Africa 1899–1902   Mons   Le Cateau   Retreat from Mons
Marne 1914   Aisne 1914   La Bassee 1914   Marne 1914   Aisne 1914
La Bassee 1914   Armentieres 1914   Ypres 1915, '17   Gravenstafel
St Julien   Frezenberg   Bellewaarde   Hooge 1915   Mount Sorrel
Somme 1916, '18   Delville Wood   Guillemont   Flers-Courcelette
Morval   Le Transloy   Ancre 1916   Bapaume 1917, '18   Arras 1917
Vimy 1917   Scarpe 1917   Arleux   Langemarck 1917   Menin Road
Polygon Wood   Broodseinde   Poelcappelle   Passchendaele
Cambrai 1917, '18   St Quentin   Rosieres   Lys   Estaires   Hazebrouck
Albert 1918   Hindenburg Line   Havrincourt   Canal du Nord   Selle
Sambre   France and Flanders 1914–18   Italy 1917–18   Struma   Doiran
1917, '18   Macedonia 1915–18   Gaza   Nebi Samwil   Jerusalem
Tell' Asur   Megiddo   Sharon   Palestine 1917–18   Aden   Defence of
Escaut   Cheux   Hill 112   Mont Pincon   Noireau Crossing

Nederrijn   Opheusden   Geilenkirchen   Rhineland   Goch   Rhine   North-West Europe 1940, '44–45   Gazala   Medjez Plain   Si Abdallah   North Africa 1942–43   Cassino II   Trasimene Line   Advance to Florence   Incontro   Rimini Line   Italy 1944–45

The motto of the regiment was 'One and All', and the regimental marches were 'One and All' and 'Trelawney' (both quick). The uniform was a scarlet jacket and blue trousers with white piping and facings, and the nicknames associated with The Duke of Cornwall's Light Infantry were 'The Docs', 'The Red Feathers' (2nd Battalion), 'The Surprisers' (2nd Battalion), 'The Lacedaemonians' (2nd Battalion), and 'Murray's Bucks' (2nd Battalion), the first being an acronym of Duke of Cornwall and the second an allusion to the colour with which the regiment dyed its head-dress feathers during the American War of Independence (1775–83). Imperial regiments affiliated to The Duke of Cornwall's Light Infantry were the Battleford Light Infantry (Canada), the 46th Battalion, Australian Infantry, and the Rand Light Infantry (South Africa).

Of The Duke of Cornwall's Light Infantry the senior component was the 32nd (Cornwall) Light Infantry, which had been raised in 1702 as Colonel Edward Fox's Regiment of Marines. The title changed with the marine regiment's colonels until 1713 when this prototype regiment was disbanded. But in 1715 it was re-raised as the 32nd Regiment of Foot, changed in 1782 to the 32nd (or the Cornwall) Regiment of Foot. In 1858 this became the 32nd (Cornwall) Light Infantry in recognition of the regiment's distinguished role in the Indian Mutiny (1857–58). The battle honours of the regiment were the following:

Dettingen   Rolica   Vimiera   Corunna   Salamanca   Pyrenees   Nivelle   Nive   Orthes   Peninsula   Waterloo   Goojerat   Mooltan   Punjaub   Lucknow

The uniform was scarlet with white facings.

The junior component of The Duke of Cornwall's Light Infantry was the 46th (South Devonshire) Regiment of Foot, which had been raised in 1741 as Colonel John Price's Regiment of Foot. The name changed with the regiment's colonels until 1751, when it became the 46th Regiment of Foot. In 1782 it was restyled the 45th (or South Devonshire) Regiment of Foot. The battle honours of the regiment were the following:

Dominica   Sevastopol

The uniform was scarlet with yellow facings.

Next in seniority to The Somerset and Cornwall Light Infantry was The King's Own Yorkshire Light Infantry, formed in 1881 by the amalgamation of the 51st (2nd Yorkshire West Riding) The King's Own Light Infantry

Regiment and the 105th (Madras Light Infantry) Regiment. The battle honours of the combined regiment were the following:

Minden   Corunna   Fuentes d'Onor   Salamanca   Vittoria   Pyrenees   Nivelle   Orthes   Peninsula   Waterloo   Pegu   Ali Masjid   Afghanistan 1878–80   Burma 1885–87   Modder River   South Africa 1899–1902   Mons   Le Cateau   Retreat from Mons   Marne 1914, '18   Aisne 1914, '18   La Bassee 1914   Messines 1914, '17, '18   Ypres 1914, '15, '17, '18   Hill 60   Gravenstafel   St Julien   Frezenberg   Bellewaarde   Hooge 1915   Loos   Somme 1916, '18   Albert 1916, '18   Bazentin   Delville Wood   Pozieres   Guillemont   Flers-Courcelette   Morval   Le Transloy   Ancre 1916   Arras 1917, '18   Scarpe 1917   Langemarck 1917   Menin Road   Polygon Wood   Broodseinde   Poelcappelle   Passchendaele   Cambrai 1917, '18   St Quentin   Bapaume 1918   Lys   Hazebrouck   Bailleul   Kemmel   Scherpenberg   Tardenois   Amiens   Hindenburg Line   Havrincourt   Epehy   Canal du Nord   St Quentin Canal   Beaurevoir   Selle   Valenciennes   Sambre   France and Flanders 1914–18   Piave   Vittorio Veneto   Italy 1917–18   Struma   Macedonia 1915–17   Egypt 1915–16   Kvam   Norway 1940   Fontenay le Pesnil   Le Havre   Antwerp-Turnhout Canal   Lower Maas   North-West Europe 1944–45   Mine de Sedjenane   Argoub Sellah   North Africa 1943   Sicily 1943   Salerno   Salerno Hills   Cava di Tirreni   Volturno Crossing   Garigliano Crossing   Minturno   Monte Tuga   Anzio   Gemmano Ridge   Carpineta   Lamone Bridgehead   Italy 1943–45   Sittang 1942   Burma 1942

The motto of the regiment was 'Cede Nullis' (Yield to None), and the regimental marches were 'Jockey to the Fair' (traditional, quick) and 'The Keel Row' (traditional, slow). The uniform was a dark green jacket and blue trousers with white piping and blue facings, and the nickname associated with The King's Own Yorkshire Light Infantry was 'The Koylis'. Imperial regiments affiliated to The King's Own Yorkshire Light Infantry were the Saskatoon Light Infantry (Canada) and the 51st Battalion, Australian Infantry.

The 51st (2nd Yorkshire West Riding) The King's Own Yorkshire Light Infantry Regiment could trace its origins to 1755, when Colonel Robert Napier raised the 53rd Regiment of Foot, otherwise known as Napier's Regiment of Foot. In 1757 this was renumbered the 51st Regiment of Foot, and in 1782 became the 51st (2nd Yorkshire, West Riding) Regiment of Foot. In 1809 the regiment became a light infantry unit with the designation 51st (2nd Yorkshire West Riding) Regiment of Foot (Light Infantry), this title being modified in 1821 to the 51st (2nd Yorkshire West Riding) The King's Own Light Infantry Regiment. The battle honours of the regiment were the following:

Minden Corunna Fuentes d'Onor Salamanca Vittoria Pyrenees Nivelle Orthes Peninsula Waterloo Pegu Ali Masjid Afghanistan 1878–80

The regimental marches were 'The Jockey of York' (traditional, quick) and 'The Keel Row' (traditional, slow), and the uniform was scarlet with blue facings.

The junior partner in The King's Own Yorkshire Light Infantry was the 105th (Madras Light Infantry) Regiment, which had been raised in 1839 as the 2nd Madras European Regiment (Light Infantry) of the army of the Honourable East India Company. In 1858 the regiment became the 2nd (Madras) Light Infantry Regiment, and this was in 1861 transferred to the British army establishment as the 105th (Madras Light Infantry) Regiment. The regiment had no battle honours, its motto was 'Cede Nullis' (Yield to None), and the uniform was scarlet with buff facings.

Third in seniority among the regiments that went into The Light Infantry in 1968 was The King's Shropshire Light Infantry, itself the result of the amalgamation in 1881 of the 53rd (Shropshire) Regiment of Foot and the 85th King's Light Infantry. The battle honours of the combined regiment were the following:

Nieuport Tournay St Lucia 1796 Talavera Fuentes d'Onor Salamanca Vittoria Pyrenees Nivelle Nive Toulouse Peninsula Bladensburg Aliwal Sobraon Goojerat Punjaub Lucknow Afghanistan 1879–80 Egypt 1882 Suakin 1885 Paardeberg South Africa 1899–1902 Aisne 1914, '18 Armentieres 1914 Ypres 1915, '17 Gravenstafel St Julien Frezenberg Bellewaarde Hooge 1915 Mount Sorrel Somme 1916, '18 Albert 1916, '18 Bazentin Delville Wood Guillemont Flers-Courcelette Morval Le Transloy Ancre 1916 Arras 1917, '18 Scarpe 1917 Arleux Hill 70 Langemarck 1917 Menin Road Polygon Wood Passchendaele Cambrai 1917, '18 St Quentin Bapaume 1918 Rosieres Lys Estaires Messines 1918 Hazebrouck Bailleul Kemmel Bethune Bligny Hindenburg Line Epehy Canal du Nord Selle Valenciennes Sambre France and Flanders 1914–18 Doiran 1917, '18 Macedonia 1915–18 Gaza Jerusalem Jericho Tell' Asur Palestine 1917–18 Defence of Escaut Dunkirk 1940 Normandy Landing Odon Caen Bourgebus Ridge Troarn Mont Pincon Souleuvre Le Perier Ridge Falaise Antwerp Nederrijn Venraij Rhineland Hochwald Ibbenburen Lingen Aller Bremen North-West Europe 1940, '44–45 Gueriat el Atach Ridge Tunis Djebel Bou Aoukaz 1943 II North Africa 1943 Anzio Campoleone Carroceto Gothic Line Monte Ceco Monte Grande Italy 1943–45 Kowang-San Hill 227 I Korea 1951–53

The motto of the regiment was 'Auctore Splendore Resurgo' (I Rise Again with Greater Splendour), and the regimental marches were 'Owd Towler' (Shields, quick), and 'The 53rd March' (anonymous, slow) and 'The Daughter of the Regiment' (Donizetti, slow). The uniform was a dark green jacket with white piping and blue trousers with a dark green stripe, and the nicknames associated with The King's Shropshire Light Infantry were 'The Brickdusts' (1st Battalion), 'The Old Five-and-Threepennies' (1st Battalion), 'The Elegant Extracts' (2nd Battalion), 'The Old Brickdusts' (2nd Battalion) and 'The Young Bucks' (2nd Battalion), the 'brickdust' referring to the colour of the 53rd's facings and 'The Young Bucks' to the county in which the 85th was raised. No imperial regiments were affiliated to The King's Shropshire Light Infantry.

Within The King's Shropshire Light Infantry the senior component was the 53rd (Shropshire) Regiment of Foot, first raised in 1755 as the 55th Regiment of Foot, but renumbered the 53rd Regiment of Foot in 1757. In 1782 the regiment became the 53rd (or the Shropshire) Regiment of Foot. The battle honours of the regiment were the following:

> Nieuport Tournay St Lucia Talavera Salamanca Vittoria
> Pyrenees Nivelle Toulouse Peninsula Aliwal Sobraon
> Punjaub Goojerat Lucknow

The regimental march was 'Old Towler' (Shields, quick), and the uniform was scarlet with scarlet facings.

The junior component of The King's Shropshire Light Infantry was the 85th King's Light Infantry, which had been raised in 1793 as the 85th Regiment of Foot (or Buck's Volunteers), and in 1808 transformed into the 85th Regiment of Foot (Buck's Volunteers) (Light Infantry). In 1815 this became the 85th King's Light Infantry. The battle honours of the regiment were the following:

> Fuentes d'Onor Nive Peninsula Bladensburg Afghanistan 1879–80

The motto of the regiment was 'Auctore Splendore Resurgo' (I Rise Again with Greater Splendour), and the regimental march was 'Daughter of the Regiment' (Donizetti, quick). The uniform was scarlet with blue facings.

The most junior of the regiments amalgamated into The Light Infantry in 1968 was The Durham Light Infantry, itself the result of the amalgamation in 1881 of the 68th (Durham) Light Infantry and the 106th Bombay Light Infantry. The battle honours of the combined regiment were the following:

> Salamanca Vittoria Pyrenees Nivelle Orthes Peninsula Alma
> Inkerman Sevastopol Reshire Bushire Koosh-Ab Persia New
> Zealand Relief of Ladysmith South Africa 1899–1902 Aisne 1914, '18
> Armentieres 1914 Ypres 1915, '17, '18 Gravenstafel St Julien
> Frezenberg Bellewaarde Hooge 1915 Loos Somme 1916, '18

Albert 1916, '18 Bazentin Delville Wood Pozieres Guillemont
Flers-Courcelette Morval Le Transloy Ancre Heights Arras
1917, '18 Scarpe 1917 Arleux Hill 70 Messines 1917 Pilckem
Langemarck 1917 Menin Road Polygon Wood Broodseinde
Passchendaele Cambrai 1917, '18 St Quentin Rosieres Lys
Estaires Hazebrouck Bailleul Kemmel Scherpenberg Marne
1918 Tardenois Bapaume 1918 Hindenburg Line Havrincourt
Epehy Canal du Nord St Quentin Canal Beaurevoir Courtrai
Selle Sambre France and Flanders 1914–18 Piave
Vittorio Veneto Italy 1917–18 Macedonia 1916–18 Egypt 1915–16
NW Frontier India 1915, '16–17 Archangel 1918–19 Afghanistan
1919 Dyle Arras Counter Attack St Omer-La Bassee
Dunkirk 1940 Villers Bocage Tilly sur Seulles Defence of Rauray
St Pierre la Vielle Gheel Roer Ibbenburen North-West
Europe 1940, '44–45 Syria 1941 Halfaya 1941 Tobruk 1941 Relief
of Tobruk Gazala Gabr el Fachri Zt El Mrasses Mersa Matruh
Point 174 El Alamein Mareth Sedjenane I El Kourzia North Africa
1940–43 Landing in Sicily Solarino Primosole Bridge Sicily 1943
Salerno Volturno Crossing Teano Monte Camino Monte Tuga
Gothic Line Gemmano Ridge Cosina Canal Crossing
Pergola Ridge Cesena Sillaro Crossing Italy 1943–45 Malta 1942
Donbaik Kohima Mandalay Burma 1943–45 Korea 1952–53

The motto of the regiment was 'Faithful', and the regimental marches were 'The Light Barque' (quick), 'Old 68th' (slow), and 'The Keel Row' and 'Monymusk' (double). The uniform was a dark green jacket and blue trousers with white piping and dark green facings, and the nickname associated with The Durham Light Infantry was 'The Faithful Durhams'. Imperial regiments affiliated to The Durham Light Infantry were the Winnipeg Light Infantry (Canada), the Canterbury Regiment (New Zealand) and the Nelson, Marlborough and West Coast Regiment (New Zealand).

Of the two regiments that went to form The Durham Light Infantry the senior was the 68th (Durham) Light Infantry, originally raised in 1756 as the 2nd Battalion of the 23rd Regiment of Foot, but then given its own identity in 1768 as the 68th Regiment of Foot. In 1782 this became the 68th (or the Durham) Regiment of Foot, and in 1808 the regiment became the 68th (Durham) Light Infantry. The battle honours of the regiment were the following:

Salamanca Vittoria Pyrenees Nivelle Orthes Peninsula Alma
Inkerman Sevastopol New Zealand

The regimental marches were 'The Light Barque' (quick), 'Prince Regent' (slow), and 'The Keel Row' and 'Monymusk' (double). The uniform was scarlet with dark green facings, and the nickname associated with the 68th (Durham) Light Infantry was 'The Faithfuls'.

The 68th (Durham) Light Infantry's junior partner was the 106th Bombay Light Infantry, originally raised by the army of the Honourable East India Company as the 2nd Bombay European Regiment of Foot but converted firstly, in 1840, to the 2nd Bombay European Light Infantry and secondly, in 1855, to the 2nd European Regiment, Bombay Light Infantry. In 1861 the regiment came onto the British establishment as the 106th Bombay Light Infantry, whose battle honours were the following:

Reshire   Bushire   Koosh-Ab   Persia

The regimental marches were 'Ap Shenkin' and 'The Light Barque' (quick), 'In the Garb of Old Gaul' (slow), and 'The Keel Row' and 'Monymusk' (double). The uniform was scarlet with white facings, and the nickname associated with the 106th Bombay Light Infantry was 'The Busters'.

REGIMENTS OF INFANTRY 9

The Prince of Wales's Own Regiment of Yorkshire (14th and 15th)

Colonel-in-Chief

Honorary Major-General HRH The Duchess of Kent

Colonel

Major-General H. M. Tillotson

Battle honours

Namur 1695 Blenheim Ramillies Oudenarde Malplaquet Louisburg Quebec 1759 Martinique 1762 Havannah St Lucia 1778 Martinique 1794, 1809 Tournay Corunna Guadaloupe 1810 Java Waterloo Bhurtpore India Sevastopol New Zealand Afghanistan 1879–80 Relief of Ladysmith South Africa 1899–1902 Aisne 1914, '18 Armentieres 1914 Neuve Chapelle Ypres 1915, '17, '18 Gravenstafel St Julien Frezenberg Bellewaarde Aubers Hooge 1915 Loos Somme 1916, '18 Albert 1916, '18 Bazentin Delville Wood Pozieres Flers-Courcelette Morval Thiepval Le Transloy Ancre Heights Ancre 1916 Arras 1917, '18 Scarpe 1917, '18 Arleux Oppy Bullecourt Hill 70 Messines 1917, '18 Pilckem Langemarck 1917 Menin Road Polygon Wood Broodseinde

Poelcappelle Passchendaele Cambrai 1917, '18 St Quentin
Bapaume 1918 Rosieres Villers Bretonneux Lys Estaires
Hazebrouck Bailleul Kemmel Scherpenberg Marne 1918
Tardenois Amiens Drocourt-Queant Hindenburg Line
Havrincourt Epehy Canal du Nord St Quentin Canal Selle
Valenciennes Sambre France and Flanders 1914–18 Piave
Vittorio Veneto Italy 1917–18 Struma Doiran 1917 Macedonia
1915–18 Suvla Landing at Suvla Scimitar Hill Gallipoli 1915 Egypt
1915–16 Withdrawal to Escaut Defence of Escaut Defence of Arras
French Frontier 1940 Ypres-Comines Canal Dunkirk 1940
Normandy Landing Tilly sur Seulles Odon Caen
Bourgebus Ridge Troarn Mont Pincon St Pierre la Vielle Gheel
Nederrijn Aam Venraij Rhineland Schaddenhof Brinkum
Bremen North-West Europe 1940, '44–45 Jebel Dafeis Keren
Ad Teclesan Abyssinia 1940–41 Gazala Cauldron Mersa Matruh
Defence of Alamein Line El Alamein Mareth Wadi Zigzaou
Akarit North Africa 1940–43 Primosole Bridge Sicily 1943
Pegu 1942 Yenangyaung 1942 North Arakan Maungdaw
Defence of Sinzweya Imphal Bishenpur Kanglatongbi Meiktila
Capture of Meiktila Defence of Meiktila Rangoon Road Pyawbwe
Sittang 1945 Burma 1942–45

Regimental headquarters

3/3A Tower Street, York, Yorkshire.

Regimental museum

3/3A Tower Street, York, Yorkshire.

Regimental marches

(quick) Ça Ira (Becourt), and The Yorkshire Lass (traditional)
(slow) God Bless the Prince of Wales (Richards) and March of the
XV Regiment (Anonymous)

Regimental motto

Nec Aspera Terrent (Nor do Difficulties Deter)

Nicknames

see below

Uniform

Scarlet with white piping and facings

Allied regiments

Les Voltigeurs de Quebec (Canada)
1st Battalion The Royal New Brunswick Regiment (Carleton and York) (Canada)
The Royal Montreal Regiment (Canada)
The Falkland Islands Defence Force

Regimental history

The Prince of Wales's Own Regiment of Yorkshire was created in April 1958 by the amalgamation of The West Yorkshire Regiment (The Prince of Wales's Own) and The East Yorkshire Regiment (The Duke of York's Own).

Just the senior of these two components was The West Yorkshire Regiment (The Prince of Wales's Own), which had been raised in 1685 as Colonel Sir Edward Hales's Regiment of Foot. Thereafter the name of the regiment changed with its colonels until 1751, when it became the 14th Regiment of Foot. The regiment then underwent a series of county affiliations, changing in 1782 to the 14th (or the Bedfordshire) Regiment of Foot, in 1876 to the 14th (Buckinghamshire) (Prince of Wales's Own) Regiment of Foot, and then in 1881 to The Prince of Wales's Own (West Yorkshire Regiment) which in 1920 became The West Yorkshire Regiment (The Prince of Wales's Own). The battle honours of the regiment were the following:

Namur 1695   Tournay   Corunna   Java   Waterloo   Bhurtpore   India   Sevastopol   New Zealand   Afghanistan 1879–80   Relief of Ladysmith   South Africa 1899–1902   Aisne 1914, '18   Armentieres 1914   Neuve Chapelle   Aubers   Hooge 1915   Loos   Somme 1916, '18   Albert 1916, '18   Bazentin   Pozieres   Flers-Courcelette   Morval   Thiepval   Le Transloy   Ancre Heights   Ancre 1916   Arras 1917, '18   Scarpe 1917, '18   Bullecourt   Hill 70   Messines 1917, '18   Ypres 1917, '18   Pilckem   Langemarck 1917   Menin Road   Polygon Wood   Poelcappelle   Passchendaele   Cambrai 1917, '18   St Quentin   Rosieres   Villers Bretonneux   Lys   Hazebrouck   Bailleul   Kemmel   Marne 1918   Tardenois   Amiens   Bapaume 1918   Drocourt-Queant   Hindenburg Line   Havrincourt   Epehy   Canal du Nord   Selle   Valenciennes   Sambre   France and Flanders 1914–18   Piave   Vittorio Veneto   Italy 1917–18   Suvla   Landing at Suvla   Scimitar Hill   Gallipoli 1915   Egypt 1915–16   North-West Europe 1940   Jebel Dafeis

Keren   Ad Teclesan   Abyssinia 1940–41   Cauldron   Defence of Alamein Line   North Africa 1940–42   Pegu 1942   Yenangyaung 1942   North Arakan   Maungdaw   Defence of Sinzweya   Imphal   Bishenpur   Kanglatongbi   Meiktila   Capture of Meiktila   Defence of Meiktila   Rangoon Road   Pyawbwe   Sittang 1945   Burma 1942–45

The motto of the regiment was 'Nec Aspera Terrent' (Nor do Difficulties Deter), and the regimental marches were 'Ça Ira' (Becourt, quick) and 'God Bless the Prince of Wales' (Richards, slow). The uniform was scarlet with buff piping and facings, and the nicknames associated with The West Yorkshire Regiment were 'The Powos', 'The Old and Bold' and 'Calvert's Entire', the first being an acronym of Prince of Wales's Own. Imperial regiments affiliated to The West Yorkshire Regiment were the Royal Montreal Regiment (Canada), the 14th Battalion, Australian Infantry, and the Waikato Regiment (New Zealand).

The West Yorkshire Regiment's junior partner in The Prince of Wales's Own Yorkshire Regiment was The East Yorkshire Regiment (The Duke of York's Own), which had been raised in 1685 as Sir William Clifton's Regiment of Foot. The regiment changed its name with its colonels until 1751, when it became the 15th Regiment of Foot. In 1782 the county affiliation was made with the change of title to the 15th (or the Yorkshire East Riding) Regiment of Foot, and further changes refined this to The East Yorkshire Regiment in 1881, and to The East Yorkshire Regiment (The Duke of York's Own) in 1935. The battle honours of the regiment were the following:

Blenheim   Ramillies   Oudenarde   Malplaquet   Louisburg   Quebec 1759   Martinique 1762   Havannah   St Lucia 1778   Martinique 1794, 1809   Guadaloupe 1810   Afghanistan 1879–80   South Africa 1900–02   Aisne 1914, '18   Armentieres 1914   Ypres 1915, '17, '18   Gravenstafel   St Julien   Frezenberg   Bellewaarde   Hooge 1915   Loos   Somme 1916, '18   Albert 1916, '18   Bazentin   Delville Wood   Pozieres   Flers-Courcelette   Morval   Thiepval   Ancre Heights   Ancre 1916   Arras 1917, '18   Scarpe 1917, '18   Arleux   Oppy   Messines 1917, '18   Pilckem   Langemarck 1917   Menin Road   Polygon Wood   Broodseinde   Poelcappelle   Passchendaele   Cambrai 1917, '18   St Quentin   Bapaume 1918   Rosieres   Lys   Estaires   Hazebrouck   Kemmel   Scherpenberg   Amiens   Hindenburg Line   Epehy   Canal du Nord   St Quentin Canal   Selle   Sambre   France and Flanders 1914–18   Struma   Doiran 1917   Macedonia 1915–18   Suvla   Landing at Suvla   Scimitar Hill   Gallipoli 1915   Egypt 1915–16   Withdrawal to Escaut   Defence of Escaut   Defence of Arras   French Frontier 1940   Ypres-Comines Canal   Dunkirk 1940   Normandy Landing   Tilly sur Seulles   Odon   Caen   Bourgebus Ridge   Troarn   Mont Pincon   St Pierre la Vielle   Gheel   Nederrijn   Aam   Venraij   Rhineland   Schaddenhof   Brinkum   Bremen   North-West Europe 1940, '44–45

Gazala   Mersa Matruh   Defence of Alamein Line   El Alamein
Mareth   Wadi Zagzaou   Akarit   North Africa 1942–43
Primosole Bridge   Sicily 1943   Sittang 1945   Burma 1945

The motto of the regiment was 'Honi Soit Qui Mal y Pense' (Evil be to Him who Evil Thinks), and the regimental marches were 'The Yorkshire Lass' (quick) and 'The XV von England' (slow). The uniform was scarlet with white piping and facings, and the nicknames associated with The East Yorkshire Regiment were 'The Snappers' and 'The Poona Guards', the first in reference to the time in the American War of Independence (1775–83) when the regiment was out of ammunition and snapped its musket locks to deter the approaching Americans.

REGIMENTS OF INFANTRY 10

The Green Howards (Alexandra, Princess of Wales's Own Yorkshire Regiment) (19th)

Colonel-in-Chief

HM King Olav V of Norway

Colonel

Major-General P. A. Iuge

Battle honours

Malplaquet Belleisle Alma Inkerman Sevastopol Tirah Relief of Kimberley Paardeberg South Africa 1899–1902 Ypres 1914, '15, '17 Langemarck 1914, '17 Gheluvelt Neuve Chapelle St Julien Frezenberg Bellewaarde Aubers Festubert 1915 Loos Somme 1916, '18 Albert 1916 Bazentin Pozieres Flers-Courcelette Morval Thiepval Le Transloy Ancre Heights Ancre 1916 Arras 1917, '18 Scarpe 1917, '18 Messines 1917, '18 Pilckem Menin Road Polygon Wood Broodseinde Poelcappelle Passchendaele Cambrai 1917, '18 St Quentin Bapaume 1918 Rosieres Lys Estaires Hazebrouck Kemmel Scherpenberg Aisne 1918 Drocourt-Queant Hindenburg Line Canal du Nord Beaurevoir Selle Valenciennes Sambre France and Flanders 1914–18

Piave   Vittorio Veneto   Italy 1917–18   Suvla   Landing at Suvla   Scimitar Hill   Gallipoli 1915   Egypt 1916   Archangel 1918   Afghanistan 1919   Otta   Norway 1940   Defence of Arras   Dunkirk 1940   Normandy Landing   Tilly sur Seulles   St Pierre la Vielle   Gheel   Nederrijn   North-West Europe 1940, '44–45   Gazala   Defence of Alamein Line   El Alamein   Mareth   Akarit   North Africa 1942–43   Landing in Sicily   Lentini   Sicily 1943   Minturno   Anzio   Italy 1943–44   Arakan Beaches   Burma 1945

Regimental headquarters

Trinity Church Square, The Market Place, Richmond, North Yorkshire.

Regimental museum

Trinity Church Square, The Market Place, Richmond, North Yorkshire.

Regimental marches

(quick) The Bonnie English Rose
(slow) Maria Theresa

Regimental motto

Honi Soit Qui Mal y Pense (Evil be to Him who Evil Thinks)

Nicknames

none

Uniform

Scarlet with grass green piping and facings

Allied regiments

The Rocky Mountain Rangers (Canada)
The Queen's York Rangers (1st American Regiment) (Canada)

Regimental history

The Green Howards is one of the few unamalgamated infantry regiments in the British army, and can find its origins in the companies of foot raised in 1688 by Colonel Francis Luttrell to aid the newly-arrived William III. In

1689 these companies were joined into Colonel Luttrell's Regiment of Foot, which subsequently changed name with its colonels until 1751, when it became the 19th Regiment of Foot. In 1782 it became the 19th (1st Yorkshire North Riding) Regiment of Foot. In 1875 the regiment became the 19th (1st Yorkshire North Riding Regiment) (The Princess of Wales's Own), and in 1902 Alexandra, Princess of Wales's Own Yorkshire Regiment. The definitive title, The Green Howards (Alexandra, Princess of Wales's Own Yorkshire Regiment) was adopted in 1921 to regularise the name by which the regiment was universally known, 'Howard' being the name of one of its more celebrated commanding officers, who chose the 'Green' facings to differentiate the regiment from The Buffs, which was at the time also commanded by a Howard. The only imperial regiment affiliated to The Green Howards was the York Rangers (Canada).

REGIMENTS OF INFANTRY 11

The Royal Highland Fusiliers (Princess Margaret's Own Glasgow and Ayrshire Regiment) (21st, 71st and 74th)

Colonel-in-Chief

HRH The Princess Margaret Countess of Snowdon

Colonel

Major-General R. L. S. Green

Battle honours

Blenheim Ramillies Oudenarde Malplaquet Dettingen Belleisle Carnatic Hindoostan Sholinghur Mysore Gibraltar 1780–83 Martinique 1794 Seringapatam Assaye Cape of Good Hope 1806 Rolica Vimiera Corunna Busaco Fuentes d'Onor Almarez Ciudad Rodrigo Badajoz Salamanca Vittoria Pyrenees Nivelle Nive Orthes Toulouse Peninsula Bladensburg Waterloo South Africa 1851–53 Alma Inkerman Sevastopol Central India South Africa 1879 Tel-el-Kebir Egypt 1882 Burmah 1885–87 Tirah Modder River Relief of Ladysmith South Africa 1899–1902 Mons Le Cateau Retreat from Mons Marne 1914 Aisne 1914 La Bassee

1914 Ypres 1914, '15, '17, '18 Langemarck 1914, '17 Gheluvelt
Nonne Bosschen Givenchy 1914 Neuve Chapelle St Julien Aubers
Festubert 1915 Loos Somme 1916, '18 Albert 1916, '18 Bazentin
Delville Wood Pozieres Flers-Courcelette Le Transloy
Ancre Heights Ancre 1916, '18 Arras 1917, '18 Vimy 1917
Scarpe 1917, '18 Arleux Messines 1917, '18 Pilckem Menin Road
Polygon Wood Passchendaele Cambrai 1917, '18 St Quentin
Bapaume 1918 Rosieres Lys Estaires Hazebrouck Bailleul
Kemmel Bethune Scherpenberg Amiens Drocourt-Queant
Hindenburg Line Havrincourt Canal du Nord St Quentin Canal
Beaurevoir Courtrai Selle Sambre France and Flanders 1914–18
Doiran 1917, '18 Macedonia 1916–18 Helles Gallipoli 1915–16
Rumani Egypt 1916–17 Gaza El Mughar Nebi Samwil Jerusalem
Jaffa Tell' Asur Palestine 1917–18 Tigris 1916 Kut al Amara 1917
Sharqat Mesopotamia 1916–18 Murman 1919 Archangel 1919
Defence of Arras Ypres-Comines Canal Somme 1940 Withdrawal
to Seine Withdrawal to Cherbourg Odon Fontenay le Pesnil
Cheux Defence of Rauray Esquay Mont Pincon Quarry Hill
Estray Falaise La Vie Crossing La Touques Crossing Seine 1944
Aart Nederrijn Best Le Havre Antwerp-Turnhout Canal Scheldt
South Beveland Walcheren Causeway Lower Maas Meijel
Venlo Pocket Roer Ourthe Rhineland Reichswald Cleve Goch
Moyland Wood Weeze Rhine Ibbenburen Dreierwalde Aller
Uelzen Bremen Artlenberg North-West Europe 1940, '44–45
Jebel Shiba Barentu Keren Massawa Abyssinia 1941 Gazala
Cauldron Mersa Matruh Fuka North Africa 1940–42 Landing in
Sicily Sicily 1943 Sangro Garigliano Crossing Minturno Anzio
Advance to Tiber Italy 1943, '44, 45 Madagascar Adriatic
Middle East 1942, '44 Athens Greece 1944–45 North Arakan
Razabil Pinwe Shweli Mandalay Burma 1944–45

Regimental headquarters

518 Sauchiehall Street, Glasgow, Scotland.

Regimental museum

518 Sauchiehall Street, Glasgow, Scotland.

Regimental marches

(quick) The British Grenadiers (traditional), and
Whistle o'er the Lave o't (traditional)

(slow) In the Garb of Old Gaul (Reid), and March of the 21st Regiment (anonymous)

Regimental motto

Nemo Me Impune Lacessit (No one Provokes me with Impunity)

Nicknames

see below

Uniform

Blue doublet and Mackenzie trews with blue facings

Allied regiments

The Highland Fusiliers of Canada
1st Battalion The Royal New Zealand Infantry Regiment
11th Battalion The Baluch Regiment (Pakistan)

Regimental history

The Royal Highland Fusiliers (Princess Margaret's Own Glasgow and Ayrshire Regiment) came into existence in January 1959 through the amalgamation of The Royal Scots Fusiliers and The Highland Light Infantry (City of Glasgow Regiment).

The senior of the components of The Royal Highland Fusiliers was The Royal Scots Fusiliers, which had been raised in 1678 as The Earl of Mar's Regiment of Foot. Thereafter the name of the regiment changed with its colonels, and in 1691 the regiment changed role slightly, becoming Colonel O'Farrell's Fuzileers. In 1707 the regiment became the North British Fuzileers, and in 1713 the Royal Regiment of North British Fuzileers. Further revision followed in 1751, when the regiment was restyled the 21st Regiment of Foot (or Royal North British Fuzileers), and this title remained in force until 1871, when the regiment became the 21st (Royal Scots Fusiliers) Regiment of Foot, changed in 1881 to The Royal Scots Fusiliers. The battle honours of the regiment were the following:

Blenheim   Ramillies   Oudenarde   Malplaquet   Dettingen   Belleisle   Martinique 1794   Bladensburg   Alma   Inkerman   Sevastopol   South Africa 1879   Burmah 1885–87   Tirah   Relief of Ladysmith   South Africa 1899–1902   Mons   Le Cateau   Retreat from Mons   Marne 1914   Aisne 1914   La Bassee 1914   Ypres 1914, '17, '18   Langemarck 1914

Gheluvelt Nonne Bosschen Neuve Chapelle Aubers Festubert 1915 Loos Somme 1916, '18 Albert 1914, '18 Bazentin Delville Wood Pozieres Flers-Courcelette Le Transloy Ancre Heights Ancre 1916 Arras 1917, '18 Scarpe 1917, '18 Arleux Messines 1917 Pilckem Menin Road Polygon Wood St Quentin Bapaume 1918 Rosieres Lys Estaires Hazebrouck Bailleul Bethune Scherpenberg Drocourt-Queant Hindenburg Line Canal du Nord Courtrai Selle France and Flanders 1914–18 Doiran 1917, '18 Macedonia 1916–18 Helles Gallipoli 1915–16 Rumani Egypt 1916–17 Gaza El Mughar Nebi Samwil Jerusalem Jaffa Tell' Asur Palestine 1917–18 Defence of Arras Ypres-Comines Canal Somme 1940 Withdrawal to Seine Odon Fontenay le Pesnil Cheux Defence of Rauray Mont Pincon Estray Falaise La Vie Crossing La Touques Crossing Aart Nederrijn Best Le Havre Antwerp-Turnhout Canal Scheldt South Beveland Lower Maas Meijel Venlo Pocket Roer Rhineland Reichswald Cleve Goch Rhine Dreierwalde Uelzen Bremen Artlenberg North-West Europe 1940, '44–45 Landing in Sicily Sicily 1943 Sangro Garigliano Crossing Minturno Anzio Advance to Tiber Italy 1943–44 Madagascar Middle East 1942 North Arakan Razabil Pinwe Shweli Mandalay Burma 1944–45

The motto of the regiment was 'Honi Soit Qui Mal y Pense' (Evil be to Him who Evil Thinks), and the regimental marches were 'The British Grenadiers' (traditional, quick) and 'In the Garb of Old Gaul' (Reid, slow). The uniform was a blue doublet and Hunting (Erskine) trews with blue facings, and nicknames associated with The Royal Scots Fusiliers were 'The Earl of Mar's Greybreeks' and 'The Fusil Jocks'. Imperial regiments affiliated to The Royal Scots Fusiliers were the Scots Fusiliers (Canada), the 23rd/21st Battalion, Australian Infantry, and Prince Alfred's Guards (South Africa).

The Highland Light Infantry (City of Glasgow Regiment), junior partner to The Royal Scots Fusiliers in The Royal Highland Fusiliers, was itself the result of the 1881 amalgamation of the 71st (Highland Light Infantry) Regiment of Foot and the 74th (Highlanders) Regiment of Foot as The Highland Light Infantry, which became the Highland Light Infantry (City of Glasgow Regiment) during 1923. The battle honours of the combined regiment were the following:

Carnatic Hindoostan Sholinghur Mysore Gibraltar 1780–83 Seringapatam Assaye Cape of Good Hope 1806 Rolica Vimiera Corunna Busaco Fuentes d'Onor Ciudad Rodrigo Badajoz Almaraz Salamanca Vittoria Pyrenees Nivelle Nive Orthes Toulouse Peninsula Waterloo South Africa 1851–53 Sevastopol Central India Tel-el-Kebir Egypt 1882 Modder River South Africa

1899–1902   Mons   Retreat from Mons   Marne 1914   Aisne 1914   La Bassee 1914   Ypres 1914, '15, '17, '18   Langemarck 1914, '17   Gheluvelt   Nonne Bosschen   Givenchy 1914   Neuve Chapelle   St Julien   Aubers   Festubert 1915   Loos   Somme 1916, '18   Albert 1916, '18   Bazentin   Delville Wood   Pozieres   Flers-Courcelette   Le Transloy   Ancre Heights   Ancre 1916, '18   Arras 1917, '18   Vimy 1917   Scarpe 1917, '18   Arleux   Pilckem   Menin Road   Polygon Wood   Passchendaele   Cambrai 1917, '18   St Quentin   Bapaume 1918   Lys Estaires   Messines 1918   Hazebrouck   Bailleul   Kemmel   Amiens   Drocourt-Queant   Hindenburg Line   Havrincourt   Canal du Nord   St Quentin Canal   Beaurevoir   Courtrai   Selle   Sambre   France and Flanders 1914–18   Gallipoli 1915–16   Rumani   Egypt 1916–17   Gaza   El Mughar   Nebi Samwil   Jaffa   Palestine 1917–18   Tigris 1916   Kut al Amara 1917   Sharqat   Mesopotamia 1916–18   Murman 1919   Archangel 1919   Withdrawal to Cherbourg   Odon   Cheux   Esquay   Mont Pincon   Quarry Hill   Estry   Falaise   Seine 1944   Aart   Nederrijn   Best   Scheldt   Lower Maas   South Beveland   Walcheren Causeway   Asten   Roer   Ourthe   Rhineland   Reichswald   Goch   Moyland Wood   Weeze   Rhine   Ibbenburen   Dreierwalde   Aller   Uelzen   Bremen   Artlenberg   North-West Europe 1940, '44–45   Jebel Shiba   Barentu   Keren   Massawa   Abyssinia 1941   Gazala   Cauldron   Mersa Matruh   Fuka   North Africa 1940–42   Landing in Sicily   Sicily 1943   Italy 1943, '45   Athens   Greece 1944–45   Adriatic   Middle East 1944

The motto of the regiment was 'Montis Insignia Calpe' (from the badge of Gibraltar), and the regimental marches were 'Whistle o'er the Lave o't' (traditional, quick) and 'Blue Bonnets o'er the Border' (traditional, slow). The uniform was a piper green doublet with buff facings, and MacKenzie kilt, and the nicknames associated with The Highland Light Infantry were 'The Pig and Whistle Infantry', 'The Glesga Keelies' or 'The Glesga Kilties' (1st Battalion) and 'The Assayes' (2nd Battalion), the reference to Assaye being in remembrance of the 74th Foot's part in the Battle of Assaye (1803), when all the regiment's officers were killed or wounded and the regiment was finally commanded by a quartermaster.

The 71st (Highland Light Infantry) Regiment of Foot was the senior of the two regiments that went to make the Highland Light Infantry in 1881, and had itself been raised in 1777 as the 73rd (Highland) Regiment of Foot, though often called MacLeod's Highlanders after Lord MacLeod who raised the regiment. In 1786 the regiment was renumbered as the 71st (Highland) Regiment of Foot, and in 1808 became the 71st (Glasgow Highland) Regiment of Foot. Thereafter two rapid changes followed, to the 71st (Glasgow Highland) Regiment of Foot (Light Infantry) in 1809 and to the 71st (Highland) Regiment of Foot (Light Infantry) in 1810. From this time onward the regiment was popularly called the 71st Highland Light Infantry, which became formal in 1855 when the title 71st (Highland Light Infantry) Regiment of Foot was accorded. The battle honours of the regiment were the following:

 Carnatic Sholinghur Mysore Hindoostan Cape of Good Hope 1806 Rolica Vimiera Corunna Fuentes d'Onor Almaraz Vittoria Pyrenees Nive Orthes Peninsula Waterloo Sevastopol Central India

The uniform was scarlet with buff facings.

 The 74th (Highlanders) Regiment of Foot was the 71st's junior partner in The Highland Light Infantry, and had been raised in 1787 by Major-General Sir Archibald Campbell as the 74th (Highland) Regiment of Foot. In 1816 this became the 74th Regiment of Foot, and two changes in the 1840s revised this to the 74th (Highland) Regiment of Foot in 1845 and to the 74th (Highlanders) Regiment of Foot in 1847. The battle honours of the regiment were the following:

 Assaye (with the Elephant) Seringapatam Busaco Fuentes d'Onor Ciudad Rodrigo Badajoz Salamanca Vittoria Pyrenees Nivelle Orthes Toulouse Peninsula South Africa 1851–53

The uniform was scarlet with white facings.

REGIMENTS OF INFANTRY 12

The Cheshire Regiment (12th)

Colonel-in-Chief
HRH The Prince of Wales

Colonel
Brigadier W. K. L. Prosser

Battle honours

Louisburg   Martinique 1762   Havannah   Meeanee   Hyderabad   Scinde   South Africa 1900–02   Mons   Le Cateau   Retreat from Mons   Marne 1914, '18   Aisne 1914, '18   La Bassee 1914   Armentieres 1914   Ypres 1914, '15, '17, '18   Nonne Bosschen   Hill 60   Gravenstafel   St Julien   Frezenberg   Bellewaarde   Loos   Somme 1916, '18   Albert 1916, '18   Bazentin   Delville Wood   Pozieres   Guillemont   Flers-Courcelette   Morval   Thiepval   Le Transloy   Ancre Heights   Ancre 1916   Arras 1917, '18   Vimy 1917   Scarpe 1917, '18   Oppy   Messines 1917, '18   Pilckem   Langemarck 1917   Menin Road   Polygon Wood   Broodseinde   Poelcappelle   Passchendaele   Cambrai 1917, '18   St Quentin   Bapaume 1918   Rosieres   Lys   Estaires   Hazebrouck   Bailleul   Kemmel   Scherpenberg   Soissonnais-Ourcq   Hindenburg Line   Canal du Nord   Courtrai   Selle   Valenciennes   Sambre   France and Flanders 1914–18   Italy 1917–18   Struma   Doiran 1917   Suvla   Scimitar Hill   Gallipoli 1915   Egypt 1915–17   Gaza   El Mughar   Jerusalem   Jericho   Tell' Asur   Palestine 1917–18   Tigris 1916

Kut al Amara 1917   Baghdad   Mesopotamia 1916-18   Dyle
Withdrawal to Escaut   St Omer-La Bassee   Wormhoudt   Cassel
Dunkirk 1940   Normandy Landing   Mont Pincon   St Pierre la Vielle
Gheel   Nederrijn   Aam   Aller   North-West Europe 1940, '44-45
Sidi Barrani   Capture of Tobruk   Gazala   Mersa Matruh
Defence of Alamein Line   Deir el Shein   El Alamein   Mareth
Wadi Zeus East   Wadi Zigzaou   Akarit   Wadi Akarit East   Enfidaville
North Africa 1940-43   Landing in Sicily   Primosole Bridge
Simeto Bridgehead   Sicily 1943   Sangro   Salerno   Santa Lucia
Battipaglia   Volturno Crossing   Monte Maro   Teano   Monte Camino
Garigliano Crossing   Minturno   Damiano   Anzio   Rome
Gothic Line   Coriano   Gemmano Ridge   Savignano   Senio Floodbank
Rimini Line   Ceriano Ridge   Valli di Comacchio   Italy 1943-45
Malta 1941-42

Regimental headquarters

The Castle, Chester, Cheshire.

Regimental museum

The Castle, Chester, Cheshire.

Regimental marches

(quick) Wha wadna fecht for Charlie? (traditional)
(slow) The 22nd Regiment Slow March 1772 (anonymous)

Regimental motto

Ich Dien (I Serve)

Nicknames

The Lightning Conductors, The Red Knights, The Old Two Twos, The Peep-of-Day Boys, The Specimens

Uniform

Scarlet with buff piping and facings

Allied regiment

2nd Battalion The Nova Scotia Highlanders (Cape Breton) (Canada)

Regimental history

A regiment that has remained unamalgamated throughout its history, The Cheshire Regiment can trace its origins as far back as 1689, when it was raised as The Duke of Norfolk's Regiment of Foot. The regiment then changed its name with its colonels until 1751, when it became the 22nd Regiment of Foot, a title changed in 1782 to the 22nd (or the Cheshire) Regiment of Foot. In 1881 this was revised to The Cheshire Regiment. The 'Charlie' of the regimental quick march refers to Sir Charles Napier, whom the regiment served in the conquest of Sind during 1843, in the process winning the unique battle honours 'Meeanee', 'Hyderabad' and 'Scinde'. Imperial regiments affiliated to The Cheshire Regiment were the Cape Breton Highlanders (Canada) and the 22nd Battalion, Australian Infantry.

REGIMENTS OF INFANTRY 13

The Royal Welch Fusiliers (23rd)

Colonel-in-Chief

HM The Queen

Colonel

Brigadier A. C. Vivian

Battle honours

Namur 1695   Blenheim   Ramillies   Oudenarde   Malplaquet   Dettingen   Minden   Egypt (with the Sphinx)   Corunna   Martinique 1809   Albuhera   Badajoz   Salamanca   Vittoria   Pyrenees   Nivelle   Orthes   Toulouse   Peninsula   Waterloo   Alma   Inkerman   Sevastopol   Lucknow   Ashantee 1873-74   Burmah 1885-87   Relief of Ladysmith   South Africa 1899-1902   Pekin 1900   Mons   Le Cateau   Retreat from Mons   Marne 1914   Aisne 1914, '18   La Bassee 1914   Messines 1914, '17, '18   Armentieres 1914   Ypres 1914, '17, '18   Langemarck 1914, '17   Gheluvelt   Givenchy 1914   Neuve Chapelle   Aubers   Festubert 1915   Loos   Somme 1916, '18   Albert 1916, '18   Bazentin   Delville Wood   Pozieres   Guillemont   Flers-Courcelette   Morval   Le Transloy   Ancre Heights   Ancre 1916, '18   Arras 1917   Scarpe 1917   Arleux   Bullecourt   Pilckem   Menin Road   Polygon Wood   Broodseinde   Poelcappelle   Passchendaele   Cambrai 1917, '18   St Quentin   Bapaume 1918   Lys   Bailleul   Kemmel   Scherpenberg   Hindenburg Line   Havrincourt   Epehy   St Quentin

Canal Beaurevoir Selle Valenciennes Sambre France and Flanders 1914–18 Piave Vittorio Veneto Italy 1917–18 Doiran 1917, '18 Macedonia 1915–18 Suvla Sari Bair Landing at Suvla Scimitar Hill Gallipoli 1915–16 Rumani Egypt 1915–17 Gaza El Mughar Jerusalem Jericho Tell' Asur Megiddo Nablus Palestine 1917–18 Tigris 1916 Kut al Amara 1917 Baghdad Mesopotamia 1916–18 Dyle Defence of Escaut St Omer-La Bassee Caen Esquay Falaise Nederrijn Lower Maas Venlo Pocket Ourthe Rhineland Reichswald Goch Weeze Rhine Ibbenburen Aller North-West Europe 1940, '44–45 Madagascar Middle East 1942 Donbaik North Arakan Kohima Mandalay Ava Burma 1943–45

Regimental headquarters

Hightown Barracks, Wrexham, Clwyd, Wales.

Regimental museum

Queen's Tower, The Castle, Caernarfon, Gwynedd, Wales.

Regimental marches

(quick) The British Grenadiers (traditional)
(slow) War Song of the Men of Glamorgan (traditional), and
Forth to the Battle (anonymous)

Regimental mottoes

Ich Dien (I Serve), and Nec Aspera Terrent (Nor Do Difficulties Deter)

Nicknames

The Nanny Goats, The Royal Goats

Uniform

Scarlet with blue facings

Allied regiments

Royal 22e Regiment (Canada)
3rd Battalion The Frontier Force Regiment (Pakistan)
4th Battalion The Royal Malay Regiment

Regimental history

Another regiment that has never been amalgamated, The Royal Welch Fusiliers was originally raised in 1689 as Lord Herbert of Cherbury's Regiment of Foot, and the regiment subsequently changed name with its colonels until 1702, when it became the Welsh Regiment of Fuzileers, in 1713 changed to The Royal Regiment of Welsh Fuzileers and in 1714 to The Prince of Wales's Own Royal Regiment of Welsh Fuzileers. Further changes followed in 1727, when the regiment became The Royal Welch Fusiliers, and in 1751 when it became the 23rd (Royal Welch Fusiliers) Regiment of Foot. Thereafter the name remained unaltered for 130 years, until the 1881 army reforms brought in the title The Royal Welsh Fusiliers, which was revised in 1920 to The Royal Welch Fusiliers. The nicknames refer to the regiment's mascot, a goat which is now provided by the sovereign. Imperial regiments affiliated to The Royal Welch Fusiliers were the Royal 22e Regiment (Canada), the 1st Battalion, Australian Infantry, and the Pretoria Regiment (Princess Alice's Own) (South Africa).

REGIMENTS OF INFANTRY 14

The Royal Regiment of Wales (24th/41st Foot)

Colonel-in-Chief

HRH The Prince of Wales

Colonel

Major-General L. A. H. Napier

Battle honours

Blenheim Ramillies Oudenarde Malplaquet Belleisle Martinique 1762 St Vincent 1797 Egypt (with the Sphinx) Cape of Good Hope 1806 India Talavera Bourbon Busaco Fuentes d'Onor Java Salamanca Detroit Queenstown Miami Vittoria Pyrenees Nivelle Niagara Orthes Peninsula Waterloo Ava Candahar 1842 Ghuznee 1842 Cabool 1842 Chillianwallah Goojerat Punjaub Alma Inkerman Sevastopol South Africa 1877–79 Burmah 1885–87 Relief of Kimberley Paardeberg South Africa 1899–1902 Mons Retreat from Mons Marne 1914 Aisne 1914, '18 Ypres 1914, '15, '17, '18 Langemarck 1914, '17 Gheluvelt Nonne Bosschen Givenchy 1914 Gravenstafel St Julien Frezenberg Bellewaarde Aubers Loos Somme 1916, '18 Albert 1916, '18 Bazentin Pozieres Flers-Courcelette Morval Ancre Heights Ancre 1916, '18 Arras 1917, '18 Scarpe 1917 Messines 1917, '18 Pilckem Menin Road

Polygon Wood   Broodseinde   Poelcappelle   Passchendaele
Cambrai 1917, '18   St Quentin   Bapaume 1918   Lys   Estaires
Hazebrouck   Bailleul   Kemmel   Bethune   Scherpenberg   Drocourt-
Queant   Hindenburg Line   Havrincourt   Epehy   St Quentin Canal
Beaurevoir   Courtrai   Selle   Valenciennes   Sambre   France and
Flanders 1914–18   Struma   Doiran 1917, '18   Macedonia 1915–18
Helles   Landing at Suvla   Scimitar Hill   Gallipoli 1915–16   Egypt
1915–17   Gaza   El Mughar   Jerusalem   Jericho   Tell' Asur   Megiddo
Nablus   Palestine 1917–18   Aden   Tigris 1916   Kut al Amara 1917
Baghdad   Mesopotamia 1916–18   Tsingtao   Norway 1940   Normandy
Landing   Sully   Odon   Caen   Bourgebus Ridge   Mont Pincon
Souleuvre   Le Perier Ridge   Falaise   Risle Crossing   Antwerp
Nederrijn   Le Havre   Antwerp-Turnhout Canal   Scheldt
Lower Maas   Venlo Pocket   Zetten   Ourthe   Rhineland   Reichswald
Weeze   Hochwald   Rhine   Ibbenburen   Aller   Arnhem 1945
North-West Europe 1944–45   Benghazi   Gazala   North Africa 1940–42
Sicily 1943   Coriano   Croce   Rimini Line   Ceriano Ridge
Argenta Gap   Italy 1943–45   Crete   Canea   Withdrawal to Sphakia
Middle East 1941   North Arakan   Mayu Tunnels   Pinwe
Kyaukmyaung Bridgehead   Shweli   Myitson   Maymyo
Rangoon Road   Sittang 1945   Burma 1944–45   Korea 1951–52

Regimental headquarters

Maindy Barracks, Cardiff, Wales.

Regimental museums

(The South Wales Borderers) The Barracks, Brecon, Powys, Wales.
(The Welch Regiment) The Castle, Cardiff, Wales.

Regimental marches

(quick) Men of Harlech (traditional)
(slow) Scipio (Handel)

Regimental motto

Gwell Angau Na Chywilydd (Better Death than Dishonour)

Nicknames

see below

Uniform

Scarlet with grass green piping and facings

Allied regiments

The Ontario Regiment RCAC (Canada)
The Royal New South Wales Regiment (Australia)

Regimental history

The Royal Regiment of Wales (24th/41st Foot) was formed in June 1969 by the amalgamation of The South Wales Borderers (24th Foot) and The Welch Regiment (41st and 69th Foot). The official mascot of the regiment is a goat.

The South Wales Borderers (24th Foot) was the senior of the two components, able to trace its history to 1689, when Sir Edward Dering's Regiment of Foot was raised. The regiment subsequently changed name with its colonels, and was ranked as the 24th Foot in 1747. The regiment was retitled the 24th Regiment of Foot in 1751, and in 1782 became the 24th (or 2nd Warwickshire) Regiment of Foot. The Welsh association followed in 1881, when the regiment became The South Wales Borderers. The battle honours of the regiment were the following:

Blenheim   Ramillies   Oudenarde   Malplaquet   Egypt (with the Sphinx)   Cape of Good Hope 1806   Talavera   Busaco   Fuentes d'Onor   Salamanca   Vittoria   Pyrenees   Nivelle   Orthes   Peninsula   Chillianwallah   Goojerat   Punjaub   South Africa 1877–79   Burmah 1885–87   South Africa 1900–02   Mons   Retreat from Mons   Marne 1914   Aisne 1914, '18   Ypres 1914, '17, '18   Langemarck 1914, '17   Gheluvelt   Nonne Bosschen   Givenchy 1914   Aubers   Loos   Somme 1916, '18   Albert 1916, '18   Bazentin   Pozieres   Flers-Courcelette   Morval   Ancre Heights   Ancre 1916   Arras 1917, '18   Scarpe 1917   Messines 1917, '18   Pilckem   Menin Road   Polygon Wood   Broodseinde   Poelcappelle   Passchendaele   Cambrai 1917, '18   St Quentin   Bapaume 1918   Lys   Estaires   Hazebrouck   Bailleul   Kemmel   Bethune   Scherpenberg   Drocourt-Queant   Hindenburg Line   Havrincourt   Epehy   St Quentin Canal   Beaurevoir   Courtrai   Selle   Valenciennes   Sambre   France and Flanders 1914–18   Doiran 1917, '18   Macedonia 1915–18   Helles   Landing at Helles   Krithia   Suvla   Sari Bair   Scimitar Hill   Gallipoli 1915–16   Egypt 1916   Tigris 1916   Kut al Amara 1917   Baghdad   Mesopotamia 1916–18   Tsingtao   Norway 1940   Normandy Landing   Sully   Caen   Falaise   Risle Crossing   Le Havre   Antwerp-Turnhout Canal   Scheldt   Zetten   Arnhem 1945   North-West Europe 1944–45   Gazala

North Africa 1942   North Arakan   Mayu Tunnels   Pinwe   Shweli   Myitson   Burma 1944–45

The regiment had no motto, and the regimental march was 'March of the Men of Harlech' (traditional, quick). The uniform was scarlet with grass green facings, and the nicknames associated with The South Wales Borderers were 'Howard Greens' and 'The Bengal Tigers'. Imperial regiments affiliated to The South Wales Borderers were the 18th and 24th Battalions, Australian Infantry.

The Welch Regiment (41st and 69th) was the junior partner to The South Wales Borderers in The Royal Regiment of Wales, and was itself the result of an 1881 amalgamation of the 41st (The Welsh) Regiment of Foot and the 69th (South Lincolnshire) Regiment of Foot. The battle honours of the combined regiment were the following:

Belleisle   Martinique 1762   St Vincent 1797   India   Bourbon   Java   Detroit   Queenstown   Miami   Niagara   Waterloo   Ava   Candahar 1842   Ghuznee 1842   Cabool 1842   Alma   Inkerman   Sevastopol   Relief of Kimberley   Paardeberg   South Africa 1899–1902   Mons   Retreat from Mons   Marne 1914   Aisne 1914, '18   Ypres 1915, '16, '17   Langemarck 1914, '17   Gheluvelt   Nonne Bosschen   Givenchy 1914   Gravenstafel   St Julien   Frezenberg   Bellewaarde   Aubers   Loos   Somme 1916, '18   Albert 1916, '18   Bazentin   Pozieres   Flers-Courcelette   Morval   Ancre Heights   Ancre 1916, '18   Messines 1917, '18   Pilckem   Menin Road   Polygon Wood   Broodseinde   Poelcappelle   Passchendaele   Cambrai 1917, '18   St Quentin   Bapaume 1918   Lys   Estaires   Hazebrouck   Bailleul   Kemmel   Bethune   Scherpenberg   Arras 1918   Drocourt-Queant   Hindenburg Line   Epehy   St Quentin Canal   Beaurevoir   Selle   Valenciennes   Sambre.   France and Flanders 1914–18   Struma   Doiran 1917, '18   Macedonia 1915–18   Suvla   Sari Bair   Landing at Suvla   Scimitar Hill   Gallipoli 1915   Egypt 1915–17   Gaza   El Mughar   Jerusalem   Jericho   Tell' Asur   Megiddo   Nablus   Palestine 1917–18   Tigris 1916   Kut al Amara 1917   Baghdad   Mesopotamia 1916–18   Falaise   Lower Maas   Reichswald   North-West Europe 1944–45   Benghazi   North Africa 1940–42   Sicily 1943   Coriano   Croce   Rimini Line   Ceriano Ridge   Argenta Gap   Italy 1943–45   Crete   Canea   Withdrawal to Sphakia   Middle East 1941   Kyaukmyaung Bridgehead   Maymyo   Rangoon Road   Sittang 1945   Burma 1944–45   Korea 1951–52

The motto of the regiment was 'Gwell Angau Na Chywilydd' (Better Death than Dishonour), and the regimental march was 'Ap Shenkin' (traditional, quick). The uniform was scarlet with white facings, and the nicknames associated with The Welch Regiment were 'The Invalids', 'Wardour's Horse', 'The Ups and Downs' (2nd Battalion) and 'The Agamemnons' (2nd

Battalion), the first because the 41st was raised as a regiment of invalids, the third because the 69th's numerical designation was the same upside down, and the last in commemoration of the 69th's marine service under Nelson in HMS *Agamemnon*. Imperial regiments affiliated to The Welch Regiment were the Ontario Regiment (Canada) and the 45th Battalion, Australian Infantry.

The 41st (The Welsh) Regiment was raised as an invalid unit at Chelsea in 1719 as Colonel Fielding's Regiment of Foot, and the regiment subsequently changed its title with its colonels until 1747, when it became The Royal Invalids (41st Regiment of Foot), changed in 1751 to the 41st Regiment of Foot, or Invalids, and again changed in 1782 to the 41st (Royal Invalids) Regiment of Foot. In 1787 the revised title the 41st Regiment of Foot was adopted, and in 1831 this became the 41st (The Welsh) Regiment of Foot. The battle honours of the regiment were the following:

> Detroit   Queenstown   Miami   Niagara   Ava   Candahar 1842
> Ghuznee 1842   Cabool 1842   Alma   Inkerman   Sevastopol

The motto of the regiment was 'Gwell Angua Na Chyliwydd' (Better Death than Dishonour), and the uniform was scarlet with white facings.

The 69th (South Lincolnshire) Regiment had been raised in 1756 as the 2nd Battalion of the 24th Foot, but became a separate entity as the 69th Regiment of Foot in 1758, and the 69th (or South Lincolnshire) Regiment of Foot in 1782. The battle honours of the regiment were the following:

> St Vincent   Bourbon   Java   Waterloo   India

The uniform was scarlet with Lincoln green facings.

REGIMENTS OF INFANTRY 15

The King's Own Scottish Borderers (25th)

Colonel-in-Chief

HRH The Princess Alice Duchess of Gloucester

Colonel

Brigadier R. W. Riddle

Battle honours

Namur 1695   Minden   Egmont-op-Zee   Egypt (with the Sphinx)   Martinique 1809   Afghanistan 1878–80   Chitral   Tirah   Paardeberg   South Africa 1900–02   Mons   Le Cateau   Retreat from Mons   Marne 1914, '18   Aisne 1914   La Bassee 1914   Messines 1914   Ypres 1914, '15, '17, '18   Nonne Bosschen   Hill 60   Gravenstafel   St Julien   Frezenberg   Bellewaarde   Loos   Somme 1916, '18   Albert 1916, '18   Bazentin   Delville Wood   Pozieres   Guillemont   Flers-Courcelette   Morval   Le Transloy   Ancre Heights   Arras 1917, '18   Vimy 1917   Scarpe 1917, '18   Arleux   Pilckem   Langemarck 1917   Menin Road   Polygon Wood   Broodseinde   Poelcappelle   Passchendaele   Cambrai 1917, '18   St Quentin   Lys   Estaires   Hazebrouck   Kemmel   Soissonnais-Ourcq   Bapaume 1918   Drocourt-Queant   Hindenburg Line   Epehy   Canal du Nord   Courtrai   Selle   Sambre   France and Flanders 1914–18   Italy 1917–18   Helles   Landing at Helles   Krithia

Suvla Scimitar Hill Gallipoli 1915–16 Rumani Egypt 1916 Gaza El Mughar Nebi Samwil Jaffa Palestine 1917–18 Dunkirk 1940 Cambes Odon Cheux Defence of Rauray Caen Esquay Troarn Mont Pincon Estry Aart Nederrijn Arnhem 1944 Best Scheldt Flushing Venraij Meijel Venlo Pocket Roer Rhineland Reichswald Cleve Goch Rhine Ibbenburen Lingen Dreierwalde Uelzen Bremen Artlenberg North-West Europe 1940, '44–45 North Arakan Buthidaung Ngakyedauk Pass Imphal Kanglatongbi Ukhrul Meiktila Irrawaddy Kama Burma 1943, '45 Kowang-San Maryang-San Korea 1951–52

Regimental headquarters

The Barracks, Berwick-on-Tweed, Northumberland.

Regimental museum

The Barracks, Berwick-on-Tweed, Northumberland.

Regimental marches

(quick) Blue Bonnets o'er the Border (traditional)
(slow) In the Garb of Old Gaul (Reid, regimental band), and
The Borderers (traditional, piper and drums)

Regimental mottoes

In Veritate Religionis Confido (In the Truth of Religion I Trust), and
Nisi Dominus Frustra (Unless the Lord be with us All is in Vain)

Nicknames

The KOSBs, The Botherers, The Kokky Olly-Birds

Uniform

Blue doublet and Leslie trews with blue facings

Allied regiments

1st Battalion The Royal New Brunswick Regiment (Carleton and York) (Canada)
25th Battalion The Royal Queensland Regiment (Australia)
5th Battalions The Royal Malay Regiment

Regimental history

The King's Own Scottish Borderers was raised in 1689 as The Earl of Leven's Regiment of Foot, its task of defending Edinburgh against the forces of ex-King James II being discernible in its alternative name, The Edinburgh Regiment. The name of the regiment subsequently changed with its colonels until 1751, when it became the 25th (Edinburgh) Regiment of Foot. In 1782 this was changed to the 25th (or the Sussex) Regiment of Foot, though the Scots connection was restored in 1802 when the regiment became the 25th (or King's Own Borderers) Regiment of Foot, changed in 1881 to The King's Own Borderers, and in 1887 to The King's Own Scottish Borderers. Imperial regiments affiliated to The King's Own Scottish Borderers were the Saint John Fusiliers (Canada) and the 25th Battalion, Australian Infantry.

REGIMENTS OF INFANTRY 16

The Cameronians (Scottish Rifles) (26th and 90th)

Colonel-in-Chief

none

Colonel

Brigadier D. B. Riddell-Webster

Battle honours

Blenheim Ramillies Oudenarde Malplaquet Mandora Egypt (with the Sphinx) Corunna Martinique 1809 Guadaloupe 1810 China South Africa 1846–47 Sevastopol Lucknow Abyssinia South Africa 1877–79 Relief of Ladysmith South Africa 1899–1902 Mons Le Cateau Retreat from Mons Marne 1914, '18 Aisne 1914 La Bassee 1914 Armentieres 1914 Neuve Chapelle Aubers Loos Somme 1916, '18 Albert 1916 Bazentin Pozieres Flers-Courcelette Le Transloy Ancre Heights Arras 1917, '18 Scarpe 1917, '18 Arleux Ypres 1917, '18 Pilckem Langemarck 1917 Menin Road Polygon Wood Passchendaele St Quentin Rosieres Avre Lys Hazebrouck Bailleul Kemmel Scherpenberg Soissonnais-Ourcq Drocourt-Queant Hindenburg Line Epehy Canal du Nord St Quentin Canal Cambrai 1918 Courtrai Selle Sambre France and Flanders 1914–18 Doiran 1917, '18 Macedonia 1915–18 Gallipoli

1915–16 Rumani Egypt 1916–17 Gaza El Mughar Nebi Samwil Jaffa Palestine 1917–18 Ypres-Comines Canal Odon Cheux Caen Mont Pincon Estry Nederrijn Best Scheldt South Beveland Walcheren Causeway Asten Roer Rhineland Reichswald Moyland Rhine Dreierwalde Bremen Artlenburg North-West Europe 1940, '44–45 Landing in Sicily Simeto Bridgehead Sicily 1943 Garigliano Crossing Anzio Advance to Tiber Italy 1943–44 Pegu 1942 Paungde Yenangyaung 1942 Chindits 1944 Burma 1942, '44

Regimental headquarters

Mote Hill, Muir Street, Hamilton, Lanarkshire, Scotland.

Regimental museums

Mote Hill, Muir Street, Hamilton, Lanarkshire, Scotland.

Regimental marches

(quick) Within a Mile of Edinboro' Town (anonymous)
(slow) In the Garb of Old Gaul (Reid)

Regimental motto

Nemo Me Impune Lacessit (No one Provokes me with Impunity)

Nickname

The Perthshire Grey-Breeks (2nd Battalion)

Uniform

Rifle green doublet and Douglas trews

Allied regiments

The Otago and Southland Regiment (New Zealand)
2nd Battalion The Ghana Regiment of Infantry
7th Duke of Edinburgh's Own Gurkha Rifles (affiliated regiment)

Regimental history

The Cameronians (Scottish Rifles) was formed in 1881 by the amalgamation of the 26th (Cameronian) Regiment of Foot and the 90th Light Infantry

Regiment, Perthshire Volunteers. In 1968 the regiment was offered the choice of amalgamation or disbandment: it opted for the latter, and now exists only as a Territorial Army cadre, although the regiment's name and battle honours still feature in the Army List.

The senior of the two regiments that went to form The Cameronians (Scottish Rifles) was the 26th (Cameronian) Regiment of Foot, which had been raised in 1689 as The Earl of Angus's Regiment of Foot, although it was known right from its beginning as The Cameronians. The regiment changed its title with its colonels until 1751, when it became the 26th Regiment of Foot. In 1782 this became the 26th (or Cameronian) Regiment of Foot. The battle honours of the regiment were the following:

> Blenheim   Ramillies   Oudenarde   Malplaquet   Egypt (with the Sphinx)   Corunna   China (with the Dragon)   Abyssinia
> South Africa 1846–47

The regimental march was 'Within a Mile of Edinboro' Town' (quick), and the uniform was scarlet with yellow facings.

The 26th's junior partner was the 90th Light Infantry Regiment, Perthshire Volunteers, which had been raised in 1794 by Colonel Thomas Graham as the 90th Regiment of Foot (or Perthshire Volunteers), a title changed in 1815 to the 90th Light Infantry Regiment, Perthshire Volunteers. The battle honours of the regiment were the following:

> Mandora   Egypt (with the Sphinx)   Martinique   Guadaloupe 1810
> Sevastopol   Lucknow

The regimental marches were 'The Gathering of the Grahams' (traditional, quick) and 'The Garb of Old Gaul' (Reid, slow), and the uniform was scarlet with buff facings.

REGIMENTS OF INFANTRY 17

The Royal Irish Rangers (27th [Inniskilling], 83rd and 87th)

Colonel-in-Chief

none

Colonel

Brigadier M. N. S. McCord

Battle honours

Martinique 1762 Havannah St Lucia 1778, '96 India Cape of Good Hope 1806 Maida Monte Video Talavera Bourbon Busaco Barrosa Fuentes d'Onor Java Tarifa Ciudad Rodrigo Badajoz Salamanca Vittoria Pyrenees Nivelle Niagara Orthes Toulouse Peninsula Waterloo Ava South Africa 1835, '46–47 Sevastopol Central India Tel-el-Kebir Egypt 1882, '84 Relief of Ladysmith South Africa 1899–1902 Mons Le Cateau Retreat from Mons Marne 1914 Aisne 1914 La Bassee 1914 Messines 1914, '17, '18 Armentieres 1914 Ypres 1914, '15, '17, '18 Nonne Bosschen Neuve Chapelle Loos Frezenberg Aubers Festubert 1915 Gravenstafel St Julien Bellewaarde Somme 1916, '18 Albert 1916 Bazentin Pozieres Guillemont Ginchy Le Transloy Ancre Ancre Heights Arras 1917 Scarpe 1917 Pilckem Langemarck 1917 Polygon Wood Broodseinde Poelcappelle Cambrai 1917, '18

St Quentin   Rosieres   Hindenburg Line   Lys   Bailleul   Beaurevoir   Kemmel   Courtrai   Selle   Sambre   France and Flanders 1914–18   Kosturino   Struma   Macedonia 1915–17   Helles   Landing at Helles   Krithia   Suvla   Sari Bair   Landing at Suvla   Scimitar Hill   Gallipoli 1915–16   Egypt 1916   Gaza   Jerusalem   Tell' Asur   Megiddo   Nablus   Palestine 1917–18   Dyle   Withdrawal to Escaut   Defence of Arras   St Omer-La Bassee   Ypres-Comines Canal   Dunkirk 1940   Normandy Landing   Cambes   Caen   Troarn   Venlo Pocket   Rhine   Bremen   North-West Europe 1940, '44–45   Two Tree Hill   Bou Arada   Stuka Farm   Oued Zarga   Djebel Bel Mahdi   Djebel Ang   Djebel Tanngoucha   North Africa 1942–43   Landing in Sicily   Solarino   Simeto Bridgehead   Adrano   Centuripe   Salso Crossing   Simeto Crossing   Malleto   Pursuit to Messina   Sicily 1943   Termoli   Trigno   San Salvo   Sangro   Fossacesia   Garigliano Crossing   Minturno   Anzio   Cassino II   Massa Tambourini   Liri Valley   Rome   Advance to Tiber   Trasimene Line   Monte Spaduro   Monte Grande   Argenta Gap   San Nicolo Canal   Italy 1943–45   Leros   Middle East 1942   Malta 1940   Yenangyaung 1942   Donbaik   Burma 1942–43   Seoul   Imjin   Korea 1950–51

Regimental headquarters

5 Waring Street, Belfast, Northern Ireland.

Regimental museums

(The Royal Inniskilling Fusiliers) The Castle, Enniskillen, Co Fermanagh, Northern Ireland.
(The Royal Ulster Rifles) 5 Waring Street, Belfast, Northern Ireland.
(The Royal Irish Fusiliers) Sovereign's House, The Mall, Armagh, Northern Ireland.

Regimental marches

(quick) Killaloe (traditional)
(slow) Eileen Allanagh (traditional)

Regimental motto

Faugh-a-Ballagh (Clear the Way)

Nicknames

see below

Uniform

Piper green with piper green facings

Allied regiments

The Princess Louise Fusiliers (Canada)
2nd Battalion The Irish Rangers of Canada (Sudbury)
The Irish Fusiliers of Canada (Vancouver Regiment)
The Adelaide University Regiment (Australia)
2nd Battalion (Canterbury and Nelson, Marlborough and West Coast)
The Royal New Zealand Infantry Regiment
1st Battalion The Punjab Regiment (Pakistan)
9th Battalion (Wilde's) The Frontier Force Regiment (Pakistan)

Regimental history

The Royal Irish Rangers came into existence during July 1968 through the amalgamation of The Royal Inniskilling Fusiliers, The Royal Ulster Rifles, and The Royal Irish Fusiliers (Princess Victoria's). The official mascot of the regiment is an Irish wolfhound.

The senior of the three components was The Royal Inniskilling Fusiliers, itself formed in 1881 by the amalgamation of the 27th (Inniskilling) Regiment of Foot and the 108th (Madras Infantry) Regiment of Foot. The battle honours of the combined regiment were the following:

Egypt (with the Sphinx)   Martinique 1762   Havannah   St Lucia 1778, '96   Maida   Badajoz   Salamanca   Vittoria   Pyrenees   Nivelle   Orthes   Toulouse   Peninsula   Waterloo   South Africa 1835, '46–47   Central India   Relief of Ladysmith   South Africa 1899–1902   Le Cateau   Retreat from Mons   Marne 1914   Aisne 1914   Messines 1914, '17   Armentieres 1914   Aubers   Festubert 1915   Somme 1916, '18   Albert 1916   Bazentin   Guillemont   Ginchy   Ancre 1916   Arras 1917   Scarpe 1917   Ypres 1917, '18   Pilckem   Langemarck 1917   Polygon Wood   Broodseinde   Poelcappelle   Cambrai 1917, '18   St Quentin   Rosieres   Hindenburg Line   Beaurevoir   Courtrai   Selle   Sambre   France and Flanders 1914–18   Kosturino   Struma   Macedonia 1915–17   Helles   Landing at Helles   Krithia   Suvla   Landing at Suvla   Scimitar Hill   Gallipoli 1915–16   Egypt 1916   Gaza   Jerusalem   Tell' Asur   Palestine 1917–18   Defence of Arras   Ypres-Comines Canal   North-West Europe 1940   Two Tree Hill   Bou Arada   Oued Zarga   Djebel Bel Mahdi   Djebel Tanngoucha   North Africa 1942–43   Landing in Sicily   Solarino   Simeto Bridgehead   Adrano   Centuripe   Simeto Crossing   Pursuit to Messina   Sicily 1943   Termoli   Trigno   San Salvo   Sangro   Garigliano Crossing   Minturno   Anzio

Cassino II   Massa Tambourini   Liri Valley   Rome   Advance to Tiber   Trasimene Line   Monte Spaduro   Argenta Gap   Italy 1943–45   Middle East 1942   Yenangyaung 1942   Donbaik   Burma 1942–43

The motto of the regiment was 'Nec Aspera Terrent' (Neither do Difficulties Deter), and the regimental marches were 'The Sprig of Shillelagh' (Code, quick) and 'Rory O'More' (Lover, quick). The uniform was scarlet with blue piping and facings, and the nicknames associated with The Royal Inniskilling Fusiliers were 'The Skins', 'The Skillingers' and 'The Lumps' (2nd Battalion). Imperial regiments affiliated to The Royal Inniskilling Fusiliers were the Princess Louise Fusiliers (Canada) and the 27th Battalion, Australian Infantry.

In the amalgamation that made the Royal Inniskilling Fusiliers in 1881, the senior component was the 27th (Inniskilling) Regiment of Foot, which had been raised in 1689 as Colonel Zachariah Tiffin's Enniskillen Regiment of Foot. The regiment subsequently changed name with its colonels until 1751, when it became the 27th (or Inniskilling) Regiment of Foot, and this title remained unaltered up to the time of the 1881 amalgamation. The battle honours of the regiment were the following:

St Lucia 1778, '96   Egypt (with the Sphinx)   Maida   Badajoz   Salamanca   Vittoria   Pyrenees   Nivelle   Orthes   Toulouse   Peninsula   Waterloo   South Africa 1835, '46–47

The motto of the regiment was 'Nec Aspera Terrent' (Neither do Difficulties Deter), and the regimental march was 'The Sprig of Shillelagh' (Code, quick). The uniform was scarlet with buff facings, and the nickname associated with the 27th (Inniskilling) Regiment of Foot was 'The Skins'.

The 27th's junior partner was the 108th (Madras Infantry) Regiment of Foot, which had been raised in 1854 as the 3rd Madras European Regiment in the army of the Honourable East India Company. The regiment was transferred to the British army establishment in 1861 and renamed the 108th (Madras Infantry) Regiment of Foot. The sole battle honour of the regiment was the following:

Central India

The regimental march was 'Rory O'More' (Lower, quick), and the uniform was scarlet with yellow facings.

Second in seniority to The Royal Inniskilling Fusiliers in the 1968 amalgamation that formed The Royal Irish Rangers was The Royal Ulster Rifles, itself created in 1881 by the amalgamation of the 83rd (County of Dublin) Regiment of Foot and the 86th (Royal County of Down) Regiment of Foot as the Royal Irish Rifles, changed in 1921 to The Royal Ulster Rifles. The battle honours of the combined regiment were the following:

Egypt (with the Sphinx)   Cape of Good Hope 1806   Talavera   Bourbon

Busaco Fuentes d'Onor Ciudad Rodrigo Badajoz Salamanca Vittoria Nivelle Orthes Toulouse Peninsula Central India South Africa 1899–1902 Mons Le Cateau Retreat from Mons Marne 1914 Aisne 1914 La Bassee 1914 Messines 1914, '17, '18 Armentieres 1914 Ypres 1914, '15, '17, '18 Nonne Bosschen Neuve Chapelle Frezenberg Aubers Somme 1916, '18 Albert 1916 Bazentin Pozieres Guillemont Ginchy Ancre Heights Pilckem Langemarck 1917 Cambrai 1917 St Quentin Rosieres Lys Bailleul Kemmel Courtrai France and Flanders 1914–18 Kosturino Struma Macedonia 1915–17 Suvla Sari Bair Gallipoli 1915 Gaza Jerusalem Tell' Asur Palestine 1917–18 Dyle Dunkirk 1940 Normandy Landing Cambes Caen Troarn Venlo Pocket Rhine Bremen North-West Europe 1940, '44–45 Seoul Imjin Korea 1950–51

The motto of the regiment was 'Quis Separabit?' (Who Shall Separate?), and the regimental marches were 'Off, Off Said the Stranger' (Craven, quick) and 'The South Down Militia' (anonymous, quick). The uniform was a rifle green jacket and black trousers with rifle green piping and facings, and the nicknames associated with The Royal Ulster Rifles were 'The Stickies' and 'The Irish Giants'. The only imperial regiment affiliated to the Royal Ulster Rifles was the Lorne Rifles (Scottish) of Canada.

The senior of the components that went to form The Royal Ulster Rifles in 1881 was the 83rd (County of Dublin) Regiment of Foot, which had been raised in 1793 by Colonel William Fitch as the 83rd Regiment of Foot but which was sarcastically known as Fitch's Grenadiers for the generally small stature of its men. In 1859 this became the 83rd (County of Dublin) Regiment of Foot. The battle honours of the regiment were the following:

Cape of Good Hope 1806 Talavera Buscaco Fuentes d'Onor Ciudad Rodrigo Badajoz Salamanca Vittoria Nivelle Orthes Toulouse Peninsula Central India

The regimental marches were 'Garry Owen' (traditional, quick) and 'Off, Off Said the Stranger' (Craven, quick), and the uniform was scarlet with yellow facings.

The 83rd's junior partner was the 86th (Royal County of Down) Regiment of Foot, raised in 1793 by Major-General Sir Cornelius Cuyler as the 86th Regiment of Foot but popularly known as The Shropshire Volunteers for the county in which it was formed. In 1809 this regiment became the 86th (or Leinster) Regiment of Foot, and in 1812 the 86th (or The Royal County of Down) Regiment of Foot. The battle honours of the regiment were the following:

Egypt (with the Sphinx) India Bourbon Central India

The regimental march was 'St Patrick's Day' (traditional, quick), and the uniform was scarlet with blue facings.

The other major component that went into the formation of The Royal Irish Rangers was The Royal Irish Fusiliers (Princess Victoria's), itself the result of the 1881 amalgamation of the 87th (Royal Irish Fusiliers) Regiment of Foot and the 89th (Princess Victoria's) Regiment of Foot. The combined regiment was initially known as Princess Victoria's (Royal Irish Fusiliers), a title changed in 1921 to The Royal Irish Fusiliers (Princess Victoria's). The battle honours of the combined regiment were the following:

> Egypt (with the Sphinx)   Monte Video   Talavera   Barrosa   Java   Tarifa   Vittoria   Nivelle   Niagara   Orthes   Toulouse   Peninsula   Ava   Sevastopol   Tel-el-Kebir   Egypt 1882, '84   Relief of Ladysmith   South Africa 1899–1902   Le Cateau   Retreat from Mons   Marne 1914   Aisne 1914   Armentieres 1914   Ypres 1915, '17, '18   Gravenstafel   St Julien   Frezenberg   Bellewaarde   Somme 1916, '18   Albert 1916   Guillemont   Ginchy   Le Transloy   Arras 1917   Scarpe 1917   Messines 1917, '18   Langemarck 1917   Cambrai 1917   St Quentin   Rosieres   Lys   Bailleul   Kemmel   Courtrai   France and Flanders 1914–18   Kosturino   Struma   Macedonia 1915–17   Suvla   Landing at Suvla   Scimitar Hill   Gallipoli 1915   Gaza   Jersualem   Tell' Asur   Megiddo   Nablus   Palestine 1917–18   Withdrawal to Escaut   St Omer-La Bassee   Bou Arada   Stuka Farm   Oued Zarga   Djebel Bel Mahdi   Djebel Ang   Djebel Tanngoucha   Adrano   Centuripe   Salso Crossing   Simeto Crossing   Malleto   Termoli   Trigno   Sangro   Fossacesia   Cassino II   Liri Valley   Trasimene Line   Monte Spaduro   Monte Grande   Argenta Gap   San Nicolo Canal   Leros   Malta 1940

The motto of the regiment was 'Faugh-a-Ballagh' (Clear the Way), and the regimental marches were 'The British Grenadiers' (anonymous, quick) and a combined version of 'St Patrick's Day', 'Barrosa' and 'Garry Owen' (quick). The uniform was scarlet with scarlet piping and blue facings, and the nicknames associated with The Royal Irish Fusiliers were 'The Aiglers', 'The Eagle Takers', 'The Faughs', 'The Old Fogs', 'The Faugh-a-Ballagh Boys', 'The Rollickers' (2nd Battalion) and 'Blayney's Bloodhounds' (2nd Battalion), the first two in reference to the 87th Regiment of Foot's capture of the first French eagle taken in the Peninsula War. The only imperial regiment affiliated to The Royal Irish Fusiliers was the Irish Fusiliers (Vancouver Regiment) of Canada.

Senior of the regiments that went into The Royal Irish Fusiliers in 1881 was the 87th (Royal Irish Fusiliers) Regiment of Foot, which had been raised in 1793 by Colonel John Doyle as the 87th (or Prince of Wales's Irish) Regiment of Foot. In 1811 this was restyled the 87th (or Prince of Wales's Own Irish) Regiment of Foot. In January 1827 this in turn became the 87th (Prince of Wales's Own Irish Fusiliers) Regiment of Foot, changing in November of the same year to the 87th (or Royal Irish Fusiliers) Regiment of Foot. The battle honours of the regiment were the following:

Monte Video   Talavera   Barrosa   Tarifa   Vittoria   Nivelle   Orthes   Toulouse   Peninsula

The motto of the regiment was 'Faugh-a-Ballagh' (Clear the Way), and the regimental marches were 'St Patrick's Day' (traditional, quick) and 'The British Grenadiers' (anonymous, quick). The uniform was scarlet with blue facings, and the nicknames associated with the 87th were 'The Aiglers', 'The Eagle Takers', 'The Faughs', 'The Faugh-a-Ballagh Boys' and 'The Old Fogs'.

The 87th's junior partner was the 89th (Princess Victoria's) Regiment of Foot, which had been raised in 1793 by Colonel William Crosbie as the 89th Regiment of Foot. The regiment underwent a title change only once before its amalgamation into The Royal Irish Fusiliers when in 1866 it became the 89th (Princess Victoria's) Regiment of Foot. The battle honours of the regiment were the following:

Egypt (with the Sphinx)   Java   Niagara   Ava   Sevastopol

The regimental marches were 'Garry Owen' (traditional, quick) and 'Barrosa' (anonymous, quick), the uniform was scarlet with black facings, and the nicknames associated with the 89th were 'The Rollickers' and 'Blayney's Bloodhounds'.

REGIMENTS OF INFANTRY 18

The Gloucestershire Regiment (28th and 61st)

Colonel-in-Chief

HRH The Duke of Gloucester

Colonel

Major-General C. J. Waters

Battle honours

Ramillies Louisburg Guadaloupe 1759 Quebec 1759 Martinique 1762 Havannah St Lucia 1778 Egypt (with the Sphinx) Maida Corunna Talavera Busaco Barrosa Albuhera Salamanca Vittoria Pyrenees Nivelle Nives Orthes Toulouse Peninsula Waterloo Chillianwallah Goojerat Punjaub Alma Inkerman Sevastopol Delhi 1857 Defence of Ladysmith Relief of Kimberley Paardeberg South Africa 1899–1902 Mons Retreat from Mons Marne 1914 Aisne 1914, '18 Ypres 1914, '15, '17 Langemarck 1914, '17 Gheluvelt Nonne Bosschen Givenchy 1914 Gravenstafel St Julien Frezenberg Bellewaarde Aubers Loos Somme 1916, '18 Albert 1916, '18 Bazentin Delville Wood Pozieres Guillemont Flers-Courcelette Morval Ancre Heights Ancre 1916 Arras 1917, '18 Vimy 1917 Scarpe 1917 Messines 1917, '18 Pilckem Menin Road Polygon Wood Broodseinde Poelcappelle Passchendaele

THE GLOUCESTERSHIRE REGIMENT

Cambrai 1917, '18 St Quentin Bapaume 1918 Rosieres Avre Lys Estaires Hazebrouck Bailleul Kemmel Bethune Drocourt-Queant Hindenburg Line Epehy Canal du Nord St Quentin Canal Beaurevoir Selle Valenciennes Sambre France and Flanders 1914–18 Piave Vittorio Veneto Italy 1917–18 Struma Doiran 1917 Macedonia 1915–18 Suvla Sari Bair Scimitar Hill Gallipoli 1915–16 Egypt 1916 Tigris 1916 Kut al Amara 1917 Baghdad Mesopotamia 1916–18 Persia 1918 Defence of Escaut St Omer-La Bassee Wormhoudt Cassel Villers Bocage Mont Pincon Falaise Risle Crossing Le Havre Zetten North-West Europe 1940, '44–45 Taukyan Paungde Monywa 1942 North Arakan Mayu Tunnels Pinwe Shweli Myitson Burma 1942, '44–45 Hill 327 Imjin Korea 1950–51

Regimental headquarters

Custom House, 31 Commercial Road, Gloucester, Gloucestershire.

Regimental museum

Custom House, 31 Commercial Road, Gloucester, Gloucestershire.

Regimental marches

(quick) Kinnegad Slashers (traditional)
(slow) Regimental Slow March of the 28th/61st (Plummer)

Regimental motto

Honi Soit Qui Mal y Pense (Evil be to Him who Evil Thinks)

Nicknames

The Back Numbers, The Fore and Aft, The Old Braggs, The Glorious Glosters, The Slashers, The Flowers of Toulouse (2nd Battalion), The Silver-Tailed Dandies (2nd Battalion)

Uniform

Scarlet with primrose piping and facings

Allied regiments

The Royal Canadian Regiment
The Royal Western Australia Regiment
3rd Battalion The Kenya Rifles

Regimental history

The Gloucestershire Regiment came into existence in 1881 through the amalgamation of the 28th (North Gloucestershire) Regiment of Foot and the 61st (South Gloucestershire) Regiment of Foot. Imperial regiments affiliated to The Gloucestershire Regiment were the Royal Canadian Regiment (Canada), and the 28th and 56th Battalions, Australian Infantry. The nickname 'The Glorious Glosters' is of recent origin, being attributable to the stand of the regiment's 1st Battalion on the Imjin river (May 1951) during the Korean War.

Of the Gloucestershire Regiment's two components the senior was the 28th (North Gloucestershire) Regiment of Foot, which had been raised in 1694 as Colonel Gibson's Regiment of Foot. The regiment subsequently changed name with its colonels until 1742, when it became the 28th Regiment of Foot, a title changed in 1782 to the 28th (or North Gloucestershire) Regiment of Foot. The battle honours of the regiment were the following:

> Ramillies   Louisburg   Quebec 1759   Martinique 1762   Havannah
> St Lucia 1778   Egypt (with the Sphinx)   Corunna   Barrosa   Albuhera
> Vittoria   Pyrenees   Nivelle   Nive   Orthes   Toulouse   Peninsula
> Waterloo   Alma   Inkerman   Sevastopol

The regimental march was 'The Kinnegad Slashers' (traditional, quick), the uniform was scarlet with yellow facings, and the nicknames associated with the regiment were 'The Back Numbers', 'The Fore and Aft', 'The Old Braggs' and 'The Slashers', the first two in reference to the regiment's unique right to a badge at the rear of the head-dress (as well as at the front) in commemoration of the 28th's back-to-back stand at the Battle of Alexandria (1801). The size of the rear badge was increased on the head-dress of The Gloucestershire Regiment to signify the regiment's engagement with four surrounding German regiments in the Battle of Festubert (1915).

The junior partner was the 61st (South Gloucestershire) Regiment of Foot, which had been raised in 1756 as the 2nd Battalion of the 3rd (or East Kent) Regiment of Foot (The Buffs), but secured a separate existence as the 61st Regiment of Foot in 1758. The regiment's only change of title came in 1782, when it became the 61st (or South Gloucestershire) Regiment of Foot. The battle honours of the regiment were the following:

> Egypt (with the Sphinx)   Maida   Guadaloupe 1759   Talavera
> Salamanca   Pyrenees   Nivelle   Nive   Orthes   Toulouse
> Peninsula   Chillianwallah   Goojerat   Punjaub   Delhi 1857

The regimental march was 'The Highland Pipers' (traditional, quick), the uniform was scarlet with buff facings, and the nicknames associated with the regiment were 'The Flowers of Toulouse' and 'The Silver-Tailed

Dandies', the first referring to the regiment's fine performance in the Battle of Toulouse (1814), and the second having two possible origins: the wearing of silver acorns on the regiment's coat tails after the Battle of Toulouse, or the officers' continued use of long-tailed coats after other regiments had adopted short-tailed coats.

The Worcestershire and Sherwood Foresters Regiment (29th/45th Foot) (29th, 36th, 45th and 95th)

Colonel-in-Chief

HRH The Princess Royal Mrs Mark Phillips

Colonel

Brigadier P. F. B. Hargrave

Battle honours

Ramillies   Belleisle   Mysore   Hindoostan   Louisburg   Rolica   Vimiera   Corunna   Talavera   Busaco   Fuentes d'Onor   Albuhera   Ciudad Rodrigo   Badajoz   Salamanca   Vittoria   Pyrenees   Nivelle   Nive   Orthes   Toulouse   Peninsula   Ava   Ferozeshah   Sobraon   South Africa 1846–47   Chillianwallah   Goojerat   Punjaub   Alma   Inkerman   Sevastopol   Central India   Abyssinia   Egypt 1882   Tirah   South Africa 1899–1902   Mons   Le Cateau   Retreat from Mons   Marne 1914   Aisne 1914   La Bassee 1914   Armentieres 1914   Ypres 1914, '15, '17, '18   Langemarck 1914, '17   Gheluvelt   Nonne Bosschen   Neuve Chapelle   Aubers   Festubert 1915   Hooge 1915   Loos   Somme 1916, '18   Albert 1916, '18   Bazentin   Delville Wood   Pozieres   Ginchy   Flers-Courcelette   Morval   Thiepval   Le Transloy   Ancre Heights

THE WORCESTERSHIRE AND SHERWOOD FORESTERS REGIMENT

Ancre 1916   Arras 1917, '18   Vimy 1917   Scarpe 1917, '18   Arleux   Messines 1917, '18   Pilckem   Langemarck 1917   Menin Road   Polygon Wood   Broodseinde   Poelcappelle   Passchendaele   Cambrai 1917, '18   St Quentin   Bapaume 1918   Rosieres   Villers Bretonneux   Lys   Estaires   Hazebrouck   Bailleul   Kemmel   Scherpenberg   Amiens   Drocourt-Queant   Hindenburg Line   Epehy   Canal du Nord   St Quentin Canal   Beaurevoir   Courtrai   Selle   Valenciennes   Sambre   France and Flanders 1914–18   Piave   Vittorio Veneto   Italy 1917–18   Doiran 1917–18   Macedonia 1915–18   Helles   Landing at Helles   Krithia   Suvla   Sari Bair   Landing at Suvla   Scimitar Hill   Gallipoli 1915–16   Egypt 1916   Tigris 1916   Kut al Amara 1917   Baghdad   Mesopotamia 1916–18   Baku   Persia 1918   Norway 1940   Defence of Escaut   St Omer-La Bassee   Ypres-Comines Canal   Wormhoudt   Dunkirk 1940   Odon   Bourgebus Ridge   Maltot   Mont Pincon   Jurques   La Variniere   Noireau Crossing   Seine 1944   Nederrijn   Geilenkirchen   Rhineland   Goch   Rhine   North-West Europe 1940, '44–45   Gogni   Barentu   Keren   Amba Alagi   Abyssinia 1940–41   Gazala   Via Balbia   El Alamein   Djebel Guerba   Tamera   Medjez Plain   Tunis   North Africa 1941–43   Salerno   Volturno Crossing   Monte Camino   Anzio   Campoleone   Advance to Tiber   Gothic Line   Coriano   Cosina Canal Crossing   Monte Ceco   Italy 1943–45   Singapore Island   Malaya 1942   Kohima   Relief of Kohima   Naga Village   Mao Songsang   Shwebo   Mandalay   Irrawaddy   Mt Popa   Burma 1944–45

Regimental headquarters

Norton Barracks, Worcester, Worcestershire.

Regimental museums

(The Worcestershire Regiment)
City Museum, Foregate Street, Worcester, Worcestershire.
(The Sherwood Foresters)
The Castle, Nottingham, Nottinghamshire, and
City Museum, Strand, Derby, Derbyshire.

Regimental marches

(quick) Royal Windsor (Princess Augusta), and Young May Moon
(traditional)
(slow) Duchess of Kent (Duchess of Kent)

Regimental motto

Firm

Nickname

The Woofers

Uniform

Scarlet with Lincoln green piping and facings

Allied regiments

The Grey and Simcoe Foresters (Canada)
13th Battalion The Punjab Regiment (Pakistan)

Regimental history

The Worcestershire and Sherwood Foresters Regiment (29th/45th Foot) came into being during February 1970 through the amalgamation of The Worcestershire Regiment and The Sherwood Foresters (Nottinghamshire and Derbyshire Regiment). The nickname is a reference to the abbreviation WFR for the amalgamated regiment. The official mascot of the regiment is a ram.

The senior of the components was The Worcestershire Regiment, itself an 1881 amalgamation of the 29th (Worcestershire) Regiment of Foot and the 36th (Herefordshire) Regiment of Foot. The battle honours of the combined regiment were the following:

Ramillies Belleisle Mysore Hindoostan Rolica Vimiera Corunna Talavera Albuhera Salamanca Pyrenees Nivelle Nive Orthes Toulouse Peninsula Ferozeshah Sobraon Chillianwallah Goojerat Punjaub South Africa 1900–1902 Mons Le Cateau Retreat from Mons Marne 1914 Aisne 1914 La Bassee 1914 Armentieres 1914 Ypres 1914, '15, '17, '18 Langemarck 1914, '17 Gheluvelt Nonne Bosschen Neuve Chapelle Aubers Festubert 1915 Loos Somme 1916, '18 Albert 1916 Bazentin Delville Wood Pozieres Le Transloy Ancre Heights Ancre 1916 Arras 1917 Scarpe 1917 Arleux Messines 1917, '18 Pilckem Menin Road Polygon Wood Broodseinde Poelcappelle Passchendaele Cambrai 1917, '18 St Quentin Bapaume 1918 Rosieres Villers Bretonneux Lys Estaires Hazebrouck Bailleul Kemmel Scherpenberg Hindenburg Line Canal du Nord St Quentin Canal Beaurevoir Courtrai Selle Valenciennes Sambre France and

Flanders 1914–18   Piave   Vittorio Veneto   Italy 1917–18   Doiran 1917–18   Macedonia 1915–18   Helles   Landing at Helles   Krithia   Suvla   Sari Bair   Landing at Suvla   Scimitar Hill   Gallipoli 1915–16   Egypt 1916   Tigris 1916   Kut al Amara 1917   Baghdad   Mesopotamia 1916–18   Baku   Persia 1918   Defence of Escaut   St Omer-La Bassee   Wormhoudt   Odon   Bourgebus Ridge   Maltot   Mont Pincon   Jurques   La Variniere   Noireau Crossing   Seine 1944   Nederrijn   Geilenkirchen   Rhineland   Goch   Rhine   North-West Europe 1940, '44–45   Gogni   Barentu   Keren   Amba Alagi   Abyssinia 1940–41   Gazala   Via Balbia   North Africa 1941–42   Kohima   Relief of Kohima   Naga Village   Mao Songsang   Shwebo   Mandalay   Irrawaddy   Mt Popa   Burma 1944–45

The motto of the regiment was 'Firm', and the regimental marches were 'Royal Windsor' (Princess Augusta, quick) and 'Duchess of Kent' (Duchess of Kent, slow). The uniform was scarlet with grass green (emerald) piping and facings, and the nicknames associated with The Worcestershire Regiment were 'The Firms', 'The Guards of the Line', 'The Saucy Greens', 'The Vein Openers', 'The Ever-Sworded 29th' and 'The Old and Bold'. The only imperial regiment affiliated to The Worcestershire Regiment was the 29th Battalion, Australian Infantry.

Within The Worcestershire Regiment the senior component was the 29th (Worcestershire) Regiment of Foot, which had been raised in 1694 as Colonel Farrington's Regiment of Foot. In 1698 the regiment was reduced to cadre status, with the officers on half-pay, but was revived in 1702 as Brigadier-General Farrington's Regiment of Foot. The name of the regiment subsequently changed with its colonels until 1751, when it became the 29th Regiment of Foot. In 1782 this title was changed to the 29th (or the Worcestershire) Regiment of Foot. The battle honours of the regiment were the following:

Ramillies   Rolica   Vimiera   Talavera   Albuhera   Peninsula   Ferozeshah   Sobraon   Chillianwallah   Goojerat   Punjaub

The regimental marches were 'Royal Windsor' (Princess Augusta, quick) and 'Duchess of Kent' (Duchess of Kent, slow). The uniform was scarlet with yellow facings, and the nicknames associated with the 29th were 'The Old and Bold' and 'The Ever-Sworded 29th'.

The 29th's junior partner in The Worcestershire Regiment was the 36th (Herefordshire) Regiment of Foot, which had been raised in 1701 as Viscount Charlemont's Regiment of Foot. The regiment subsequently changed its title with its colonels until 1751, when it became the 36th Regiment of Foot, a title changed in 1782 to the 36th (or the Herefordshire) Regiment of Foot. The battle honours of the regiment were the following:

Mysore   Hindoostan   Rolica   Vimiera   Corunna   Salamanca   Pyrenees   Nivelle   Nive   Orthes   Toulouse   Peninsula

The motto of the regiment was 'Firm', and the regimental march was 'The Lincolnshire Poacher' (traditional, quick). The uniform was scarlet with grass green facings, and the nicknames associated with the 36th were 'The Firms' and 'The Saucy Greens'.

The junior partner to The Worcestershire Regiment in the 1970 amalgamation to form The Worcestershire and Sherwood Foresters Regiment was The Sherwood Foresters (Nottinghamshire and Derbyshire Regiment), itself the result of the 1881 amalgamation of the 45th (Nottinghamshire-Sherwood Foresters) Regiment of Foot and the 95th (Derbyshire) Regiment of Foot. The combined regiment was at first (May 1881) styled The Derbyshire Regiment (Sherwood Foresters), but later (July 1881) restyled The Sherwood Foresters (Derbyshire Regiment). In 1902 this became The Sherwood Foresters (Nottinghamshire and Derbyshire Regiment). The battle honours of the combined regiment were the following:

Louisburg   Rolica   Vimiera   Talavera   Busaco   Fuentes d'Onor   Ciudad Rodrigo   Badajoz   Salamanca   Vittoria   Pyrenees   Nivelle   Nive   Orthes   Toulouse   Peninsula   Ava   South Africa 1846–47   Alma   Inkerman   Sevastopol   Central India   Abyssinia   Egypt 1882   Tirah   South Africa 1899–1902   Aisne 1914, '18   Armentieres 1914   Neuve Chapelle   Aubers   Hooge 1915   Loos   Somme 1916, '18   Albert 1916, '18   Bazentin   Delville Wood   Pozieres   Ginchy   Flers-Courcelette   Morval   Thiepval   Le Transloy   Ancre Heights   Ancre 1916   Arras 1917, '18   Vimy 1917   Scarpe 1917, '18   Messines 1917   Ypres 1917, '18   Pilckem   Langemarck 1917   Menin Road   Polygon Wood   Broodseinde   Poelcappelle   Passchendaele   Cambrai 1917, '18   St Quentin   Bapaume 1918   Rosieres   Villers Bretonneux   Lys   Bailleul   Kemmel   Scherpenberg   Amiens   Drocourt-Queant   Hindenburg Line   Epehy   Canal du Nord   St Quentin Canal   Beaurevoir   Courtrai   Selle   Sambre   France and Flanders 1914–18   Piave   Italy 1917–18   Suvla   Landing at Suvla   Scimitar Hill   Gallipoli 1915   Egypt 1916   Norway 1940   St Omer-La Bassee   Ypres-Comines Canal   Dunkirk 1940   North-West Europe 1940   Gazala   El Alamein   Djebel Guerba   Tamera   Medjez Plain   Tunis   North Africa 1942–43   Salerno   Volturno Crossing   Monte Camino   Anzio   Campoleone   Advance to Tiber   Gothic Line   Coriano   Cosina Canal Crossing   Monte Ceco   Italy 1943–45   Singapore Island   Malaya 1942

The motto of the regiment was 'Honi Soit Qui Mal y Pense' (Evil be to Him who Evil Thinks), and the regimental marches were 'The Young May Moon' and 'I'm 95' (traditional and anonymous, quick) and 'The Crich Memorial' (slow). The uniform was scarlet with Lincoln green piping and facings, and the nicknames associated with The Sherwood Foresters (Nottinghamshire and Derbyshire Regiment) were 'The Old Stubborns' (1st Battalion), 'The Sweeps' and 'The Hosiers'. The imperial regiments affiliated to The Sherwood Foresters (Nottinghamshire and Derbyshire Regiment) were the Manitoba Rangers (Canada) and the Simcoe Foresters (Canada).

The senior partner in The Sherwood Foresters (Nottinghamshire and Derbyshire Regiment) was the 45th (Nottinghamshire–Sherwood Foresters) Regiment of Foot, which had been raised in 1741 as Colonel Houghton's Regiment of Foot. The regiment subsequently changed name with its colonels until 1751, when it became the 45th Regiment of Foot. In 1779 this title was changed to the 45th (or Nottinghamshire) Regiment of Foot, and in 1866 to the 45th (Nottinghamshire–Sherwood Foresters) Regiment of Foot. The battle honours of the regiment were the following:

Louisburg   Rolica   Vimiera   Talavera   Busaco   Fuentes d'Onor   Ciudad Rodrigo   Badajoz   Salamanca   Vittoria   Pyrenees   Nivelle   Orthes   Toulouse   Peninsula   Ava   South Africa 1846–47   Abyssinia

The regimental march was 'The Young May Moon' (traditional, quick). The uniform was scarlet with Lincoln green facings, and the nicknames associated with the 45th were 'The Old Stubborns' and 'The Hosiers', the former in reference to the regiment's impressive performance in the Peninsula War and the latter to the regiment's association with Nottingham, centre of the British hosiery trade.

Junior to the 45th was the 95th (Derbyshire) Regiment of Foot, which had been raised in 1823 by Colonel Sir John Halkett as the 95th Regiment of Foot, a title changed in 1823 to the 95th (or Derbyshire) Regiment of Foot. The battle honours of the regiment were the following:

Alma   Inkerman   Sevastopol   Central India

The regimental march was 'I'm 95' (anonymous, quick). The uniform was scarlet with yellow facings, and the nickname associated with the 95th was 'The Nails'.

REGIMENTS OF INFANTRY 20

The Queen's Lancashire Regiment (30th, 40th, 47th, 59th, 81st and 82nd)

Colonel-in-Chief

HM The Queen

Colonel

Major-General D. Houston

Battle honours

Gibraltar 1704–05 Louisburg Quebec 1759 Belleisle Martinique 1762 Havannah St Lucia 1778 Egypt (with the Sphinx) Cape of Good Hope 1806 Maida Monte Video Rolica Vimiera Corunna Talavera Java Tarifa Badajoz Salamanca Vittoria St Sebastian Pyrenees Nivelle Nive Niagara Orthes Toulouse Peninsula Waterloo Ava Bhurtpore Candahar 1842 Ghuznee 1842 Cabool 1842 Maharajpore Alma Inkerman Sevastopol Lucknow Canton New Zealand Ali Masjid Ahmad Khel Afghanistan 1878–80 Chitral Defence of Kimberley Relief of Ladysmith South Africa 1899–1902 Mons Le Cateau Retreat from Mons Marne 1914, '18 Aisne 1914, '18 La Bassee 1914 Messines 1914, '17, '18 Armentieres 1914 Ypres 1914, '15, '17, '18 Langemarck 1914, '17 Gheluvelt Nonne Bosschen Givenchy 1914 Neuve Chapelle St Julien Frezenberg Bellewaarde Aubers Festubert 1915 Loos

THE QUEEN'S LANCASHIRE REGIMENT

Somme 1916, '18   Albert 1916, '18   Bazentin   Pozieres   Guillemont   Ginchy   Flers-Courcelette   Morval   Le Transloy   Ancre Heights   Ancre 1916, '18   Arras 1917, '18   Vimy 1917   Scarpe 1917, '18   Arleux   Oppy   Pilckem   Menin Road   Polygon Wood   Broodseinde   Poelcappelle   Passchendaele   Cambrai 1917, '18   St Quentin   Bapaume 1918   Rosieres   Villers Bretonneux   Lys   Estaires   Hazebrouck   Bailleul   Kemmel   Bethune   Scherpenberg   Soissonais-Ourcq   Drocourt-Queant   Hindenburg Line   Epehy   Canal du Nord   St Quentin Canal   Courtrai   Selle   Valenciennes   Sambre   France and Flanders 1914-18   Kosturino   Doiran 1917, '18   Macedonia 1915-18   Helles   Krithia   Suvla   Sari Bair   Gallipoli 1915   Rumani   Egypt 1915-17   Gaza   Nebi Samwil   Jerusalem   Jaffa   Tell' Asur   Palestine 1917-18   Tigris 1916   Kut al Amara 1917   Baghdad   Mesopotamia 1916-18   Kilimanjaro   East Africa 1914-16   Baluchistan 1918   Afghanistan 1919   Defence of Escaut   Dunkirk 1940   Normandy Landing   Odon   Caen   Bourgebus Ridge   Troarn   Falaise   Nederrijn   Lower Maas   Venraij   Ourthe   Rhineland   Reichswald   Weeze   Hochwald   Rhine   Ibbenburen   Aller   Bremen   North-West Europe 1940, '44-45   Banana Ridge   Djebel Kesskiss   Medjez Plain   Gueriat et Atach Ridge   Gab Gab Gap   Djebel Bou Aoukaz 1943 I   North Africa 1943   Anzio   Rome   Fiesole   Gothic Line   Monte Gamberaldi   Monte Ceco   Monte Grande   Italy 1944-45   Madagascar   Middle East 1942   Johore   Batu Pahat   Singapore Island   Malaya 1941-42   North Arakan   Mayu Tunnels   Kohima   Pinwe   Meiktila   Nyaungu Bridgehead   Letse   Irrawaddy   Burma 1943-45

Regimental headquarters

Fulwood Barracks, Preston, Lancashire.

Regimental museum

Fulwood Barracks, Preston, Lancashire.

Regimental marches

(quick) L'Attaque, and The Red Rose
(slow) Long Live Elizabeth

Regimental motto

Loyally I Serve

Nicknames

see below

Uniform

Scarlet with blue piping and facings

Allied regiments

The West Nova Scotia Regiment (Canada)
The Loyal Edmonton Regiment (4th Battalion Princess Patricia's Canadian Light Infantry) (Canada)
The Royal Tasmania Regiment (Australia)
7th Battalion (Wellington [City of Wellington's Own] and Hawke's Bay) The Royal New Zealand Infantry Regiment
8th Battalion The Punjab Regiment (Pakistan)
14th Battalion The Punjab Regiment (Pakistan)
2nd Battalion The Royal Malay Regiment

Regimental history

The Queen's Lancashire Regiment was created in March 1970 by the amalgamation of The Lancashire Regiment (Prince of Wales's Volunteers) and The Loyal Regiment (North Lancashire).

The senior component of this amalgamation was The Lancashire Regiment (Prince of Wales's Volunteers), itself the result of a 1958 amalgamation of The East Lancashire Regiment and The South Lancashire Regiment (The Prince of Wales's Volunteers). The regimental march of the combined regiment was an arrangement of 'L'Attaque' and 'God Bless the Prince of Wales', and the uniform was scarlet with white piping and facings.

Within The Lancashire Regiment the senior partner was The East Lancashire Regiment, itself the result of yet another amalgamation, in this instance during 1881 between the 30th (1st Cambridgeshire) Regiment of Foot, which was often known as the 30th of Foot (1st Cambridgeshire Regiment), and the 59th (2nd Nottinghamshire) Regiment of Foot. The combined regiment was initially known as The West Lancashire Regiment, a designation changed later in 1881 to The East Lancashire Regiment. The battle honours of the combined regiment were the following:

Gibraltar 1704–05   Belleisle   Egypt (with the Sphinx)   Cape of Good Hope 1806   Corunna   Java   Badajoz   Salamanca   Vittoria   St Sebastian   Nive   Peninsula   Waterloo   Bhurtpore   Alma   Inkerman   Sevastopol   Canton   Ahmad Khel   Afghanistan 1878–80   Chitral   South Africa 1900–02   Le Cateau   Retreat from Mons   Marne 1914

Aisne 1914, '18   Armentieres 1914   Neuve Chapelle   Ypres 1915, '17, '18   St Julien   Frezenberg   Bellewaarde   Aubers   Somme 1916, '18   Albert 1916, '18   Bazentin   Pozieres   Le Transloy   Ancre Heights   Ancre 1916, '18   Arras 1917, '18   Vimy 1917   Scarpe 1917, '18   Arleux   Oppy   Messines 1917   Pilckem   Langemarck 1917   Menin Road   Polygon Wood   Broodseinde   Poelcappelle   Passchendaele   St Quentin   Bapaume 1918   Rosieres   Villers Bretonneux   Lys   Estaires   Hazebrouck   Bailleul   Kemmel   Hindenburg Line   Canal du Nord   Cambrai 1918   Selle   Valenciennes   Sambre   France and Flanders 1914-18   Kosturino   Doiran 1917, '18   Macedonia 1915-18   Helles   Krithia   Suvla   Sari Bair   Gallipoli 1915   Rumani   Egypt 1915-17   Tigris 1916   Kut al Amara 1917   Baghdad   Mesopotamia 1916-17   Defence of Escaut   Dunkirk 1940   Caen   Falaise   Nederrijn   Lower Maas   Ourthe   Rhineland   Reichswald   Weeze   Rhine   Ibbenburen   Aller   North-West Europe 1940, '44-45   Madagascar   North Arakan   Pinwe   Burma 1943-45

The motto of the regiment was 'Spectamur Agendo' (By Our Deeds are we Known), and the regimental marches were 'L'Attaque' (quick) and 'God Bless the Prince of Wales' (Richards, slow). The uniform was scarlet with white piping and facings, and the nicknames associated with The East Lancashire Regiment were 'The Three Tens', 'The Triple Xs' and 'The Lillywhites'. The only imperial regiment affiliated to The East Lancashire Regiment was the 59th Battalion, Australian Infantry.

Within The East Lancashire Regiment the senior partner was the 30th (1st Cambridgeshire) Regiment of Foot, which had been raised in 1689 by Viscount Castleton as Lord Castleton's Regiment of Foot. By 1698 it had become Colonel Saunderson's Regiment of Foot, but was disbanded in that year only to be re-raised in 1702 as Colonel Saunderson's Regiment of Marines. Thereafter the regiment changed name with its colonels up to 1714, when it became General Wills's Regiment of Foot, subsequently again changing its name with its colonels up to 1751, when it became the 30th Regiment of Foot. The only other change followed in 1782, when the regiment became the 30th (1st Cambridgeshire) Regiment of Foot. The battle honours of the regiment were the following:

Egypt (with the Sphinx)   Badajoz   Salamanca   Peninsula   Waterloo   Alma   Inkerman   Sevastopol

The motto of the regiment was 'Spectamur Agendo' (By Our Deeds are we Known), and the regimental march was 'L'Attaque' (quick). The uniform was scarlet with yellow facings, and the nicknames associated with the 30th were 'The Three Tens', 'The Triple X's' and 'The Yellow Bellies'.

The 30th's junior partner in The East Lancashire Regiment was the 59th (2nd Nottinghamshire) Regiment of Foot, which had been raised in 1755 by Colonel Sir Charles Montagu as the 61st Regiment of Foot. In 1757 the regiment was renumbered as the 59th Regiment of Foot, and the only other title change up to the time of the regiment's amalgamation with the 30th in 1881 was to the 59th (2nd Nottinghamshire) Regiment of Foot in 1782. The regiment's battle honours were the following:

> Cape of Good Hope 1806   Corunna   Java   Vittoria   St Sebastian   Nive   Peninsula   Bhurtpore   Canton   Ahmad Khel   Afghanistan 1878–80

The regimental march was 'Lancashire Lad' (traditional, quick). The uniform was scarlet with white facings, and the nickname associated with the 59th was 'The Lillywhites'.

Junior partner to The East Lancashire Regiment in the 1958 amalgamation to create The Lancashire Regiment (Prince of Wales's Volunteers) was The South Lancashire Regiment (The Prince of Wales's Volunteers), itself also the result of earlier amalgamation in 1881 between the 40th (2nd Somersetshire) Regiment of Foot and the 82nd Regiment of Foot (Prince of Wales's Volunteers). The regiment resulting from this amalgamation was at first known as The Prince of Wales's Volunteers (South Lancashire), a title changed in 1938 to The South Lancashire Regiment (The Prince of Wales's Volunteers). The battle honours of the combined regiment were the following:

> Louisburg   Martinique 1762   Havannah   St Lucia 1778   Egypt (with the Sphinx)   Monte Video   Rolica   Vimiera   Corunna   Talavera   Badajoz   Salamanca   Vittoria   Pyrenees   Nivelle   Orthes   Toulouse   Peninsula   Niagara   Waterloo   Candahar 1842   Ghuznee 1842   Cabool 1842   Maharajpore   Sevastopol   Lucknow   New Zealand   Relief of Ladysmith   South Africa 1899–1902   Mons   Le Cateau   Retreat from Mons   Marne 1914   Aisne 1914, '18   La Bassee 1914   Messines 1914, '17, '18   Armentieres 1914   Ypres 1914, '15, '17, '18   Nonne Bosschen   St Julien   Frezenberg   Bellewaarde   Somme 1916, '18   Albert 1916   Bazentin   Pozieres   Guillemont   Ginchy   Flers-Courcelette   Morval   Le Transloy   Ancre Heights   Ancre 1916   Arras 1917, '18   Scarpe 1917, '18   Pilckem   Langemarck 1917   Menin Road   Polygon Wood   Passchendaele   Cambrai 1917, '18   St Quentin   Bapaume 1918   Rosieres   Lys   Estaires   Hazebrouck   Bailleul   Kemmel   Scherpenberg   Drocourt-Queant   Hindenburg Line   Canal du Nord   Courtrai   Selle   Sambre   France and Flanders 1914–18   Doiran 1917, '18   Macedonia 1915–18   Baluchistan 1918   Afghanistan 1919   Dunkirk 1940   Normandy Landing   Odon   Bourgebus Ridge   Troarn   Falaise   Venraij   Rhineland   Hochwald   Bremen   North-West Europe 1940, '44–45   Madagascar   Middle East 1942

North Arakan Mayu Tunnels Kohima Meiktila Nyaungu Bridgehead Letse Irrawaddy Burma 1943–45

The motto of the regiment was 'Ich Dien' (I Serve), and the regimental marches were 'God Bless the Prince of Wales' (Richards, quick) and 'The Lancashire Witches' (traditional, slow). The uniform was scarlet with buff piping and facings, and the nicknames associated with The South Lancashire Regiment were 'The Fighting Fortieth' and 'The Excellers', the latter referring to the regiment's number in Roman numerals (XL). The imperial regiments affiliated to The South Lancashire Regiment were the Princess of Wales's Own Regiment (Canada), the Annapolis Regiment (Canada), the 40th Battalion, Australian Infantry, and the Hawke's Bay Regiment (New Zealand).

The senior of the components that went to form The South Lancashire Regiment was the 40th (2nd Somersetshire) Regiment of Foot, which had been raised from independent infantry companies in Nova Scotia during 1717 as Colonel Phillips's Regiment of Foot. The regiment subsequently changed name with its colonels until 1751, when it was designated the 40th Regiment of Foot before becoming the 40th (2nd Somersetshire) Regiment of Foot in 1782. The battle honours of the regiment were the following:

Louisburg Egypt (with the Sphinx) Monte Video Rolica Vimiera Talavera Badajoz Salamanca Vittoria Pyrenees Nivelle Orthes Toulouse Peninsula Waterloo Candahar Ghuznee 1842 Cabool 1842 Maharajpore New Zealand

The regimental march was 'The Somerset Poacher' (traditional, quick). The uniform was scarlet with buff facings, and the nicknames associated with the 40th were 'The Fighting Fortieth' and 'The Excellers'.

The 40th's junior partner in The South Lancashire Regiment was the 82nd Regiment of Foot (Prince of Wales's Volunteers), which had been raised in 1793 by Colonel Charles Leigh as the 82nd Regiment of Foot (or Prince of Wales's Volunteers), a title that remained unmodified up to the time of the 1881 amalgamation. The battle honours of the regiment were the following:

Rolica Vimiera Vittoria Pyrenees Nivelle Orthes Peninsula Niagara Sevastopol Lucknow

The motto of the regiment was 'Ich Dien' (I Serve), and the regimental march was 'God Bless the Prince of Wales' (Richards, quick). The uniform was scarlet with yellow facings, and there were no nicknames associated with the 82nd.

The other regiment that went with The Lancashire Regiment to create The Queen's Lancashire Regiment in 1970 was The Loyal Regiment (North

Lancashire), itself the creation of an 1881 amalgamation that linked the 47th (Lancashire) Regiment of Foot and the 81st (Loyal Lincoln Volunteers) Regiment of Foot as The Loyal North Lancashire Regiment, a title changed in 1921 to The Loyal Regiment (North Lancashire). The battle honours of the combined regiment were the following:

Louisburg   Quebec 1759   Maida   Corunna   Tarifa   Vittoria   St Sebastian   Nive   Peninsula   Ava   Alma   Inkerman   Sevastopol   Ali Masjid   Afghanistan 1878–79   Defence of Kimberley   South Africa 1899–1902   Mons   Retreat from Mons   Marne 1914, '18   Aisne 1914, '18   Ypres 1914, '15, '17, '18   Langemarck 1914   Gheluvelt   Nonne Bosschen   Givenchy 1914   Aubers   Festubert 1915   Loos   Somme 1916, '18   Albert 1916   Bazentin   Pozieres   Guillemont   Ginchy   Flers-Courcelette   Morval   Ancre Heights   Ancre 1916   Arras 1917, '18   Scarpe 1917   Arleux   Messines 1917   Pilckem   Menin Road   Polygon Wood   Poelcappelle   Passchendaele   Cambrai 1917, '18   St Quentin   Bapaume 1918   Lys   Estaires   Bailleul   Kemmel   Bethune   Scherpenberg   Soissonais–Ourcq   Drocourt–Queant   Hindenburg Line   Epehy   Canal du Nord   St Quentin Canal   Courtrai   Selle   Sambre   France and Flanders 1914–18   Doiran 1917   Macedonia 1917   Suvla   Sari Bair   Gallipoli 1915   Egypt 1916   Gaza   Nebi Samwil   Jerusalem   Jaffa   Tell 'Asur   Palestine 1917–18   Tigris 1916   Kut al Amara 1917   Baghdad   Mesopotamia 1916–18   Kilimanjaro   East Africa 1914–16   Dunkirk 1940   North-West Europe 1940   Banana Ridge   Djebel Kesskiss   Medjez Plain   Gueriat el Atach Ridge   Djebel Bou Aoukaz 1943 I   North Africa 1943   Anzio   Rome   Fiesole   Gothic Line   Monte Gamberaldi   Monte Ceco   Monte Grande   Italy 1944–45   Johore Batu Pahat   Singapore Island   Malaya 1941–42

The motto of the regiment was 'Loyauté M'Oblige' (Loyalty Binds Me), and the regimental march was 'The Red Rose' (traditional, quick). The uniform was scarlet with white piping and facings, and the nickname associated with The Loyal Regiment was 'The Lancashire Lads'. Imperial regiments affiliated with The Loyal Regiment were the Edmonton Regiment (Canada), the 47th Battalion, Australian Infantry, and the Kimberley Regiment (South Africa).

Of the two regiments that went to form The Loyal North Lancashire Regiment in 1881, the senior was the 47th (Lancashire) Regiment of Foot, which had been raised in 1741 as Colonel Mordaunt's Regiment of Foot. The regiment changed title with its colonels until 1751, when it became the 47th Regiment of Foot, modified in 1782 to the 47th (or the Lancashire) Regiment of Foot. The battle honours of the regiment were the following:

Louisburg Quebec 1759 Tarifa Vittoria St Sebastian Peninsula
Ava Alma Inkerman Sevastopol

The regimental march was 'The Mountain Rose' (traditional, quick). The uniform was scarlet with white facings, and the nicknames associated with the 47th were 'Wolfe's Own' and 'The Cauliflowers', the former in remembrance of the regiment's service with General Wolfe in the capture of Quebec (1759), and the latter is scathing reference to the regiment's red rose badge.

Junior to the 47th in The Loyal North Lancashire Regiment was the 81st (Loyal Lincoln Volunteers) Regiment of Foot, which had been raised in 1793 by Major-General Albemarle Bertie, as the 83rd (Loyal Lincolnshire Volunteer) Regiment of Foot. In 1794 the regiment was redesignated the 81st Regiment of Foot, and in 1832 became the 81st (Loyal Lincoln Volunteers) Regiment of Foot. The battle honours of the regiment were the following:

Maida Corunna Peninsula Ali Masjid Afghanistan 1878-80

The motto of the regiment was 'Mox Surgere Victor' (Soon to Rise as Victor), and the regimental march was 'The Lincolshire Poacher' (traditional, quick). The uniform was scarlet with buff facings, and the nickname associated with the 81st was 'The Loyals'.

REGIMENTS OF INFANTRY 21

The Duke of Wellington's Regiment (West Riding) (33rd and 76th)

Colonel-in-Chief

Colonel (Honorary Brigadier) The Duke of Wellington

Colonel

Lieutenant-General Sir Charles Huxtable

Battle honours

Dettingen   Mysore   Seringapatam   Ally Ghur   Delhi 1803   Leswarree   Deig   Hindoostan (with the Elephant)   Corunna   Nive   Peninsula   Waterloo   Alma   Inkerman   Sevastopol   Abyssinia   Relief of Kimberley   South Africa 1900–02   Mons   Le Cateau   Retreat from Mons   Marne 1914, '18   Aisne 1914   La Bassee 1914   Ypres 1914, '15, '17   Nonne Bosschen   Hill 60   Gravenstafel   St Julien   Aubers   Somme 1916, '18   Albert 1916, '18   Bazentin   Delville Wood   Pozieres   Flers-Courcelette   Morval   Thiepval   Le Transloy   Ancre Heights   Arras 1917, '18   Scarpe 1917, '18   Arleux   Bullecourt   Messines 1917, '18   Langemarck 1917   Menin Road   Polygon Wood   Broodseinde   Poelcappelle   Passchendaele   Cambrai 1917, '18   St Quentin   Ancre 1918   Lys   Estaires   Hazebrouck   Bailleul   Kemmel   Bethune   Scherpenberg   Tardenois   Amiens   Bapaume 1918   Drocourt-Queant   Hindenburg Line   Havrincourt   Epehy   Canal du Nord   Selle

Valenciennes Sambre France and Flanders 1914–18 Piave Vittorio Veneto Italy 1917–18 Suvla Landing at Suvla Scimitar Hill Gallipoli 1915 Egypt 1916 Afghanistan 1919 Dunkirk 1940 St Valery-en-Caux Tilly sur Seulles Odon Fontenay le Pesnil North-West Europe 1940, '44–45 Banana Ridge Medjez Plain Gueriat el Atach Ridge Tunis Djebel Bou Aoukaz 1943 North Africa 1943 Anzio Campoleone Rome Monte Ceco Italy 1943–45 Sittang 1942 Paungde Kohima Chindits 1944 Burma 1942–44 The Hook 1953 Korea 1952–53

Regimental headquarters

Wellesley Park, Highroad Well, Halifax, Yorkshire.

Regimental museum

Bankfield Museum, Boothtown Road, Halifax, Yorkshire.

Regimental march

(quick) The Wellesley

Regimental motto

Virtutis Fortuna Comes (Fortune is the Companion of Bravery)

Nicknames

The Dukies, The Have-a-Cake Lads

Uniform

Scarlet with scarlet piping and facings

Allied regiments

Les Voltigeurs de Quebec (Canada)
10th Battalion The Baluch Regiment (Pakistan)

Regimental history

The Duke of Wellington's Regiment (West Riding) was formed in 1881 by the amalgamation of the 33rd (Duke of Wellington's Regiment) and the 76th Regiment of Foot. The amalgamated regiment's initial title was The

Duke of Wellington's (West Riding Regiment), changed in 1921 to The Duke of Wellington's Regiment (West Riding). Imperial regiments affiliated with The Duke of Wellington's (West Riding Regiment) were the Yorkton Regiment (Canada) and the 33rd Battalion, Australian Infantry.

The senior of the current regiment's components was the 33rd (Duke of Wellington's Regiment), which had been raised in 1702 as The Earl of Huntingdon's Regiment of Marines. The name of the regiment subsequently changed with its colonels until 1751, when it became the 33rd Regiment of Foot. In 1782 this was changed to the 33rd (or 1st Yorkshire West Riding) Regiment of Foot, and in 1853 Queen Victoria gave permission for the regiment to be named after its most distinguished former officer as the 33rd (Duke of Wellington's Regiment), the only British regiment now named for a person not of royal blood. The battle honours of the regiment were the following:

Dettingen   Seringapatam   Waterloo   Alma   Inkerman   Sevastopol
Abyssinia

The motto of the regiment was 'Virtutis Fortuna Comes' (Fortune is the Companion of Bravery), and the regimental march was 'The Wellesley' (quick). The uniform was scarlet with scarlet facings, and the nicknames associated with the 33rd were 'The Dukes' and 'The Have-a-Cake Lads', the latter for a recruiting officer's practice of proffering an oatcake on the tip of his sword.

The 33rd's junior partner was the 76th Regiment of Foot, which had been raised originally in 1787 by Colonel Thomas Musgrave as the 76th Regiment of Foot (also known as The Hindoostan Regiment up to 1812) at the expense of the Honourable East India Company for service in India. The name of the regiment remained unaltered until its amalgamation with the 33rd in 1881, and the regiment's battle honours were the following:

Hindoostan (with the Elephant)   Mysore   Ally Ghur   Delhi 1803
Leswarree   Deig   Corunna   Nive   Peninsula

The regimental marches were 'Scotland the Brave' (traditional, quick) and 'Logie o'Buchan' (traditional, slow). The uniform was scarlet with scarlet facings, and nicknames associated with the 76th were 'The Immortals', 'The Pigs' and 'The Old Seven and Sixpennies', the first in reference to the regiment's performance in the storming of Bangalore in the 3rd Mysore War (1789–92), which resulted in the award of the Elephant honour badge, the second in soldierly misappreciation of the Elephant, and the last in reference to the regiment's numerical designation.

REGIMENTS OF INFANTRY 22

The Royal Hampshire Regiment (37th and 67th)

Colonel-in-Chief

HRH The Princess of Wales

Colonel

General Sir David Fraser

Battle honours

Blenheim Ramillies Oudenarde Malplaquet Dettingen Minden Belleisle Tournay Barrosa Peninsula India (with the Tiger) Taku Forts Pekin 1860 Charasiah Kabul 1879 Afghanistan 1879–80 Burmah 1885–87 Paardeberg South Africa 1900–02 Le Cateau Retreat from Mons Marne 1914, '18 Aisne 1914 Armentieres 1914 Ypres 1915, '17, '18 St Julien Frezenberg Bellewaarde Somme 1916, '18 Albert 1916 Guillemont Ginchy Flers-Courcelette Thiepval Le Transloy Ancre Heights Ancre 1916 Arras 1917, '18 Vimy 1917 Scarpe 1917, '18 Messines 1917, '18 Pilckem Langemarck 1917 Menin Road Polygon Wood Broodseinde Poelcappelle Passchendaele Cambrai 1917, '18 St Quentin Bapaume 1918 Rosieres Lys Estaires Hazebrouck Bailleul Kemmel Bethune Tardenois Drocourt-Queant Hindenburg Line Havrincourt Canal du Nord Courtrai Selle Valenciennes Sambre France and

Flanders 1914–18   Italy 1917–18   Kosturino   Struma   Doiran 1917, '18   Macedonia 1915–18   Helles   Landing at Helles   Krithia   Suvla   Sari Bair   Landing at Suvla   Scimitar Hill   Gallipoli 1915–16   Egypt 1915–17   Gaza   El Mughar   Nebi Samwil   Jerusalem   Jaffa   Tell 'Asur   Megiddo   Sharon   Palestine 1917–18   Aden   Shaiba   Kut al Amara 1915, '17   Tigris 1916   Baghdad   Sharqat   Mesopotamia 1915–18   Persia 1918–19   Archangel 1919   Siberia 1918–19   Dunkirk 1940   Normandy Landing   Tilly sur Seulles   Caen   Hill 112   Mont Pincon   Jurques   St Pierre la Vielle   Nederrijn   Roer   Rhineland   Goch   Rhine   North-West Europe 1940, '44–45   Tebourba Gap   Sidi Nsir   Hunt's Gap   Montagne Farm   Fondouk   Pichon   El Kourzia   Ber Rabai   North Africa 1940–43   Landing in Sicily   Regalbuto   Sicily 1943   Landing at Porto San Venere   Salerno   Salerno Hills   Battipaglia   Cava di Tirreni   Volturno Crossing   Garigliano Crossing   Damiano   Monte Ornito   Cerasola   Cassino II   Massa Vertecchi   Trasimene Line   Advance to Florence   Gothic Line   Monte Gridolfo   Montegaudio   Coriano   Montilgallo   Capture of Forli   Cosina Canal Crossing   Lamone Crossing   Pideura   Rimini Line   Montescudo   Frisoni   Italy 1943–45   Athens   Greece 1944–45   Malta 1941–42

Regimental headquarters

Serle's House, Southgate Street, Winchester, Hampshire.

Regimental museum

Serle's House, Southgate Street, Winchester, Hampshire.

Regimental march

(quick) The Hampshire (anonymous)

Regimental motto

Honi Soit Qui Mal y Pense (Evil be to Him who Evil Thinks)

Nickname

The Tigers

Uniform

Scarlet with yellow piping and facings

Allied regiments

49th (Sault Ste Marie) Field Artillery Regiment (Canada)
5th Battalion (Wellington, West Coast and Taranaki) The Royal New Zealand Infantry Regiment

Regimental history

The Royal Hampshire Regiment came into existence during 1881 through the amalgamation of the 37th (North Hampshire) Regiment of Foot and the 67th (South Hampshire) Regiment of Foot to create The Hampshire Regiment, which in 1946 became The Royal Hampshire Regiment. In 1969 it was planned that The Royal Hampshire Regiment and The Gloucestershire Regiment should amalgamate into The Royal Regiment of Gloucestershire and Hampshire; however, The Royal Hampshire Regiment instead opted to reduce to a one-company cadre and thus maintain its separate existence, and was later allowed to grow to battalion strength. Imperial regiments affiliated with The Hampshire Regiment were the Sault Ste Marie Regiment (Canada) and the Wellington West Coast Regiment (New Zealand).

The senior of The Royal Hampshire Regiment's two predecessors was the 37th (North Hampshire) Regiment of Foot, which had been raised in 1702 as Colonel Meredith's Regiment of Foot. The regiment subsequently changed name with its colonels until 1751, when it became the 37th Regiment of Foot. In 1782 this was further revised to the 37th (or North Hampshire) Regiment of Foot. The battle honours of the regiment were the following:

Blenheim   Ramillies   Oudenarde   Malplaquet   Dettingen   Minden
Peninsula

The regimental march was 'The Highland Piper' (traditional, quick). The uniform was scarlet with yellow facings, and there were no nicknames associated with the 37th.

The 37th's junior partner was the 67th (South Hampshire) Regiment of Foot, which had been raised in 1756 as the 2nd Battalion of the 20th Regiment of Foot but secured a separate existence two years later as the 67th Regiment of Foot. In 1782 this became the 67th (or South Hampshire) Regiment of Foot. The battle honours of the regiment were the following:

Belleisle   Barrosa   Peninsula   India (with the Tiger)   Taku Forts
Pekin 1860   Charasiah   Kabul 1879   Afghanistan 1879–80

The regimental march was 'We'll gang nae mair to yon Toon' (traditional, quick). The uniform was scarlet with yellow facings, and the nickname associated with the 67th was 'The Royal Tigers' in reference to the Tiger honour badge awarded for the regiment's services in India in the first quarter of the nineteenth century.

REGIMENTS OF INFANTRY 23

The Staffordshire Regiment (The Prince of Wales's) (38th, 64th, 80th and 98th)

Colonel-in-Chief

none

Colonel

Lieutenant-General Sir Derek Boorman

Battle honours

Guadaloupe 1759   Martinique 1762   Martinique 1794   Egypt (with the Sphinx)   St Lucia 1803   Surinam   Monte Video   Rolica   Vimiera   Corunna   Busaco   Badajoz   Salamanca   Vittoria   St Sebastian   Nive   Peninsula   China (with the Dragon)   Ava   Mookdee   Ferozeshah   Sobraon   Punjaub   Pegu   Alma   Inkerman   Sevastopol   Reshire   Bushire   Koosh-Ab   Persia   Lucknow   Central India   South Africa 1878–79   Egypt 1882   Kirbekan   Nile 1884–85   Hafir   South Africa 1900–02   Mons   Retreat from Mons   Marne 1914   Aisne 1914, '18   Armentieres 1914   Ypres 1914, '17, '18   Langemarck 1914, '17   Gheluvelt   Nonne Bosschen   Neuve Chapelle   Bellewaarde   Aubers   Festubert 1915   Loos   Somme 1916, '18   Albert 1916, '18   Bazentin   Delville Wood   Pozieres   Guillemont   Flers-Courcelette

THE STAFFORDSHIRE REGIMENT

Morval Thiepval Ancre Heights Ancre 1916 Bapaume 1917, '18 Arras 1917, '18 Scarpe 1917, '18 Arleux Bullecourt Hill 70 Messines 1917, '18 Pilckem Menin Road Polygon Wood Broodseinde Poelcappelle Passchendaele Cambrai 1917, '18 St Quentin Rosieres Avre Lys Bailleul Kemmel Scherpenberg Drocourt-Queant Hindenburg Line Havrincourt Canal du Nord St Quentin Canal Beaurevoir Courtrai Selle Valenciennes Sambre France and Flanders 1914–18 Piave Vittorio Veneto Italy 1917–18 Suvla Sari Bair Landing at Suvla Scimitar Hill Gallipoli 1915–16 Egypt 1916 Tigris 1916 Kut al Amara 1917 Baghdad Mesopotamia 1916–18 Baku Persia 1918 NW Frontier India 1915 Afghanistan 1919 Dyle Defence of Escaut Ypres-Comines Canal Caen Orne Noyers Mont Pincon Brieux Bridgehead Falaise Arnhem 1944 North-West Europe 1940, '44 Sidi Barrani Djebel Kesskiss Medjez Plain Gueriat el Atach Ridge Gab Gab Gap North Africa 1940, '43 Landing in Sicily Sicily 1943 Anzio Carroceto Rome Advance to Tiber Gothic Line Marradi Italy 1943–45 Chindits 1944 Burma 1943, '44

Regimental headquarters

Whittington Barracks, Lichfield, Staffordshire.

Regimental museum

Whittington Barracks, Lichfield, Staffordshire.

Regimental marches

(quick) The Staffordshire Regiment (traditional)
(slow) God Bless the Prince of Wales (Richards)

Regimental motto

Honi Soit Qui Mal y Pense (Evil be to Him who Evil Thinks)

Nicknames

see below

Uniform

Scarlet with yellow piping and facings

Allied regiments

4e Battalion Royal 22e Régiment (Chateauguay) (Canada)
2nd Battalion The Royal Victoria Regiment (Australia)
The Antigua and Barbuda Defence Force
7th Battalion The Baluch Regiment (Pakistan)
The Jamaica Regiment

Regimental history

The Staffordshire Regiment (The Prince of Wales's) came into existence in January 1959 through the amalgamation of The South Staffordshire Regiment and The North Staffordshire Regiment.

The South Staffordshire Regiment was created in 1881 by the amalgamation of the 38th (1st Staffordshire) Regiment of Foot and the 80th Regiment of Foot (Staffordshire Volunteers). The battle honours of the combined regiment were the following:

Guadaloupe 1759   Martinique 1762   Monte Video   Egypt (with the Sphinx)   Rolica   Vimiera   Corunna   Busaco   Badajoz   Salamanca   Vittoria   St Sebastian   Nive   Peninsula   Ava   Mookdee   Ferozeshah   Sobraon   Pegu   Alma   Inkerman   Sevastopol   Lucknow   Central India   South Africa 1878–79   Egypt 1882   Kirbekan   Nile 1884–85   South Africa 1900–02   Mons   Retreat from Mons   Marne 1914   Aisne 1914, '18   Ypres 1914, '17   Langemarck 1914, '17   Gheluvelt   Nonne Bosschen   Neuve Chapelle   Aubers   Festubert 1915   Loos   Somme 1916, '18   Albert 1916, '18   Bazentin   Delville Wood   Pozieres   Flers-Courcelette   Morval   Thiepval   Ancre 1916   Bapaume 1917, '18   Arras 1917, '18   Scarpe 1917, '18   Arleux   Bullecourt   Hill 70   Messines 1917, '18   Menin Road   Polygon Wood   Broodseinde   Poelcappelle   Passchendaele   Cambrai 1917, '18   St Quentin   Lys   Bailleul   Kemmel   Scherpenberg   Drocourt-Queant   Hindenburg Line   Havrincourt   Canal du Nord   St Quentin Canal   Beaurevoir   Selle   Sambre   France and Flanders 1914–18   Piave   Vittorio Veneto   Italy 1917–18   Suvla   Landing at Suvla   Scimitar Hill   Gallipoli 1915   Egypt 1916   Caen   Noyers   Falaise   Arnhem 1944   North-West Europe 1940, '44   Sidi Barrani   North Africa 1940   Landing in Sicily   Sicily 1943   Italy 1943   Chindits 1944   Burma 1944

The motto of the regiment was 'Honi Soit Qui Mal y Pense' (Evil be to Him who Evil Thinks), and the regimental marches were 'Come Lasses and Lads' (traditional, quick) and 'The 80th' (anonymous, slow). The uniform was scarlet with white (changed to yellow in 1935) piping and facings, and the nicknames associated with The South Staffordshire Regiment were

'The Pump and Tortoise Brigade', 'The Staffordshire Knots' and 'The Staffordshire Volunteers'. Imperial regiments affiliated with The South Staffordshire Regiment were the Colchester and Hants Regiment (Canada) and the 53rd Battalion, Australian Infantry.

Within The South Staffordshire Regiment the senior component was the 38th (1st Staffordshire) Regiment of Foot, which had been raised in 1705 as Colonel Lillingston's Regiment of Foot. The regiment subsequently changed title with its colonels until 1751, when it became the 38th Regiment of Foot, a title amended in 1782 to the 38th (or 1st Staffordshire) Regiment of Foot, which had been raised in 1705 as Colonel Lillingston's Regiment of Foot. The regiment subsequently changed title with its colonels until 1751, when it became the 38th Regiment of Foot, a title amended in 1782 to the 38th (or 1st Staffordshire) Regiment of Foot. The battle honours of the regiment were the following:

Monte Video   Rolica   Vimiera   Corunna   Busaco   Badajoz
Salamanca   Vittoria   St Sebastian   Nive   Peninsula   Ava   Alma
Inkerman   Sevastopol   Lucknow

The regimental march was 'Over the Hills and Far Away' (traditional, quick).

The uniform was scarlet with yellow facings, and the nickname associated with the 38th was 'The Pump and Tortoise Brigade'.

The 38th's junior partner was the 80th Regiment of Foot (Staffordshire Volunteers), which had been raised by Lieutenant-Colonel Lord Paget in 1793 as the 80th Regiment of Foot (or Staffordshire Volunteers), a title that remained unaltered during the regiment's existence as a separate entity. The battle honours of the regiment were the following:

Egypt (with the Sphinx)   Mookdee   Ferozeshah   Sobraon   Pegu
Central India   South Africa 1878–79

The regimental marches were 'Come Lasses and Lads' (traditional, quick) and 'In the Garb of Old Gaul' (Reid, slow). The uniform was scarlet with yellow facings, and the nicknames associated with the 80th were 'The Staffordshire Knots' and 'The Staffordshire Volunteers', the former for the Staffordshire knot incorporated in their badge.

The North Staffordshire Regiment (The Prince of Wales's) was junior partner to The South Staffordshire Regiment in the formation of The Staffordshire Regiment during 1959. The North Staffordshire Regiment had come into existence during 1881 through the amalgamation of the 64th (2nd Staffordshire) Regiment of Foot and the 98th (Prince of Wales's) Regiment of Foot. The amalgamated regiment was initially designated The Prince of Wales's (North Staffordshire Regiment), but in 1921 this was changed to The North Staffordshire Regiment (The Prince of Wales's). The battle honours of the combined regiment were the following:

THE STAFFORDSHIRE REGIMENT

Guadaloupe 1759 Martinique 1794 St Lucia 1803 Surinam China (with the Dragon) Punjaub Reshire Bushire Koosh-Ab Persia Lucknow Hafir South Africa 1900–02 Aisne 1914, '18 Armentieres 1914 Loos Somme 1916, '18 Albert 1916, '18 Bazentin Delville Wood Pozieres Guillemont Ancre Heights Ancre 1916 Arras 1917 Scarpe 1917 Arleux Messines 1917, '18 Ypres 1917, '18 Pilckem Langemarck 1917 Menin Road Polygon Wood Broodseinde Poelcappelle Passchendaele Cambrai 1917, '18 St Quentin Bapaume 1918 Rosieres Avre Lys Bailleul Kemmel Hindenburg Line Havrincourt Canal du Nord St Quentin Canal Beaurevoir Courtrai Selle Valenciennes Sambre France and Flanders 1914–18 Suvla Sari Bair Gallipoli 1915–16 Egypt 1916 Tigris 1916 Kut al Amara 1917 Baghdad Mesopotamia 1916–18 Baku Persia 1918 NW Frontier India 1915 Afghanistan 1919 Dyle Defence of Escaut Ypres-Comines Canal Caen Orne Noyers Mont Pincon Brieux Bridgehead North-West Europe 1940, '44 Djebel Kesskiss Medjez Plain Gueriat el Atach Ridge Gab Gab Gap North Africa 1943 Anzio Carroceto Rome Advance to Tiber Gothic Line Marradi Italy 1944–45 Burma 1943

The motto of the regiment was 'Ich Dien' (I Serve), and the regimental marches were 'The Days We Went A-Gipsying' (traditional, quick) and 'God Bless the Prince of Wales' (Richards, slow). The uniform was scarlet with white (changed to black in 1937) piping and facings, and the nickname associated with The North Staffordshire Regiment was 'The Black Knots'. The only imperial regiment affiliated to The North Staffordshire Regiment was Le Régiment de Chateaugnay (Canada).

The 64th (2nd Staffordshire) Regiment of Foot was the senior of the two regiments that went to form The North Staffordshire Regiment in 1881. This had been raised in 1758 by Colonel John Barrington as the 64th Regiment of Foot, a title changed in 1782 to the 64th (or 2nd Staffordshire) Regiment of Foot. The battle honours of the regiment were the following:

St Lucia 1803 Surinam Reshire Bushire Koosh-Ab Persia Lucknow

The regimental march was 'Romaika' (quick). The uniform was scarlet with black facings, and the nickname associated with the 64th was 'The Black Knots'.

The 64th's junior partner was the 98th (Prince of Wales's) Regiment of Foot, which had been raised in 1824 as the 98th Regiment of Foot, a title changed in 1876 to the 98th (Prince of Wales's) Regiment of Foot. The battle honours of the regiment were the following:

China (with the Dragon) Punjaub

The regimental march was 'God Bless the Prince of Wales' (Richards, quick). The uniform was scarlet with white facings, and there was no nickname associated with the 98th.

REGIMENTS OF INFANTRY 24

The Black Watch (Royal Highland Regiment) (42nd and 73rd)

Colonel-in-Chief

HM Queen Elizabeth The Queen Mother

Colonel

Major-General A. L. Watson

Battle honours

Gaudaloupe 1759 Martinique 1762 Havannah North America 1763–64 Mangalore Mysore Seringapatam Egypt (with the Sphinx) Corunna Busaco Fuentes d'Onor Salamanca Pyrenees Nivelle Nive Orthes Toulouse Peninsula Waterloo South Africa 1846–47, '51–53 Alma Sevastopol Lucknow Ashantee 1873–74 Tel-el-Kebir Egypt 1882, '84 Kirbekan Nile 1884–85 Paardeberg South Africa 1899–1902 Retreat from Mons Marne 1914, '18 Aisne 1914 La Bassee 1914 Ypres 1914, '17, '18 Langemarck 1914 Gheluvelt Nonne Bosschen Givenchy 1914 Neuve Chapelle Aubers Festubert 1915 Loos Somme 1916, '18 Albert 1916 Bazentin Delville Wood Pozieres Flers-Courcelette Morval Thiepval Le Transloy Ancre Heights Ancre 1916 Arras 1917, '18 Vimy 1917 Scarpe 1917, '18 Arleux Pilckem Menin Road Polygon Wood Poelcappelle Passchendaele Cambrai 1917, '18 St Quentin

Bapaume 1918   Rosieres   Lys   Estaires   Messines 1918   Hazebrouck   Kemmel   Bethune   Scherpenberg   Soissonnais-Ourcq   Tardenois   Drocourt-Queant   Hindenburg Line   Epehy   St Quentin Canal   Beaurevoir   Courtrai   Selle   Sambre   France and Flanders 1914–18   Doiran 1917   Macedonia 1915–18   Egypt 1916   Gaza   Jerusalem   Tell' Asur   Megiddo   Sharon   Damascus   Palestine 1917–18   Tigris 1916   Kut al Amara 1917   Baghdad   Mesopotamia 1915–17   Defence of Arras   Ypres-Comines Canal   Dunkirk 1940   Somme 1940   St Valery-en-Caux   Saar   Breville   Odon   Fontenay le Pesnil   Defence of Rauray   Caen   Falaise   Falaise Road   Le Vie Crossing   Le Havre   Lower Maas   Venlo Pocket   Ourthe   Rhineland   Reichswald   Goch   Rhine   North-West Europe 1940, '44–45   Barkasan   British Somaliland 1940   Tobruk 1941   Tobruk Sortie   El Alamein   Advance on Tripoli   Medenine   Zemlet el Lebene   Mareth   Akarit   Wadi Akarit East   Djebel Roumana   Medjez Plain   Si Mediene   Tunis   North Africa 1941–43   Landing in Sicily   Vizzini   Sferro   Gerbini   Adrano   Sferro Hills   Sicily 1943   Cassino II   Liri Valley   Advance to Florence   Monte Scalari   Casa Fortis   Rimini Line   Casa Fabbri Ridge   Savio Bridgehead   Italy 1944–45   Athens   Greece 1944–45   Crete   Heraklion   Middle East 1941   Chindits 1944   Burma 1944   The Hook 1952   Korea 1952–53

Regimental headquarters

Balhousie Castle, Perth, Perthshire, Scotland.

Regimental museum

Balhousie Castle, Perth, Perthshire, Scotland.

Regimental marches

(quick) All the Blue Bonnets are over the Border (traditional, regimental band), and Hielan' Laddie (traditional, pipes and drums)
(slow) In the Garb of Old Gaul (Reid, regimental band), and My Home and Highland Cradle Song (both traditional, pipes and drums)

Regimental motto

Nemo Me Impune Lacessit (No one Provokes me with Impunity)

Nickname

The Watch

Uniform

Piper green doublet and Black Watch kilt with blue facings

Allied regiments

The Prince Edward Island Regiment (Canada)
The Black Watch (Royal Highland Regiment) of Canada
The Lanark and Renfrew Scottish Regiment (Canada)
The Royal Queensland Regiment (Australia)
The Royal New South Wales Regiment (Australia)
1st and 2nd Squadron, New Zealand Scottish, Royal New Zealand Armoured Corps

Regimental history

The Black Watch (Royal Highland Regiment) is the senior Highland regiment, and came into existence during 1881 through the amalgamation of the 42nd Royal Highland Regiment of Foot (The Black Watch) and the 73rd (Perthshire) Regiment of Foot. The amalgamated regiment was at first designated The Black Watch (Royal Highlanders), but this was modified to The Black Watch (Royal Highland Regiment) during 1936. Imperial regiments affiliated to The Black Watch were The Lanark and Renfrew Scottish Regiment (Highlander) and the Prince Edward Island Highlanders (both of Canada), the 30th Battalion, Australian Infantry, the Transvaal Scottish (South Africa) and the New Zealand Scottish (New Zealand).

The senior of the two regiments that went to form The Black Watch in 1881 was the 42nd Royal Highland Regiment of Foot (The Black Watch), which had been raised in 1739 by Lord Crawford from independent companies of Highlanders loyal to the British crown. The regiment was initially styled The Earl of Crawford's Regiment of Foot, and was also known as The Highland Regiment. It was ranked as the 43rd Foot, but was renumbered as the 42nd Foot in 1749. Up to 1751 the regiment changed name with its colonels, but in that year became the 42nd Regiment of Foot, a title modified in 1758 to the 42nd (The Royal Highland) Regiment of Foot, and in 1861 to the 42nd Royal Highland Regiment of Foot (The Black Watch). The battle honours of the regiment were the following:

Guadaloupe 1759   Martinique 1762   Havannah   North America 1763–64   Egypt (with the Sphinx)   Corunna   Busaco   Fuentes d'Onor   Salamanca   Pyrenees   Nivelle   Nive   Orthes   Toulouse   Peninsula   Waterloo   Alma   Sevastopol   Lucknow   Ashantee 1873–74

The motto of the regiment was 'Nemo Me Impune Lacessit' (No one Provokes me with Impunity), and the regimental marches were 'Highland Laddie' (traditional, quick) and 'In the Garb of Old Gaul' (Reid, slow). The uniform was a scarlet doublet and Black Watch kilt with blue facings, and the nicknames associated with the 42nd Royal Highland Regiment of Foot were 'The Watch' and 'The Forty Twas'.

The 42nd's junior partner was the 73rd (Perthshire) Regiment of Foot, which had been raised in 1779 as the 2nd Battalion of the 42nd before securing in 1786 an independent existence as the 73rd (Highland) Regiment of Foot. In 1806 this became the 73rd Regiment of Foot, and in 1862 the 73rd (Perthshire) Regiment of Foot. The battle honours of the regiment were the following:

> Mangalore   Mysore   Seringapatam   Waterloo
> South Africa 1846-47, '51-53

The regimental march was 'My Love is like a Red, Red Rose' (traditional, quick). The uniform was scarlet with dark green facings, and there was no motto or nickname associated with the 73rd.

REGIMENTS OF INFANTRY 25

The Duke of Edinburgh's Royal Regiment (Berkshire and Wiltshire) (49th, 62nd, 66th and 99th)

Colonel-in-Chief

Field-Marshal HRH The Prince Philip Duke of Edinburgh

Colonel

Major-General D. T. Crabtree

Battle honours

Louisburg   St Lucia 1778   Egmont-op-Zee   Copenhagen   Douro   Talavera   Albuhera   Queenstown   Vittoria   Pyrenees   Nivelle   Nive   Orthes   Peninsula   China (with the Dragon)   New Zealand   Ferozeshah   Sobraon   Alma   Inkerman   Sevastopol   Pekin 1860   Kandahar 1880   Afghanistan 1879–80   Egypt 1882   Tofrek   Suakin 1885   South Africa 1879, 1899–1902   Mons   Le Cateau   Retreat from Mons   Marne 1914   Aisne 1914, '18   La Bassee 1914   Messines 1914, '17, '18   Armentieres 1914   Ypres 1914, '17   Langemarck 1914, '17   Gheluvelt   Nonne Bosschen   Neuve Chapelle   Aubers   Festubert 1915   Loos   Somme 1916, '18   Albert 1916, '18   Bazentin   Delville Wood   Pozieres   Flers-Courcelette   Morval   Thiepval   Le Transloy   Ancre Heights   Ancre 1916, '18   Arras 1917, '18   Scarpe 1917, '18

Arleux   Pilckem   Menin Road   Polygon Wood   Broodseinde
Poelcappelle   Passchendaele   Cambrai 1917, '18   St Quentin
Bapaume 1918   Rosieres   Avre   Villers Bretonneux   Lys
Hazebrouck   Bailleul   Kemmel   Bethune   Scherpenberg   Amiens
Hindenburg Line   Havrincourt   Epehy   Canal du Nord
St Quentin Canal   Beaurevoir   Selle   Valenciennes   Sambre
France and Flanders 1914–18   Piave   Vittorio Veneto   Italy 1917–18
Doiran 1917, '18   Macedonia 1915–18   Suvla   Sari Bair
Gallipoli 1915–16   Gaza   Nebi Samwil   Jerusalem   Megiddo   Sharon
Palestine 1917–18   Tigris 1916   Kut al Amara 1917   Baghdad
Mesopotamia 1916–18   Dyle   Defence of Arras   St Omer-La Bassee
Ypres-Comines Canal   Dunkirk 1940   Normandy Landing
Odon   Caen   Hill 112   Bourgebus Ridge   Maltot   Mont Pincon
La Variniere   Seine 1944   Nederrijn   Roer   Rhineland   Cleve
Goch   Xanten   Rhine   Bremen   North-West Europe 1940, '44–45
Solarino   Simeto Bridgehead   Pursuit to Messina   Sicily 1943
Monte Camino   Calabritto   Garigliano Crossing   Minturno   Damiano
Anzio   Carroceto   Rome   Advance to Tiber   Italy 1943–45
Middle East 1942   Donbaik   North Arakan   Point 551   Mayu Tunnels
Nyakyedauk Pass   Kohima   Mao Songsang   Shwebo
Kyaukmyaung Bridgehead   Mandalay   Fort Dufferin   Rangoon Road
Toungoo   Burma 1942–45

Regimental headquarters

The Wardrobe, 58 The Close, Salisbury, Wiltshire.

Regimental museum

The Wardrobe, 58 The Close, Salisbury, Wiltshire.

Regimental marches

(quick) The Farmer's Boy (traditional)
(slow) Auld Robin Grey (traditional)

Regimental motto

Honi Soit Qui Mal y Pense (Evil be to Him who Evil Thinks)

Nicknames

see below

Uniform

Scarlet with white piping and blue facings

Allied regiments

The Lincoln and Welland Regiment (Canada)
The Algonquin Regiment (Canada)
7th Battalion (Wellington [City of Wellington's Own] and Hawke's Bay)
The Royal New Zealand Infantry Regiment
13th Battalion The Frontier Force Regiment (Pakistan)

Regimental history

The Duke of Edinburgh's Royal Regiment (Berkshire and Wiltshire) came into existence in June 1959 through the amalgamation of The Royal Berkshire Regiment (Princess Charlotte of Wales's) and The Wiltshire Regiment (Duke of Edinburgh's).

The Royal Berkshire Regiment (Princess Charlotte of Wales's) was itself the result of an 1881 amalgamation between the 49th (Princess Charlotte of Wales's or Hertfordshire) Regiment of Foot and the 66th (Berkshire) Regiment of Foot, initially becoming Princess Charlotte of Wales's (Berkshire Regiment), then in 1885 Princess Charlotte of Wales's (Royal Berkshire Regiment), and finally in 1921 The Royal Berkshire Regiment (Princess Charlotte of Wales's). The battle honours of the combined regiment were the following:

St Lucia 1778   Egmont-op-Zee   Copenhagen   Douro   Talavera   Albuhera   Queenstown   Vittoria   Pyrenees   Nivelle   Nive   Orthes   Peninsula   Alma   Inkerman   Sevastopol   Kandahar 1880   Afghanistan 1879–80   Egypt 1882   Tofrek   Suakin 1885   China (with the Dragon)   South Africa 1899–1902   Mons   Retreat from Mons   Marne 1914   Aisne 1914, '18   Ypres 1914, '17   Langemarck 1914, '17   Gheluvelt   Nonne Bosschen   Neuve Chapelle   Aubers   Festubert 1915   Loos   Somme 1916, '18   Albert 1916, '18   Bazentin   Delville Wood   Pozieres   Flers-Courcelette   Morval   Thiepval   Le Transloy   Ancre Heights   Ancre 1916, '18   Arras 1917, '18   Scarpe 1917, '18   Arleux   Pilckem   Polygon Wood   Broodseinde   Poelcappelle   Passchendaele   Cambrai 1917, '18   St Quentin   Bapaume 1918   Rosieres   Avre   Villers Bretonneux   Lys   Hazebrouck   Bethune   Amiens   Hindenburg Line   Havrincourt   Epehy   Canal du Nord   St Quentin Canal   Selle   Valenciennes   Sambre   France and Flanders 1914–18   Piave   Vittorio Veneto   Italy 1917–18   Doiran 1917, '18   Macedonia 1915–18   Dyle   St Omer-La Bassee   Dunkirk 1940   Normandy Landing   Rhine   North-West Europe 1940, '44–45   Pursuit to Messina   Sicily 1943   Monte Camino   Calabritto   Garigliano Crossing   Damiano   Anzio   Carroceto   Italy 1943–45   Donbaik   Kohima   Mao Songsang   Shwebo   Kyaukmyaung Bridgehead   Mandalay   Fort Dufferin   Rangoon Road   Toungoo   Burma 1942–45

The motto of the regiment was 'Honi Soit Qui Mal y Pense' (Evil be to Him who Evil Thinks), and the regimental marches were 'The Dashing White Sergeant' (anonymous, quick) and 'The Farmer's Boy' (traditional, quick). The uniform was scarlet with white piping and blue facings, and the nicknames associated with The Royal Berkshire Regiment were 'The Biscuit Boys' and 'The Brave Boys of Berks', the former in reference to the regiment's base at Reading, home of the English biscuit trade. Imperial regiments affiliated to The Royal Berkshire Regiment were the Lincoln and Welland Regiment (Canada), the 49th Battalion, Australian Infantry, and the Hawke's Bay Regiment (New Zealand).

Senior component in the amalgamation to create The Royal Berkshire Regiment was the 49th (Princess Charlotte of Wales's or Hertfordshire) Regiment of Foot, which had been raised during 1743 in Jamaica by the governor, Colonel Edward Trelawny, by combining several independent garrison companies as Colonel Trelawny's Regiment of Foot, otherwise known as The Jamaica Volunteers and ranked as the 63rd Foot. In 1748 the regiment became the 49th Regiment of Foot, in 1782 the 49th (or Hertfordshire) Regiment of Foot, and in 1816 the 49th (Princess Charlotte of Wales's or Hertfordshire) Regiment of Foot. The battle honours of the regiment were the following:

St Lucia 1778   Egmont-op-Zee   Copenhagen   China (with the Dragon)   Queenstown   Alma   Inkerman   Sevastopol

The regimental march was 'The Dashing White Sergeant' (anonymous, quick). The uniform was scarlet with green facings, and there were no nicknames associated with the 49th.

The 49th's junior partner was the 66th (Berkshire) Regiment of Foot, which had been raised in 1755 as the 2nd Battalion of the 19th Regiment of Foot (Green Howards) before gaining a separate existence as the 66th Regiment of Foot in 1758. In 1782 the regiment became the 66th (or Berkshire) Regiment of Foot. The battle honours of the regiment were the following:

Douro   Talavera   Albuhera   Vittoria   Pyrenees   Nivelle   Nive   Orthes   Peninsula   Kandahar 1880   Afghanistan 1879–80

The regimental marches were 'The Farmer's Boy' (traditional, quick) and 'Young May Moon' (traditional, quick). The uniform was scarlet with white piping and gosling green facings, and there were no nicknames associated with the 66th.

Junior partner to The Royal Berkshire Regiment in the amalgamation that produced The Duke of Edinburgh's Royal Regiment during 1959 was The Wiltshire Regiment (Duke of Edinburgh's), itself the result of an 1881 amalgamation between the 62nd (Wiltshire) Regiment of Foot and the 99th (Duke of Edinburgh's) Regiment of Foot. The combined regiment was known initially as The Duke of Edinburgh's (Wiltshire Regiment), a title changed in 1920 to The Wiltshire Regiment (Duke of Edinburgh's). The battle honours of the combined regiment were the following:

Louisburg   Nive   Peninsula   New Zealand   Ferozeshah   Sobraon   Sevastopol   Pekin 1860   South Africa 1879, 1900–02   Mons   Le Cateau   Retreat from Mons   Marne 1914   Aisne 1914, '18   La Bassee 1914   Messines 1914, '17, '18   Armentieres 1914   Ypres 1914, '17   Langemarck 1914   Nonne Bosschen   Neuve Chapelle   Aubers   Festubert 1915   Loos   Somme 1916, '18   Albert 1916, '18   Bazentin   Pozieres   Le Transloy   Ancre Heights   Ancre 1916   Arras 1917   Scarpe 1917   Pilckem   Menin Road   Polygon Wood   Broodseinde   Poelcappelle   Passchendaele   St Quentin   Lys   Bailleul   Kemmel   Scherpenberg   Bapaume 1918   Hindenburg Line   Epehy   Canal du Nord   St Quentin Canal   Beaurevoir   Cambrai 1918   Selle   Sambre   France and Flanders 1914–18   Doiran 1917   Macedonia 1915–18   Suvla   Sari Bair   Gallipoli 1915–16   Gaza   Nebi Samwil   Jerusalem   Megiddo   Sharon . Palestine 1917–18   Tigris 1916   Kut al Amara 1917   Baghdad   Mesopotamia 1916–18   Defence of Arras   Ypres-Comines Canal   Odon   Caen   Hill 112   Bourgebus Ridge   Maltot   Mont Pincon   La Variniere   Seine 1944   Nederrijn   Roer   Rhineland   Cleve   Goch   Xanten   Rhine   Bremen   North-West Europe 1940, '44–45   Solarino   Simeto Bridgehead   Sicily 1943   Garigliano Crossing   Minturno   Anzio   Rome   Advance to Tiber   Italy 1943–44   Middle East 1942   North Arakan   Point 551   Mayu Tunnels   Nyakyedauk Pass   Burma 1943–44

The motto of the regiment was 'Honi Soit Qui Mal y Pense' (Evil be to Him who Evil Thinks), and the regimental marches were 'The Wiltshire' (anonymous, quick) and 'Auld Robin Grey' (traditional, slow). The uniform was scarlet with buff piping and facings, and the nicknames associated with The Wiltshire Regiment were 'The Moonrakers' and 'The Springers'. Imperial regiments affiliated to The Wiltshire Regiment were the Duke of Edinburgh's Own Rifles (South Africa) and the Otago Regiment (New Zealand).

Senior of the two regiments that went to create The Wiltshire Regiment in 1881 was the 62nd (Wiltshire) Regiment of Foot, which had been raised in 1756 as the 2nd Battalion of 4th (King's Own) Regiment before securing an independent existence in 1758 as the 62nd Regiment of Foot. In 1782 this became the 62nd (or Wiltshire) Regiment of Foot. The battle honours of the regiment were the following:

Louisburg   Nive   Peninsula   Ferozeshah   Sobraon   Sevastopol

The regimental marches were 'The Vly be on the Turmit' (traditional, quick) and 'May Blossoms' (traditional, slow). The uniform was scarlet with buff facings, and nicknames associated with the 62nd were 'The Moonrakers', 'The Splashers' and 'The Springers', the first in reference to an occasion when men of the regiment were caught dragging a pond with rakes during the night in a vain search for smuggled brandy, the second in reference to the regiment's defence of Carrickfergus Castle (1758) against the invading French when ammunition ran so short that buttons were fired (being commemorated by a dent or 'splash' on the regiment's buttons), and the last for the regiment's alertness in the War of American Independence (1775–83).

The 62nd's junior partner in The Wiltshire Regiment was the 99th (Duke of Edinburgh's) Regiment of Foot, which had been raised in 1824 as the 99th (or Lanarkshire) Regiment of Foot. In 1874 this became the 99th (Duke of Edinburgh's) Regiment of Foot. The battle honours of the regiment were the following:

New Zealand   Pekin 1860   South Africa 1879

The regimental marches were 'Blue Bonnets over the Border' (traditional, quick) and 'Auld Robin Grey' (traditional, slow). The uniform was scarlet with yellow facings, and the nicknames associated with the 99th were 'The Queen's Pets' and 'The Nines'.

(NOTE: When on parade with the army, The Royal Marines take precedence after The Duke of Edinburgh's Royal Regiment.)

REGIMENTS OF INFANTRY 26

The York and Lancaster Regiment (65th and 84th)

Colonel-in-Chief

none

Colonel

Brigadier R. Eccles

Battle honours

Guadaloupe 1759   Martinique 1794   India 1796–1819   Nive   Peninsula   Arabia   New Zealand   Lucknow   Tel-el-Kebir   Egypt 1882–84   Relief of Ladysmith   South Africa 1899–1902   Aisne 1914   Armentieres 1914   Ypres 1915, '17, '18   Gravenstafel   St Julien   Frezenberg   Bellewaarde   Hooge 1915   Loos   Somme 1916, '18   Albert 1916   Pozieres   Flers-Courcelette   Morval   Thiepval   Le Transloy   Ancre Heights   Ancre 1916   Arras 1917, '18   Scarpe 1917, '18   Arleux   Oppy   Messines 1917, '18   Langemarck 1917   Menin Road   Polygon Wood   Broodseinde   Poelcappelle   Passchendaele   Cambrai 1917, '18   St Quentin   Bapaume 1918   Lys   Hazebrouck   Bailleul   Kemmel   Scherpenberg   Marne 1918   Tardenois   Drocourt-Queant   Hindenburg Line   Havrincourt   Epehy   Canal du Nord   Selle   Valenciennes   Sambre   France and Flanders 1914–18   Piave   Vittorio Veneto   Italy 1917–18   Struma   Doiran 1917   Macedonia 1915–18   Suvla   Landing at Suvla   Scimitar Hill   Gallipoli 1915   Egypt 1916

Norway 1940   Odon   Fontenay le Pesnil   Caen   La Vie Crossing   La Touques Crossing   Foret de Bretonne   Le Havre   Antwerp-Tournhout Canal   Scheldt   Lower Maas   Arnhem 1945   North-West Europe 1940, '44–45   Tobruk 1941   Tobruk Sortie   Mine de Sedjenane   Djebel Kournine   North Africa 1941, '43   Landing in Sicily   Simeto Bridgehead   Pursuit to Messina   Sicily 1943   Salerno   Vietri Pass   Capture of Naples   Cava di Tirreni   Volturno Crossing   Monte Camino   Calabritto   Colle Cedro   Garigliano Crossing   Minturno   Monte Tuga   Anzio   Advance to Tiber   Gothic Line   Coriano   San Clemente   Gemmano Ridge   Carpineta   Lamone Crossing   Defence of Lamone Bridgehead   Rimini Line   San Marino   Italy 1943–45   Crete   Heraklion   Middle East 1941   Toungoo   Arakan Beaches   Chindits 1944   Burma 1943–45

Regimental headquarters

Endcliffe Hall, Endcliffe Vale Road, Sheffield, Yorkshire.

Regimental museum

Endcliffe Hall, Endcliffe Vale Road, Sheffield, Yorkshire.

Regimental marches

(quick) The York and Lancaster (Winterbottom), and
The Jockey of York (traditional)
(slow) The Regimental Slow March of the York and
Lancaster Regiment (anonymous)

Regimental motto

Honi Soit Qui Mal y Pense (Evil be to Him who Evil Thinks)

Nicknames

The Young and Lovelies, The Royal Tigers, The Tigers, The Twin Roses

Uniform

Scarlet with white facings

Allied regiments

Les Fusiliers Mont-Royal (Canada)
7th Battalion (Wellington [City of Wellington's Own] and Hawke's Bay)

The Royal New Zealand Infantry Regiment
7th Battalion The Royal Malay Regiment

Regimental history

The York and Lancaster Regiment came into existence in 1881 through the amalgamation of the 65th (2nd Yorkshire, North Riding) Regiment of Foot and the 84th (York and Lancaster) Regiment of Foot. In the rationalization of the British army in the late 1960s the regiment refused the suggestion of amalgamation and was disbanded in December of that year, though the regiment's title and battle honours are still included in the Army List. Imperial regiments affiliated to The York and Lancaster Regiment were Les Fusiliers Mont-Royal (Canada) and the Wellington Regiment (New Zealand).

The senior of The York and Lancaster Regiment's two components was the 65th (2nd Yorkshire, North Riding) Regiment of Foot, which had been raised in 1756 as the 2nd Battalion of the 12th Regiment of Foot before securing an independent existence in 1758 as the 65th Regiment of Foot. In 1782 this became the 65th (2nd Yorkshire, North Riding) Regiment of Foot, a title that remained unaltered until the regiment's amalgamation into The York and Lancaster Regiment in 1881. The battle honours of the regiment were the following:

Guadaloupe 1759   Martinique 1794   India   Arabia   New Zealand

The regimental marches were 'The York and Lancaster' (Winterbottom, quick) and 'War March of the Priests' (Mendelssohn, slow). The uniform was scarlet with white facings, and the nicknames associated with the 65th were 'The Royal Tigers' and 'The Tigers'.

The 65th's junior partner was the 84th (York and Lancaster) Regiment of Foot, which had been raised in 1794 as the 84th Regiment of Foot, and became the 84th (York and Lancaster) Regiment of Foot in 1809. The battle honours of the regiment were the following:

Nive   Peninsula   India (with the Royal Tiger)   Lucknow

The regimental march was 'The Jockey of York' (traditional, quick). The uniform was scarlet with yellow facings, and the nicknames associated with the 84th were 'The Royal Tigers' and 'The Tigers' for, like the 65th, the regiment had served illustriously in India between 1796 and 1816.

REGIMENTS OF INFANTRY 27

The Queen's Own Highlanders (Seaforth and Camerons) (72nd, 78th and 79th)

Colonel-in-Chief
Field-Marshal HRH The Prince Philip Duke of Edinburgh

Colonel
Major-General J. C. O. R. Hopkinson

Battle honours

Carnatic Hindoostan Mysore Egmont-op-Zee Egypt (with the Sphinx) Assaye Cape of Good Hope 1806 Maida Corunna Busaco Fuentes d'Onor Java Salamanca Pyrenees Nivelle Nive Toulouse Peninsula Waterloo South Africa 1835 Alma Sevastopol Koosh-Ab Persia Lucknow Central India Peiwar Kotal Charasiah Kabul 1879 Kandahar 1880 Afghanistan 1878–80 Tel-el-Kebir Egypt 1882 Nile 1884–85 Chitral Atbara Khartoum Paardeberg South Africa 1899–1902 Le Cateau Retreat from Mons Marne 1914, '18 Aisne 1914 La Bassee 1914 Armentieres 1914 Ypres 1914, '15, 17, '18 Langemarck 1914 Gheluvelt Nonne Bosschen Festubert 1914, '15 Givenchy 1914 Neuve Chapelle Hill 60 Gravenstafel St Julien Frezenberg Bellewaarde Aubers

Loos   Somme 1916, '18   Albert 1916   Bazentin   Delville Wood   Pozieres   Flers-Courcelette   Morval   Le Transloy   Ancre Heights   Ancre 1916   Arras 1917, '18   Vimy 1917   Scarpe 1917, '18   Arleux   Pilckem   Menin Road   Polygon Wood   Broodseinde   Poelcappelle   Passchendaele   Cambrai 1917, '18   St Quentin   Bapaume 1918   Lys   Estaires   Messines 1918   Hazebrouck   Bailleul   Kemmel   Bethune   Soissonnais-Ourcq   Tardenois   Drocourt-Queant   Hindenburg Line   Epehy   St Quentin Canal   Courtrai   Selle   Valenciennes   Sambre   France and Flanders 1914–18   Struma   Macedonia 1915–18   Megiddo   Sharon   Palestine 1918   Tigris 1916   Kut al Amara 1917   Baghdad   Mesopotamia 1915–18   Defence of Escaut   St Omer-La Bassee   Ypres-Comines Canal   Somme 1940   Withdrawal to Seine   St Valery-en-Caux   Odon   Cheux   Caen   Troarn   Mont Pincon   Quarry Hill   Falaise   Falaise Road   Dives Crossing   La Vie Crossing   Lisieux   Nederrijn   Best   Le Havre   Lower Maas   Meijel   Venlo Pocket   Ourthe   Rhineland   Reichswald   Goch   Moyland   Rhine   Uelzen   Artlenberg   North-West Europe 1940, '44–45   Agordat   Keren   Abyssinia 1941   Sidi Barrani   Tobruk 1941, '42   Gubi II   Carmusa   Gazala   El Alamein   Advance on Tripoli   Mareth   Wadi Zigzaou   Akarit   Djebel Roumana   North Africa 1940–43   Landing in Sicily   Augusta   Francofonte   Adrano   Sferro Hills   Sicily 1943   Garigliano Crossing   Anzio   Cassino I   Poggio del Grillo   Gothic Line   Tavoleto   Coriano   Pian di Castello   Monte Reggiano   Rimini Line   San Marino   Italy 1943–45   Madagascar   Middle East 1942   Imphal   Shenam Pass   Litan   Kohima   Relief of Kohima   Naga Village   Aradura   Tengnoupal   Shwebo   Mandalay   Ava   Irrawaddy   Mt Popa   Burma 1942–45

Regimental headquarters

Cameron Barracks, Inverness, Scotland.

Regimental museum

Fort George, Ardesier, By Inverness, Scotland.

Regimental marches

(quick) arrangement of Scotland for Ever (traditional) and
The March of the Cameron Men (traditional, regimental band), and
Pibroch O'Donuil Dubh (traditional, pipes and drums)
(slow) In the Garb of Old Gaul (Reid, regimental band, and
pipes and drums)

Regimental motto

Cuidich 'n Righ (Help to the King)

Nicknames

see below

Uniform

Piper green doublet and Mackenzie (Seaforth) or Cameron of Erracht (Camerons) kilt with blue and blue facings

Allied regiments

The Cameron Highlanders of Ottawa (Canada)
The Queen's Own Cameron Highlanders of Canada
The Seaforth Highlanders of Canada
The Royal South Australia Regiment
The Royal Western Australia Regiment
7th Battalion (Wellington [City of Wellington's Own] and Hawke's Bay) The Royal New Zealand Infantry Regiment
4th Battalion (Otago and Southland) The Royal New Zealand Infantry Regiment
7th Duke of Edinburgh's Own Gurkha Rifles (affiliated regiment)

Regimental history

The Queen's Own Highlanders (Seaforth and Camerons) was formed in February 1961 through the amalgamation of The Seaforth Highlanders (Ross-shire Buffs, The Duke of Albany's) and The Queen's Own Cameron Highlanders.

The senior of these two components was The Seaforth Highlanders (Ross-Shire Buffs, The Duke of Albany's), itself created by the amalgamation in 1881 of the 72nd (or The Duke of Albany's Own Highlanders) Regiment of Foot and the 78th (Highland) Regiment of Foot (or the Ross-Shire Buffs). The battle honours of the combined regiment were the following:

Carnatic Hindoostan Mysore Assaye Cape of Good Hope 1806 Maida Java South Africa 1835 Sevastopol Koosh-Ab Persia Lucknow Central India Peiwar Kotal Charasiah Kabul 1879 Kandahar 1880 Afghanistan 1878–80 Tel-el-Kebir Egypt 1882 Chitral Atbara Khartoum Paardeberg South Africa 1899–1902 Le Cateau Retreat from Mons Marne 1914, '18 Aisne 1914 La Bassee

1914   Armentieres 1914   Festubert 1914, '15   Givenchy 1914   Neuve Chapelle   Ypres 1915, '17, '18   St Julien   Frezenberg   Bellewaarde   Aubers   Loos   Somme 1916, '18   Albert 1916   Bazentin   Delville Wood   Pozieres   Flers-Courcelette   Le Transloy   Ancre Heights   Ancre 1916   Arras 1917, '18   Vimy 1917   Scarpe 1917, '18   Arleux   Pilckem   Menin Road   Polygon Wood   Broodseinde   Poelcappelle   Passchendaele   Cambrai 1917, '18   St Quentin   Bapaume 1918   Lys   Estaires   Messines 1918   Hazebrouck   Bailleul   Kemmel   Bethune   Soissonnais-Ourcq   Tardenois   Drocourt-Queant   Hindenburg Line   Courtrai   Selle   Valenciennes   Sambre   France and Flanders 1914–18   Macedonia 1917–18   Megiddo   Sharon   Palestine 1918   Tigris 1916   Kut al Amara 1917   Baghdad   Mesopotamia 1915–18   Ypres-Comines Canal   Somme 1940   Withdrawal to Seine   St Valery-en-Caux   Odon   Cheux   Caen   Troarn   Mont Pincon   Quarry Hill   Falaise   Falaise Road   Dives Crossing   La Vie Crossing   Lisieux   Nederrijn   Best   Le Havre   Lower Maas   Meijel   Venlo Pocket   Ourthe   Rhineland   Reichswald   Goch   Moyland   Rhine   Uelzen   Artlenberg   North-West Europe 1940, '44–45   El Alamein   Advance on Tripoli   Mareth   Wadi Zigzaou   Akarit   Djebel Roumana   North Africa 1942–43   Landing in Sicily   Augusta   Francofonte   Adrano   Sferro Hills   Sicily 1943   Garigliano Crossing   Anzio   Italy 1943–44   Madagascar   Middle East 1942   Imphal   Shenam Pass   Litan   Kohima   Relief of Kohima   Naga Village   Aradura   Tengnoupal   Burma 1942–44

The motto of the regiment was 'Cuidich 'n Righ' (Help to the King), and the regimental march was 'Blue Bonnets over the Border' (traditional, quick). The uniform was a piper green coatee and Mackenzie kilt with buff facings, and the nicknames associated with The Seaforth Highlanders were 'The Macraes' and 'The King's Men', the former in commemoration of the time when a large portion of the Macrae clan joined the regiment. The two imperial regiments affiliated to The Seaforth Highlanders were the Seaforth Highlanders of Canada and the Pictou Highlanders (Canada).

Of the two regiments that went to form The Seaforth Highlanders in 1881 the senior was the 72nd (or the Duke of Albany's Own Highlanders) Regiment of Foot, which had been raised in 1778 by the Earl of Seaforth as Seaforth's Highlanders, 78th Regiment of (Highland) Foot. In 1786 this became the 72nd (Highland) Regiment of Foot, in 1809 the 72nd Regiment of Foot, and in 1823 the 72nd (or The Duke of Albany's Own Highlanders) Regiment of Foot. The battle honours of the regiment were the following:

Carnatic   Hindoostan   Mysore   Cape of Good Hope 1806   South Africa 1835   Sevastopol   Central India   Peiwar Kotal   Charasiah   Kabul 1870   Kandahar 1880   Afghanistan 1878–80

The motto of the regiment was 'Cabar Feidh' (The Antlers of the Deer), and the regimental march 'Blue Bonnets over the Border' (traditional, quick). The uniform was scarlet with yellow facings and Royal Stuart trews, and the nickname associated with the 72nd was 'The Macraes'.

The 72nd's junior partner in the 1881 amalgamation was the 78th (Highland) Regiment of Foot (or the Ross-Shire Buffs), which had been raised by Lieutenant-Colonel Francis Mackenzie in 1793 as the 78th (Highland) Regiment of Foot, joined in 1794 by the 2nd Battalion, 78th (Highland) Regiment of Foot, The Ross-Shire Buffs. The two battalions were combined in 1796 as the 78th (Highland) Regiment of Foot (or the Ross-Shire Buffs), a title that remained unaltered up to the time of the 1881 amalgamation. The battle honours of the regiment were the following:

 Assaye (with the Elephant) Maida Java Koosh-Ab Persia
  Lucknow Afghanistan 1879–80

The motto of the regiment was 'Cuidich 'n Righ' (Help to the King), and the regimental march 'Pibroch of Donuil Dubh' (traditional, quick). The uniform was scarlet and a Mackenzie of Seaforth kilt with buff facings, and there was no nickname associated with the 78th.

The Seaforth Highlanders' junior partner in the amalgamation of 1961 was The Queen's Own Cameron Highlanders, a regiment which had been raised in 1793 by Major Alan Cameron of Erracht as the 79th Regiment of Foot (or Cameronian Volunteers). In 1804 the regiment was restyled the 79th Regiment of Foot (or Cameronian Highlanders), in 1806 the 79th Regiment of Foot (or Cameron Highlanders), in 1873 the 79th Queen's Own Cameron Highlanders, and in 1881 The Queen's Own Cameron Highlanders. The battle honours of the regiment were the following:

 Egmont-op-Zee Egypt (with the Sphinx) Corunna Busaco
 Fuentes d'Onor Salamanca Pyrenees Nivelle Nive Toulouse
 Peninsula Waterloo Alma Sevastopol Lucknow Tel-el-Kebir
 Egypt 1882 Nile 1884–85 Atbara Khartoum South Africa 1900–02
 Retreat from Mons Marne 1914, '18 Aisne 1914 Ypres 1914, '15,
 '17, '18 Langemarck 1914 Gheluvelt Nonne Bosschen Givenchy 1914
 Neuve Chapelle Hill 60 Gravenstafel St Julien Frezenberg
 Bellewaarde Aubers Festubert 1915 Loos Somme 1916, '18
 Albert 1916 Bazentin Delville Wood Pozieres Flers-Courcelette
 Morval Le Transloy Ancre Heights Ancre 1916 Arras 1917, '18
 Scarpe 1917 Arleux Pilckem Menin Road Polygon Wood
 Poelcappelle Passchendaele St Quentin Bapaume 1918 Lys
 Estaires Messines 1918 Kemmel Bethune Soissonnais-Ourcq
 Drocourt-Queant Hindenburg Line Epehy St Quentin Canal
 Courtrai Selle Sambre France and Flanders 1914–18 Struma
 Macedonia 1915–18 Defence of Escaut St Omer-La Bassee Somme

1940 St Valery-en-Caux Falaise Falaise Road La Vie Crossing Le Havre Lower Maas Venlo Pocket Rhineland Reichswald Goch Rhine North-West Europe 1940, '44–45 Agordat Keren Abyssinia 1941 Sidi Barrani Tobruk 1941, '42 Gubi II Carmusa Gazala El Alamein Mareth Wadi Zigzaou Akarit Djebel Roumana North Africa 1940–43 Francofonte Adrano Sferro Hills Sicily 1943 Cassino I Poggio del Grillo Gothic Line Tavoleto Coriano Pian di Castello Monte Reggiano Rimini Line San Marino Italy 1944 Kohima Relief of Kohima Naga Village Aradura Shwebo Mandalay Ava Irrawaddy Mt Popa Burma 1944–45

The motto of the regiment was 'Honi Soit Qui Mal y Pense' (Evil be to Him who Evil Thinks), and the regimental marches were 'Highland Laddie' (traditional, quick) and 'Logie of Buchan' (traditional, slow). The uniform was a piper green coatee with blue facings and a Cameron of Erracht kilt, and the nickname associated with The Queen's Own Cameron Highlanders was 'The Camerons'. Imperial regiments affiliated to The Queen's Own Cameron Highlanders were the Queen's Own Cameron Highlanders of Canada, the Cameron Highlanders of Ottawa (Canada), and the 37th/52nd Battalion, Australian Infantry.

REGIMENTS OF INFANTRY 28

The Gordon Highlanders (75th and 92nd)

Colonel-in-Chief

HRH The Prince of Wales

Colonel

Major-General J. R. A. MacMillan

Battle honours

Mysore Seringapatam Egmont-op-Zee Mandora India (with the Tiger) Egypt (with the Sphinx) Corunna Fuentes d'Onor Almaraz Vittoria Pyrenees Nive Orthes Peninsula Waterloo South Africa 1835 Delhi 1857 Lucknow Charasiah Kabul 1879 Kandahar 1880 Afghanistan 1878–80 Tel-el-Kebir Egypt 1882, '84 Nile 1884–85 Chitral Tirah Defence of Ladysmith Paardeberg South Africa 1899–1902 Mons Le Cateau Retreat from Mons Marne 1914, '18 Aisne 1914 La Bassee 1914 Messines 1914 Armentieres 1914 Ypres 1914, '15, '17 Langemarck 1914 Gheluvelt Nonne Bosschen Neuve Chapelle Frezenberg Bellewaarde Aubers Festubert 1915 Hooge 1915 Loos Somme 1916, '18 Albert 1916, '18 Bazentin Delville Wood Pozieres Guillemont Flers-Courcelette Le Transloy Ancre 1916 Arras 1917, '18 Vimy 1917 Scarpe 1917, '18 Arleux Bullecourt Pilckem Menin Road

Polygon Wood   Broodseinde   Poelcappelle   Passchendaele
Cambrai 1917, '18   St Quentin   Bapaume 1918   Rosieres   Lys
Estaires   Hazebrouck   Bethune   Soissonnais-Ourcq   Tardenois
Hindenburg Line   Canal du Nord   Selle   Sambre   France and
Flanders 1914–18   Piave   Vittorio Veneto   Italy 1917–18   Withdrawal
to Escaut   Ypres-Comines Canal   Dunkirk 1940   Somme 1940
St Valery-en-Caux   Odon   La Vie Crossing   Lower Maas
Venlo Pocket   Rhineland   Reichswald   Cleve   Goch   Rhine
North-West Europe 1940, '44–45   El Alamein   Advance on Tripoli
Mareth   Medjez Plain   North Africa 1942–43   Landing in Sicily   Sferro
Sicily 1943   Anzio   Rome   Italy 1944–45

Regimental headquarters

Viewfield Road, Aberdeen, Scotland.

Regimental marches

(quick) Cock o' the North (traditional, regimental band and pipes and drums)
(slow) In the Garb of Old Gaul (Reid, regimental band), and St Andrew's Cross (traditional, pipes and drums)

Regimental motto

Bydand (Stand Fast)

Nicknames

see below

Uniform

Piper green doublet and Gordon kilt with yellow facings

Allied regiments

48th Highlanders of Canada
The Toronto Scottish Regiment (Canada)
5th/6th Battalion The Royal Victoria Regiment (Australia)

Regimental history

The Gordon Highlanders came into existence in 1881 through the amalgamation of the 75th (Stirlingshire) Regiment of Foot and the 92nd (Gordon

Highlanders) Regiment of Foot. Imperial regiments affiliated to The Gordon Highlanders were the 48th Highlanders of Canada, the 5th Battalion, Australian Infantry, and the Capetown Highlanders (Duke of Connaught and Strathearn's Own) of South Africa.

The senior of these components was the 75th (Stirlingshire) Regiment of Foot, which had been raised in 1787 by Colonel Robert Abercromby as the 75th (Highland) Regiment of Foot, otherwise known as Abercromby's Highlanders. In 1807 the regiment became the 75th Regiment of Foot, and in 1862 the 75th (Stirlingshire) Regiment of Foot. The battle honours of the regiment were the following:

> Mysore   Seringapatam   India (with the Tiger)   South Africa 1835
> Delhi 1857   Lucknow

The uniform was scarlet with yellow facings, and there was no nickname associated with the 75th.

Junior partner to the 75th in The Gordon Highlanders was the 92nd (Gordon Highlanders) Regiment of Foot, which had been raised in 1794 by the Duke of Gordon as the 100th Regiment of Foot, otherwise known as the Gordon Highlanders. In 1798 the regiment was renumbered the 92nd Regiment of Foot, and in 1861 became the 92nd (Gordon Highlanders) Regiment of Foot. The battle honours of the regiment were the following:

> Egmont-op-Zee   Mandora   Egypt (with the Sphinx)   Corunna
> Fuentes d'Onor   Almaraz   Vittoria   Pyrenees   Nive   Orthes
> Peninsula   Waterloo   Charasiah   Kabul 1879   Kandahar 1880
> Afghanistan 1879–80

The motto of the regiment was 'Bydand' (Stand Fast), and the regimental march was 'Cock o' the North' (traditional, quick). The uniform was scarlet with yellow facings, and the nickname associated with the 92nd was 'The Gay Gordons'.

REGIMENTS OF INFANTRY 29

The Argyll and Sutherland Highlanders (Princess Louise's) (91st and 93rd)

Colonel-in-Chief

HM The Queen

Colonel

Major-General C. D. R. Palmer

Battle honours

Cape of Good Hope 1806   Rolica   Vimiera   Corunna   Pyrenees   Nivelle   Orthes   Toulouse   Peninsula   South Africa 1846–47, '51–53   Alma   Balaklava   Sevastopol   Lucknow   South Africa 1879   Modder River   Paardeberg   South Africa 1899–1902   Mons   Le Cateau   Retreat from Mons   Marne 1914, '18   Aisne 1914   La Bassee 1914   Messines 1914, '18   Armentieres 1914   Ypres 1915, '17, '18   Gravenstafel   St Julien   Frezenberg   Bellewaarde   Festubert 1915   Loos   Somme 1916, '18   Albert 1916, '18   Bazentin   Delville Wood   Pozieres   Flers-Courcelette   Morval   Le Transloy   Ancre Heights   Ancre 1916   Arras 1917, '18   Scarpe 1917, '18   Arleux   Pilckem   Menin Road   Polygon Wood   Broodseinde   Poelcappelle   Passchendaele   Cambrai 1917, '18   St Quentin   Bapaume 1918

Rosieres Lys Estaires Hazebrouck Bailleul Kemmel Bethune Soissonnais-Ourcq Tardenois Amiens Hindenburg Line Epehy Canal du Nord St Quentin Canal Beaurevoir Courtrai Selle Sambre France and Flanders 1914–18 Italy 1917–18 Struma Doiran 1917, '18 Macedonia 1915–18 Gallipoli 1915–16 Rumani Egypt 1917–18 Somme 1940 Odon Tourmauville Bridge Caen Esquay Mont Pincon Quarry Hill Estry Falaise Dives Crossing Aart Lower Maas Meijel Venlo Pocket Ourthe Rhineland Reichswald Rhine Uelzen Artlenberg North-West Europe 1940, '44–45 Abyssinia 1941 Sidi Barrani El Alamein Medenine Akarit Djebel Azzag 1942 Kef Ouiba Pass Mine de Sedjenane Medjez Plain Longstop Hill 1943 North Africa 1940–43 Landing in Sicily Gerbini Adrano Centuripe Sicily 1943 Termoli Sangro Cassino II Liri Valley Aquino Monte Casalino Monte Spaduro Monte Grande Senio Santerno Crossing Argenta Gap Italy 1943–45 Crete Heraklion Middle East 1941 North Malaya Grik Road Central Malaya Ipoh Slim River Singapore Island Malaya 1942–42

Regimental headquarters

The Castle, Stirling, Stirlingshire, Scotland.

Regimental museum

The Castle, Stirling, Stirlingshire, Scotland.

Regimental marches

(quick) The Thin Red Line (Alford, regimental band), and The Campbells Are Coming (traditional, pipes and drums) (slow) In the Garb of Old Gaul (Reid, regimental band), and Loch Duich (traditional, pipes and drums)

Regimental mottoes

Ne Obliviscaris (Do Not Forget), and Sans Peur (Without Fear)

Nicknames

The Thin Red Line, The Rories

Uniform

Piper green doublet and Black Watch kilt with yellow facings

Allied regiments

The Argyll and Sutherland Highlanders of Canada (Princess Louise's)
The Calgary Highlanders (Canada)
The Royal New South Wales Regiment (Australia)
The Punjab Frontier Force (Pakistan)

Regimental history

The Argyll and Sutherland Highlanders (Princess Louise's) was formed in 1881 through the amalgamation of the 91st (Princess Louise's Argyllshire Highlanders) Regiment of Foot and the 93rd (Sutherland Highlanders) Regiment of Foot. The amalgamated regiment was at first designated Princess Louise's (Sutherland and Argyll Highlanders), changed in 1882 to Princess Louise's (Argyll and Sutherland Highlanders), and in 1920 to The Argyll and Sutherland Highlanders (Princess Louise's). Imperial regiments affiliated to the Argyll and Sutherland Highlanders were the Argyll and Sutherland Highlanders of Canada (Princess Louise's) and the Calgary Highlanders (Canada). The official mascot of the regiment is a Shetland pony.

Senior of the two regiments that went into the 1881 amalgamation was the 91st (Princess Louise's Argyllshire Highlanders) Regiment of Foot, which had been raised in 1794 by Colonel Duncan Campbell of Lochnell as the 98th (Argyllshire) Regiment of Foot (Highlanders). In 1798 the regiment was renumbered as the 91st (Argyllshire) Regiment of Foot (Highlanders), and in 1809 this title was changed to the 91st Regiment of Foot. In 1820 the title became the 91st (Argyllshire) Regiment of Foot, modified in 1864 to the 91st (Argyllshire Highlanders) Regiment of Foot, and in 1872 to the 91st (Princess Louise's Argyllshire Highlanders) Regiment of Foot. The battle honours of the regiment were the following:

Rolica   Vimiera   Corunna   Pyrenees   Nivelle   Nive   Orthes   Toulouse   Peninsula   South Africa 1846–47, 1851–53, 1879

The motto of the regiment was 'Ne Obliviscaris' (Do Not Forget), and the regimental march was 'The Campbells are Coming' (traditional, quick). The uniform was scarlet with yellow facings, and there was no nickname associated with the 91st.

The 91st's slightly junior partner in the 1881 amalgamation was the 93rd (Sutherland Highlanders) Regiment of Foot, which had been raised in 1799 by General William Wemyss of Wemyss as the 93rd (Highland) Regiment of Foot, a title amended only once, to the 93rd (Sutherland Highlanders) Regiment of Foot in 1861. The battle honours of the regiment were the following:

Cape of Good Hope 1806   Alma   Balaklava   Sevastopol   Lucknow

The motto of the regiment was 'Sans Peur' (Without Fear), and the regimental march was 'Highland Laddie' (traditional, quick). The uniform was a scarlet doublet and Government tartan with yellow facings, and the nicknames associated with the 93rd were 'The Thin Red Line' and 'The Rories', the former in commemoration of the 93rd's celebrated stand against the Russian cavalry at the Battle of Balaklava (1854).

REGIMENTS OF INFANTRY 30

The Parachute Regiment

Colonel-in-Chief
HRH The Prince of Wales

Colonel Commandant
General Sir Geoffrey Howlett

Battle honours
Bruneval   Normandy Landing   Pegasus Bridge   Merville Battery
Breville   Dives Crossing   La Touques Crossing   Arnhem 1944
Ourthe   Rhine   Southern France   North-West Europe 1942, '44–45
Soudia   Oudna   Djebel Azzag 1943   Djebel Alliliga   El Hadjeba
Tamera   Djebel Dahra   Kef el Debna   North Africa 1942–43
Primosole Bridge   Sicily 1943   Taranto   Orsigna   Italy 1943–44
Athens   Greece 1944–45   Falkland Islands 1982   Goose Green
Mount Longdon   Wireless Ridge

Regimental headquarters
Browning Barracks, Aldershot, Hampshire.

Regimental museum
Airborne Forces Museum, Browning Barracks, Aldershot, Hampshire.

THE PARACHUTE REGIMENT

Regimental march
(quick) Ride of the Valkyries (Wagner)

Regimental motto
Utrinque Paratus (Ready for Anything)

Nicknames
The Red Devils, The Paras

Uniform
Cambridge blue piping with maroon facings

Allied regiment
8th/9th Battalion The Royal Australian Regiment

Regimental history

The Parachute Regiment came into existence in August 1942, although it was in November 1940 that the first parachute battalion had been formed. Up to 1949 the regiment came under the administrative auspices of the Army Air Corps, and up to 1953 the regiment operated with men seconded from other regiments. The official mascot of the regiment is a Shetland pony.

The Brigade of Gurkhas

Brigade headquarters
BFPO 1, Hong Kong.

Brigade museum
Queen Elizabeth Barracks, Church Crookham, Aldershot, Hampshire.

Brigade motto
Kaphar Hunnu Bhanda Marnu Ramro (Better to Die than to Live a Coward)

Allied regiments
The Royal Australian Regiment
The Queen's Own Rifles of Canada

Brigade history
The Brigade of Gurkhas was created in January 1948 to control the four (out of 10) Gurkha regiments that were retained by the British army after the British withdrawal from India and the partitioning of that viceroyalty into the independent countries of India and Pakistan. The regiments that remained with the British army were the 2nd King Edward VII's Own Gurkha Rifles (The Sirmoor Rifles), the 6th Gurkha Rifles, the 7th Gurkha

Rifles, and the 10th Gurkha Rifles, subsequently augmented by the brigade's own specialist units (The Queen's Gurkha Engineers, The Queen's Gurkha Signals and The Gurkha Transport Regiment).

REGIMENTS OF INFANTRY 31A

2nd King Edward VII's Own Gurkha Rifles (The Sirmoor Rifles)

Colonel-in-Chief

HRH The Prince of Wales

Colonel

Lieutenant-General Sir John Chapple

Battle honours

Bhurtpore Aliwal Sobraon Delhi 1857 Kabul 1879 Kandahar 1880 Afghanistan 1878–80 Tirah Punjaub Frontier La Bassee 1914 Festubert 1914, '15 Givenchy 1914 Neuve Chapelle Aubers Loos France and Flanders 1914–15 Egypt 1915 Tigris 1916 Kut al Amara 1917 Baghdad 1915 Mesopotamia 1916, '18 Persia 1918 Baluchistan 1918 Afghanistan 1919 El Alamein Mareth Akarit Djebel el Meida Enfidaville Tunis North Africa 1942–43 Cassino I Monastery Hill Pian di Maggio Gothic Line Coriano Poggio San Giovanni Monte Reggiano Italy 1944–45 Greece 1944–45 North Malaya Jitra Central Malaya Kampar Slim River Johore Singapore Island Malaya 1941–42 North Arakan Irrawaddy Magwe Sittang 1945 Point 1433 Arakan Beaches Myebon Tamandu Chindits 1943 Burma 1943–45

Regimental marches

(quick) Lutzow's Wild Hunt, and Wha's the Steer Kimmer
(slow) God Bless the Prince of Wales (Richards)

Regimental motto

none

Nicknames

none

Uniform

Rifle green with scarlet piping and facings

Allied regiments

The Royal Brunei Armed Forces
The Royal Green Jackets (affiliated regiment)

Regimental history

The 2nd King Edward VII's Own Gurkha Rifles (The Sirmoor Rifles) came into existence in April 1815 as The Sirmoor Battalion of the army of the Honourable East India Company, and changes in designation followed quite swiftly. In 1823 the unit became the 8th or Sirmoor Local Battalion, in 1858 (on becoming part of the British army with the disbandment of the Honourable East India Company's army) The Sirmoor Rifle Regiment, in 1861 the 2nd Goorkha Regiment, in 1864 the 2nd Goorkha (The Sirmoor Rifles) Regiment, in 1876 the 2nd (The Prince of Wales's Own) Gurkha Regiment (The Sirmoor Rifles), in 1906 the 2nd King Edward's Own Gurkha Rifles (The Sirmoor Regiment), and in 1922 the 2nd King Edward VII's Own Gurkha Rifles (The Sirmoor Rifles).

REGIMENTS OF INFANTRY 31B

6th Queen Elizabeth's Own Gurkha Rifles

Colonel-in-Chief

none

Colonel

Lieutenant-General Sir Derek Boorman

Battle honours

Burmah 1885–87 Helles Krithia Suvla Sari Bair Gallipoli 1915 Suez Canal Egypt 1915–16 Khan Baghdadi Mesopotamia 1916–18 Persia 1918 NW India Frontier 1915 Afghanistan 1919 Coriano Santarcangelo Monte Chicco Lamone Crossing Senio Floodbank Medicina Gaiana Crossing Italy 1944–45 Shwebo Kyaukmyaung Bridgehead Mandalay Fort Dufferin Maymyo Rangoon Road Toungoo Sittang 1945 Chindits 1944 Burma 1944–45

Regimental marches

(quick) Young May Moon (regimental band), and
Queen Elizabeth's Own (pipes and drums)

Regimental motto

none

Nicknames

none

Uniform

Rifle green with black piping and facings

Allied regiments

14th/20th King's Hussars (affiliated regiment)
The Royal Green Jackets (affiliated regiment)

Regimental history

The 6th Queen Elizabeth's Own Gurkha Rifles was formed in 1817 as the Cuttack Legion, and then underwent a number of title changes before and after becoming part of the British army's regular establishment. In 1823 the Cuttack Legion became the Rangpur Light Infantry Battalion, in 1826 the 8th Rangpur Local Light Infantry, in 1827 the 8th Assam Light Infantry, in 1850 the 1st Assam Light Infantry, in 1861 the 46th Bengal Native Infantry and then the 42nd (Assam) Regiment of Bengal Native Infantry (Light Infantry), in 1865 the 42nd (Assam) Regiment of Bengal Native (Light Infantry), in 1886 the 42nd Goorkha Light Infantry, in 1889 the 42nd (Goorkha) Regiment of Bengal (Light) Infantry, in 1891 the 42nd Gurkha (Rifle) Regiment Bengal Infantry, in 1901 the 42nd Gurkha Rifles, in 1903 the 6th Gurkha Rifles, and in 1959 the 6th Queen Elizabeth's Own Gurkha Rifles.

REGIMENTS OF INFANTRY 31C

7th Duke of Edinburgh's Own Gurkha Rifles

Colonel-in-Chief

none

Colonel

Brigadier J. Whitehead

Battle honours

Suez Canal Egypt 1915 Megiddo Sharon Palestine 1918 Shaiba Kut al Amara 1915, '17 Ctesiphon Defence of Kut al Amara Baghdad Sharqat Mesopotamia 1915–18 Afghanistan 1919 Tobruk 1942 North Africa 1942 Cassino I Campriano Poggio del Grillo Tavoleto Montebello-Scorticata Ridge Italy 1944 Sittang 1942, '45 Pegu 1942 Kyaukse 1942 Shwegyin Imphal Bishenpur Meiktila Capture of Meiktila Defence of Meiktila Rangoon Road Pyawbwe Burma 1942–45 Falkland Islands 1982

Regimental march

(quick) Old Monmouthshire

Regimental motto

none

Nicknames

none

Uniform

Rifle green with black piping and facings

Allied regiments

The Pacific Islands Regiment Papua New Guinea
The Cameronians (Scottish Rifles) (affiliated regiment)
The Queen's Own Highlanders (Seaforth and Camerons)
(affiliated regiment)

Regimental history

The 7th Duke of Edinburgh's Own Gurkha Rifles was raised in 1902 as the 8th Gurkha Rifles, but in the following year became the 2nd Battalion of the 10th Gurkha Rifles. In 1907 the regiment secured a separate existence again, this time as the 7th Gurkha Rifles, which in 1959 became the 7th Duke of Edinburgh's Own Gurkha Rifles.

REGIMENTS OF INFANTRY 31D

10th Princess Mary's Own Gurkha Rifles

Colonel-in-Chief

none

Colonel

Major-General G. D. Johnson

Battle honours

Helles Krithia Suvla Sari Bair Gallipoli 1915 Suez Canal Egypt 1915 Sharqat Mesopotamia 1916–18 Afghanistan 1919 Iraq 1941 Deir ez Zor Syria 1941 Coriano Santarcangelo Senio Floodbank Bologna Sillaro Crossing Gaiana Crossing Italy 1944–45 Monywa 1942 Imphal Tultum Tamu Road Shenam Pass Litan Bishenpur Tengnoupal Mandalay Myinmu Bridgehead Kyaukse 1945 Meiktila Capture of Meiktila Defence of Meiktila Irrawaddy Rangoon Road Pegu 1945 Sittang 1945 Burma 1942–45

Regimental march

(quick) Hundred Pipers

255

Regimental motto

none

Nicknames

none

Uniform

Rifle green with black piping and facings

Allied regiment

The Royal Scots (The Royal Regiment) (affiliated regiment)

Regimental history

The 10th Princess Mary's Own Gurkha Rifles began life in 1887 as a military police unit, the Kubo Valley Police Battalion, but in 1890 became the 10th (Burma) Regiment Madras Infantry, in 1892 the 10th Regiment (1st Burma Rifles) Madras Infantry, in 1896 the 10th Regiment (1st Burma Gurkha Rifles) Madras Infantry, in 1901 the 10th Gurkha Rifles, and in 1949 the 10th Princess Mary's Own Gurkha Rifles.

REGIMENTS OF INFANTRY 32

The Royal Green Jackets (43rd, 52nd, King's Royal Rifle Corps, and Rifle Brigade)

Colonel-in-Chief

HM The Queen

Colonel Commandant

General Sir Roland Guy (1986, out of three)

Battle honours

Louisburg Quebec 1759 Martinique 1762 Havannah North America 1763–64 Mysore Hindoostan Martinique 1794 Copenhagen Monte Video Rolica Vimiera Corunna Martinique 1809 Talavera Busaco Barrosa Fuentes d'Onor Albuhera Ciudad Rodrigo Badajoz Salamanca Vittoria Pyrenees Nivelle Nive Orthes Toulouse Peninsula Waterloo South Africa 1846–47 Mooltan Goojerat Punjaub South Africa 1851–53 Alma Inkerman Sevastopol Delhi 1857 Lucknow Taku Forts Pekin 1860 New Zealand Ashantee 1873–74 Ali Masjid South Africa 1879 Ahmad Khel Kandahar 1880 Afghanistan 1878–80 Tel-el-Kebir Egypt 1882–84 Burmah 1885–87 Chitral Khartoum Defence of Ladysmith Relief of Kimberley Paardeberg Relief of Ladysmith South Africa

1899–1902 Mons Le Cateau Retreat from Mons Marne 1914 Aisne 1914, '18 Armentieres 1914 Ypres 1914, '15, '17, '18 Langemarck 1914, '17 Gheluvelt Nonne Bosschen Givenchy 1914 Neuve Chapelle Gravenstafel St Julien Frezenberg Bellewaarde Aubers Festubert 1915 Hooge 1915 Loos Mount Sorrel Somme 1916, '18 Albert 1916, '18 Bazentin Delville Wood Pozieres Guillemont Flers-Courcelette Morval Le Transloy Ancre Heights Ancre 1916, '18 Bapaume 1917, '18 Arras 1917, '18 Vimy 1917 Scarpe 1917, '18 Arleux Messines 1917, '18 Pilckem Menin Road Polygon Wood Broodseinde Poelcappelle Passchendaele Cambrai 1917, '18 St Quentin Rosieres Avre Villers Bretonneux Lys Hazebrouck Bailleul Kemmel Bethune Drocourt-Queant Hindenburg Line Havrincourt Epehy Canal du Nord St Quentin Canal Beaurevoir Courtrai Selle Valenciennes Sambre France and Flanders 1914–18 Piave Vittorio Veneto Italy 1917–18 Doiran 1917, '18 Macedonia 1915–18 Kut al Amara 1915 Ctesiphon Defence of Kut al Amara Tigris 1916 Khan Baghdadi Mesopotamia 1914–18 Archangel 1919 Defence of Escaut Calais 1940 Cassel Ypres-Comines Canal Normandy Landing Pegasus Bridge Villers Bocage Odon Caen Esquay Bourgebus Ridge Mont Pincon Le Perier Ridge Falaise Antwerp Hechtel Nederrijn Lower Maas Roer Ourthe Rhineland Reichswald Cleve Goch Hochwald Rhine Ibbenburen Dreierwalde Leese Aller North-West Europe 1940, '44–45 Egyptian Frontier 1940 Sidi Barrani Beda Fomm Mersa el Brega Agedabia Derna Aerodrome Tobruk 1941 Sidi Rezegh 1941 Chor es Sufan Saunnu Gazala Bir Hacheim Knightsbridge Defence of Alamein Line Ruweisat Fuka Airfield Alam el Halfa El Alamein Capture of Halfaya Pass Nofilia Tebaga Gap Enfidaville Medjez el Bab Kasserine Thala Fondouk Fondouk Pass El Kourzia Djebel Kournine Argoub el Megas Tunis Hamman Lif North Africa 1940–43 Sangro Salerno Santa Lucia Salerno Hills Cardito Teano Monte Camino Garigliano Crossing Damiano Anzio Cassino II Liri Valley Melfa Crossing Monte Rotondo Capture of Perugia Monte Malbe Arezzo Advance to Florence Gothic Line Coriano Gemmano Ridge Lamone Crossing Orsara Tossignano Argenta Gap Fossa Cembalina Italy 1943–45 Veve Greece 1941, '44, '45 Crete Middle East 1941 Arakan Beaches Tamandu Burma 1943–45

Regimental headquarters

Peninsula Barracks, Winchester, Hampshire.

Regimental museum

Peninsula Barracks, Winchester, Hampshire.

Regimental marches

(quick) arrangement of The Huntsmen's Chorus (Weber), and
The Italian Song (anonymous)
(double past) The Road to the Isles (traditional)

Regimental motto

Honi Soit Qui Mal y Pense (Evil be to Him who Evil Thinks)

Nicknames

see below

Uniform

Rifle green with black facings

Allied regiments

The British Columbia Regiment (Duke of Connaught's Own) (Canada)
Princess Patricia's Canadian Light Infantry
The Queen's Own Rifles of Canada
The Brockville Rifles (Canada)
The Royal Winnipeg Rifles (Canada)
The Regina Rifle Regiment (Canada)
The Western Australia University Regiment
The Sydney University Regiment (Australia)
The Melbourne University Regiment (Australia)
1st Battalion The Royal New Zealand Infantry Regiment
6th Battalion (Hauraki) The Royal New Zealand Infantry Regiment
The Fiji Infantry Regiment
2nd King Edward VII's Own Gurkha Rifles (The Sirmoor Rifles)
(affiliated regiment)
6th Queen Elizabeth's Own Gurkha Rifles (affiliated regiment)

Regimental history

The Royal Green Jackets was created in January 1966 through the amalgamation of the 1st Green Jackets, the 2nd Green Jackets (The King's Royal Rifle Corps) and the 3rd Green Jackets (The Rifle Brigade).

Senior of these components was the 1st Green Jackets, itself the result of the 1958 redesignation of The Oxfordshire and Buckinghamshire Light Infantry. This was in turn the result of the amalgamation in 1881 of the 43rd (Monmouthshire Light Infantry) Regiment of Foot and the 52nd (Oxfordshire Light Infantry) Regiment of Foot. The new regiment was originally designated The Oxfordshire Light Infantry, a title changed in 1908 to The Oxfordshire and Buckinghamshire Light Infantry. The battle honours of the combined regiment were the following:

Quebec 1759   Martinique 1762   Havannah   Mysore   Hindoostan   Martinique 1794   Vimiera   Corunna   Busaco   Fuentes d'Onor   Ciudad Rodrigo   Badajoz   Salamanca   Vittoria   Pyrenees   Nivelle   Nive   Orthes   Toulouse   Peninsula   Waterloo   South Africa 1851–53   Delhi 1857   New Zealand   Relief of Kimberley   Paardeberg   South Africa 1900–02   Mons   Retreat from Mons   Marne 1914   Aisne 1914   Ypres 1914, '17   Langemarck 1914, '17   Gheluvelt   Nonne Bosschen   Aubers   Festubert 1915   Hooge 1915   Loos   Mount Sorrel   Somme 1916, '18   Albert 1916, '18   Bazentin   Delville Wood   Pozieres   Guillemont   Flers-Courcelette   Morval   Le Transloy   Ancre Heights   Ancre 1916   Bapaume 1917, '18   Arras 1917   Vimy 1917   Scarpe 1917   Arleux   Menin Road   Polygon Wood   Broodseinde   Poelcappelle   Passchendaele   Cambrai 1917, '18   St Quentin   Rosieres   Avre   Lys   Hazebrouck   Bethune   Hindenburg Line   Havrincourt   Canal du Nord   Selle   Valenciennes   France and Flanders 1914–18   Piave   Vittorio Veneto   Italy 1917–18   Doiran 1917, '18   Macedonia 1915–18   Kut al Amara 1915   Ctesiphon   Defence of Kut al Amara   Tigris 1916   Khan Baghdadi   Mesopotamia 1914–18   Archangel 1919   Defence of Escaut   Cassel   Ypres-Comines Canal   Normandy Landing   Pegasus Bridge   Caen   Esquay   Lower Maas   Ourthe   Rhineland   Reichswald   Rhine   Ibbenburen   North-West Europe 1940, '44–45   Enfidaville   North Africa 1943   Salerno   Santa Lucia   Salerno Hills   Teano   Monte Camino   Garigliano Crossing   Damiano   Anzio   Coriano   Gemmano Ridge   Italy 1943–45   Arakan Beaches   Tamandu   Burma 1943–45

The motto of the regiment was 'Honi Soit Qui Mal y Pense' (Evil be to Him who Evil Thinks), and the regimental marches were 'Ein Schütze Bin Ich' (traditional, quick) and 'The Lower Castle Yard' (anonymous, quick). The uniform was a dark green jacket and blue trousers with white piping and facings, and the nicknames associated with The Oxfordshire and Buckinghamshire Light Infantry were 'Wolfe's Own' and 'The Light Bobs'. Imperial regiments affiliated to The Oxfordshire and Buckinghamshire Light Infantry were Le Régiment de Joliette (Canada), the 43rd Battalion, Australian Infantry, and the Hauraki Regiment (New Zealand).

The senior partner in The Oxfordshire and Buckinghamshire Light

Infantry was the 43rd (Monmouthshire Light Infantry) Regiment of Foot, which had been raised in 1741 as Colonel Fowke's Regiment of Foot and numbered as the 54th Foot. The regiment subsequently changed names with its colonels, and in 1748 was renumbered as the 43rd Foot. In 1751 the regiment became the 43rd Regiment of Foot, and in 1782 the 43rd (or the Monmouthshire) Regiment of Foot (Light Infantry) was accorded, and the regiment later became the 43rd (Monmouthshire Light Infantry) Regiment of Foot. The battle honours of the regiment were the following:

Quebec 1759 Martinique 1762 Havannah North America 1763–64 Vimiera Corunna Busaco Fuentes d'Onor Ciudad Rodrigo Badajoz Salamanca Vittoria Nivelle Nive Toulouse Peninsula South Africa 1851–53 New Zealand

The uniform was scarlet with white facings, and the nicknames of the 43rd were 'Wolfe's Own' and 'The Light Bobs', the former for the regiment's part in the capture of Quebec under General Thomas Wolfe in 1759, and the latter in celebration of the fact that the 43rd was the first regiment to adopt the 140/160-pace to the minute double past.

The 43rd's junior partner was the 52nd (or the Oxfordshire) Regiment of Foot (Light Infantry), which had been raised in 1755 by Colonel Hedworth Lambton as the 54th Regiment of Foot. In 1757 this was renumbered as the 52nd Regiment of Foot, and in 1782 became the 52nd (or the Oxfordshire) Regiment of Foot. In 1803 it became the 52nd (or the Oxfordshire) Regiment of Foot (Light Infantry). The battle honours of the regiment were the following:

Mysore Hindoostan Vimiera Corunna Busaco Fuentes d'Onor Ciudad Rodrigo Badajoz Salamanca Vittoria Nivelle Nive Orthes Toulouse Peninsula Waterloo Delhi 1857

The uniform was scarlet with buff facings, and there were no nicknames associated with the 52nd.

Second in seniority to the 1st Green Jackets in The Royal Green Jackets was the 2nd Green Jackets (The King's Royal Rifle Corps), created in 1958 by the redesignation of The King's Royal Rifle Corps, which had itself been raised in 1755 by the Earl of Loudon in the American colonies of Maryland, Pennsylvania and Virginia. The new regiment was initially styled the 62nd, or The Royal American Regiment of Foot, and in 1824 the 60th, or The Duke of York's Rifle Corps. Further revision followed in 1830 to the 60th, or The King's Royal Rifle Corps Regiment of Foot, and in 1881 to The King's Royal Rifle Corps. The battle honours of the corps were the following:

Louisburg Quebec 1759 Martinique 1762 Havannah North America 1763–64 Rolica Vimiera Martinique 1809 Talavera Busaco

Fuentes d'Onor Albuhera Ciudad Rodrigo Badajoz Salamanca
Vittoria Pyrenees Nivelle Nive Orthes Toulouse Peninsula
Mooltan Goojerat Punjaub South Africa 1851–53 Delhi 1857 Taku
Forts Pekin 1860 South Africa 1879 Ahmad Khel Kandahar 1880
Afghanistan 1878–80 Tel-el-Kebir Egypt 1882, '84 Chitral Defence
of Ladysmith Relief of Ladysmith South Africa 1899–1902 Mons
Retreat from Mons Marne 1914 Aisne 1914 Ypres 1914, '15, '17, '18
Langemarck 1914, '17 Gheluvelt Nonne Bosschen Givenchy 1914
Gravenstafel St Julien Frezenberg Bellewaarde Aubers
Festubert 1915 Hooge 1915 Loos Somme 1916, '18 Albert 1916,
'18 Bazentin Delville Wood Pozieres Guillemont Flers-
Courcelette Morval Le Transloy Ancre Heights Ancre 1916, '18
Arras 1917, '18 Scarpe 1917 Arleux Messines 1917, '18 Pilckem
Menin Road Polygon Wood Broodseinde Poelcappelle
Passchendaele Cambrai 1917, '18 St Quentin Rosieres Avre Lys
Bailleul Kemmel Bethune Bapaume 1918 Drocourt-Queant
Hindenburg Line Havrincourt Epehy Canal du Nord St Quentin
Canal Beaurevoir Courtrai Selle Sambre France and Flanders
1914–18 Macedonia 1915–18 Italy 1917–18 Calais 1940
Mont Pincon Falaise Roer Rhineland Cleve Goch Hochwald
Rhine Dreierwalde Aller North-West Europe 1940, '44–45
Egyptian Frontier 1940 Sidi Barrani Derna Aerodrome Tobruk 1941
Sidi Rezegh 1941 Gazala Bir Hacheim Knightsbridge Defence of
Alamein Line Ruweisat Fuka Airfield Alam el Halfa El Alamein
Capture of Halfaya Pass Nofilia Tebaga Gap Argoub el Megas
Tunis North Africa 1940–43 Sangro Arezzo Coriano
Lamone Crossing Argenta Gap Italy 1943–45 Veve
Greece 1941, '44–45 Crete Middle East 1941

The regimental motto was 'Celer et Audax' (Swift and Bold), and the regimental march was 'Lutzow's Wild Hunt' (quick). The uniform was rifle green with scarlet piping and facings, and the nicknames associated with The King's Royal Rifle Corps were 'The Green Jackets', 'The Sweeps', 'The Kaiser's Own' and 'The 60th', the first for the regiment's uniform, the second because on hot days the glove blacking tended to come off on the skin, and the third because of the resemblance of the corps' badge to the German Iron Cross decoration. Imperial regiments affiliated to The King's Royal Rifle Corps were the Regina Rifle Regiment (Canada), The King's Own Rifles of Canada, the Halifax Rifles (Canada), the Royal Rifles of Canada, the Dufferin Rifles of Canada, the Brockville Rifles (Canada), the Victoria Rifles of Canada, the Sydney University Regiment (Australia), the Kaffrarian Rifles (South Africa), and the Rhodesia Regiment (Southern Rhodesia).

The most junior of The Royal Green Jackets' components was the 3rd

Green Jackets (The Rifle Brigade), created in 1958 by redesignation of The Rifle Brigade (Princess Consort's Own). This had been raised in 1800 by Colonel Coote Manningham from rifle elements of existing regiments as the Experimental Corps of Riflemen, otherwise known as the Rifle Corps. In 1803 this was ranked as the 95th Foot and given the title the 95th or Rifle Regiment, and in 1816 this was changed to the Rifle Brigade. In 1862 this became The Prince Consort's Own Rifle Brigade, and further changes were modifications of this basic designation: in 1868 the unit became the Rifle Brigade (Prince Consort's Own), in 1881 The Prince Consort's Own (Rifle Brigade), in 1882 The Rifle Brigade (The Prince Consort's Own) and in 1920 The Rifle Brigade (Prince Consort's Own). The battle honours of the brigade were the following:

Copenhagen   Monte Video   Rolica   Vimiera   Corunna   Busaco   Barrosa   Fuentes d'Onor   Ciudad Rodrigo   Badajoz   Salamanca   Vittoria   Pyrenees   Nivelle   Nive   Orthes   Toulouse   Peninsula   Waterloo   South Africa 1846–47, '51–53   Alma   Inkerman   Sevastopol   Lucknow   Ashantee 1873–74   Ali Masjid   Afghanistan 1878–79   Burmah 1885–87   Khartoum   Defence of Ladysmith   Relief of Ladysmith   South Africa 1899–1902   Le Cateau   Retreat from Mons   Marne 1914   Aisne 1914, '18   Armentieres 1914   Neuve Chapelle   Ypres 1915, '17   Gravenstafel   St Julien   Frezenberg   Bellewaarde   Aubers   Hooge 1915   Somme 1916, '18   Albert 1916, '18   Bazentin   Delville Wood   Guillemont   Flers-Courcelette   Morval   Le Transloy   Ancre Heights   Ancre 1916, '18   Arras 1917, '18   Vimy 1917   Scarpe 1917, '18   Arleux   Messines 1917   Pilckem   Langemarck 1917   Menin Road   Polygon Wood   Broodseinde   Poelcappelle   Passchendaele   Cambrai 1917, '18   St Quentin   Rosieres   Avre   Villers Bretonneux   Lys   Hazebrouck   Bethune   Drocourt-Queant   Hindenburg Line   Havrincourt   Canal du Nord   Selle   Valenciennes   Sambre   France and Flanders 1914–18   Macedonia 1915–18   Calais 1940   Mont Pincon   Falaise   Roer   Rhineland   Cleve   Goch   Hochwald   Rhine   Dreierwalde   Aller   North-West Europe 1940, '44–45   Egyptian Frontier 1940   Sidi Barrani   Derna Aerodrome   Tobruk 1941   Sidi Rezegh 1941   Gazala   Bir Hacheim   Knightsbridge   Defence of Alamein Line   Ruweisat   Fuka Airfield   Alam el Halfa   El Alamein   Capture of Halfaya Pass   Nofilia   Tebaga Gap   Argoub el Megas   Tunis   North Africa 1940–43   Sangro   Arezzo   Coriano   Lamone Crossing   Argenta Gap   Italy 1943–44   Veve   Greece 1941, '44–45   Crete   Middle East 1941

The motto of the corps was 'Treu und Fest' (Loyal and Steadfast), and the corps march was 'I'm 95' (quick). The uniform was rifle green with black piping and facings, and the nicknames associated with The Rifle Brigade were 'The Green Jackets' and 'The Sweeps' for the same reasons that these nicknames were attributed to The King's Royal Rifle Corps. Imperial regiments affiliated to The Rifle Brigade were Princess Patricia's Canadian Light Infantry, the Royal Winnipeg Rifles (Canada), the British Columbia Regiment (Duke of Connaught's Own Rifles) of Canada, the Melbourne University Rifles (Australia), the Royal Durban Light Infantry (South Africa), and the Ceylon Tea Planters' Rifle Corps.

Special Air Service Regiment

Colonel-in-Chief

none

Colonel Commandant

none

Battle honours

North-West Europe 1944–45   Tobruk 1941   Benghazi Raid
North Africa 1940–43   Landing in Sicily   Sicily 1943   Termoli
Valli di Comacchio   Italy 1943–45   Greece 1944–45   Adriatic
Middle East 1943–44   Falkland Islands 1982

Regimental headquarters

Centre Block, Duke of York's Headquarters, Chelsea, London.

Regimental museum

none

Regimental marches

(quick) Marche du Régiment Parachutiste Belge

Regimental motto

Who Dares Wins

Nicknames

none

Uniform

none

Allied regiments

The Special Air Service Regiment (Australia)
1st New Zealand Special Air Service Squadron

Regimental history

The 1st Special Air Service Regiment was created in January 1943, although the regiment can trace its origins back to July 1941 and the formation in North Africa of special raiding parties under the designation 'L' Detachment, Special Air Service Brigade. Another British SAS regiment was raised in 1943, and in 1944 an SAS Brigade was created to control the activities of the two British, two French and one Belgian SAS regiments. In 1945 the British regiments were disbanded, and the French and Belgian regiments were taken onto the strength of the French and Belgian armies. In 1947 a Territorial Army SAS unit was raised as the 21st Special Air Service (Artists) Regiment, and in the early 1950s the demands of the Malayan Emergency led to the creation of the Malayan Scouts from 21st SAS volunteers. The Malayan Scouts became part of the British army regular establishment in 1952 as the 22nd Special Air Service Regiment, now The Special Air Service Regiment. A second TA regiment was created in 1959 as the 23rd Special Air Service Regiment.

Army Air Corps

Colonel-in-Chief

none

Colonel Commandant

General Sir Martin Farndale

Corps headquarters

Army Air Corps Centre, Middle Wallop, near Stockbridge, Hampshire.

Corps museum

Museum of Army Flying, Air Army Corps Centre, Middle Wallop, near Stockbridge, Hampshire.

Corps marches

(quick) Recce Flight
(slow) Thievish Magpie

Corps motto

none

Nicknames

none

Uniform

Light blue piping

Corps history

The original Army Air Corps was formed in 1942 to control the Glider Pilot Regiment and the Parachute Regiment, and in 1944 the Special Air Service Regiment was also subordinated to the AAC. However, in 1950 the AAC was disbanded, being re-raised in 1957 to oversee the fixed-wing units of the Air Observation Post and Light Liaison units in an army that was making increasing use of helicopters as well as fixed-wing aircraft. From 1957 to 1973 the AAC was little more than a permanent cadre supplemented by men from other regiments, but since 1973 the AAC has recruited its own personnel.

Royal Army Chaplains' Department

Departmental headquarters
Royal Army Chaplains' Department Centre, Bagshot Park, Bagshot, Surrey.

Departmental museum
none

Departmental march
Trumpet Tune (Clark)

Departmental motto
In This Sign Conquer

Nicknames
The Padres, The Sky Pilots

Uniform
Black with purple facings

Departmental history

An Army Chaplains' Department was created in 1796, initially for Church of England chaplains, although Presbyterians were admitted in 1827, Roman Catholics in 1836, Wesleyans in 1881, and Jews in 1892. The Army Chaplains' Department became the Royal Army Chaplains' Department in 1919.

Royal Corps of Transport

Colonel-in-Chief
HRH The Princess Alice Duchess of Gloucester

Colonel Commandant
Major-General W. Bate (1986, out of six)

Corps headquarters
Buller Barracks, Aldershot, Hampshire.

Corps museums
Buller Barracks, Aldershot, Hampshire, and Museum of Army Transport, Beverley, North Humberside.

Corps march
arrangement of Wait for the Wagon and Boer Trek Song

Corps motto
Nil Sine Labore (Nothing Without Work)

Nicknames

The Commos, The London Thieving Corps, The Moke Train, and The Murdering Thieves

Uniform

Blue with white stripes and facings

Corps history

In 1965 the Royal Army Service Corps was redesignated the Royal Corps of Transport. Up to 1794 all British army transport and supply services had been within the purview of the Commissary General, a department of the Treasury. In 1794, however, a Corps of Waggoners was raised under army auspices for service on the continent of Europe, becoming the Royal Waggon Corps in 1799 and the Royal Waggon Train in 1802. The Royal Waggon Train was disbanded in 1833, but in 1855 a Land Transport Corps was created, and in 1856 this became The Military Train. In 1869 The Military Train was redesignated the Army Service Corps. This contained only non-commissioned ranks, the officers being found by the Control Department. Various other changes followed until 1888, when a single Army Service Corps was created with its own specialist officers. In 1918 the Army Service Corps became the Royal Army Service Corps.

Royal Army Medical Corps

Colonel-in-Chief
HM Queen Elizabeth The Queen Mother

Colonel Commandant
Major-General R. N. Evans (1986, out of four)

Corps headquarters
Royal Army Medical College, Millbank, London.

Corps museum
Keogh Barracks, Ash Vale, Aldershot, Hampshire.

Corps march
Here's a Health unto Her Majesty

Corps motto
In Arduis Fidelis (Faithful in Adversity)

Nicknames
The Linseed Lancers, The Pills, The Poultice Wallopers

Uniform

Blue with dark cherry piping and facings

Corps history

An army-level Medical Staff Corps was created in 1855 to supersede the regimental surgeons hitherto responsible for military health, consisting solely of non-commissioned medical orderlies. In 1857 this became the Army Hospital Corps, being supplemented in 1873 by the Army Medical Staff for medical officers. In 1884 the two were united as the Medical Staff Corps. In 1898 this was restyled the Royal Army Medical Corps.

Royal Army Ordnance Corps

Colonel-in-Chief
HM The Queen

Colonel Commandant
General Sir Richard Trant (1986, out of four)

Corps headquarters
Director-General of Ordnance Services, Logistic Executive (Army), Portway, Monxton Road, Andover, Hampshire.

Corps museum
Blackdown Barracks, Deepcut, Camberley, Surrey.

Corps march
The Village Blacksmith

Corps motto
Sua Tela Tonanti (His Missiles Thundering)

Nicknames
The Ordnance, The Sugar Stick Brigade

Uniform

Blue with scarlet piping and facings

Corps history

The Royal Army Ordnance Corps can trace its ancestry back as far as 1414, when a civilian Office of Ordnance was created. In 1683 this became the Board of Ordnance, and like its predecessor this was tasked with the development, procurement, storage and issue of military ordnance, ammunition and other weapons. In 1792 the Board of Ordnance spawned a Field Train Department, and the Board itself disappeared in 1855 to be replaced in 1857 by a Military Store Department of officers only. In 1859 the Field Train Department disappeared, and was replaced in 1865 by the Military Store Staff Corps officered by the Military Store Department. In 1869 the Army Service Corps was created (*see* Royal Corps of Transport), its non-commissioned ranks being officered by men of the Control Department, which took over from the Military Store Department in 1870. In 1875 the Control Department became the Ordnance Store Department, and in 1877 the Ordnance Store Branch (from 1881 the Ordnance Store Corps) assumed control of non-commissioned ranks. In 1896 the officers came under the Army Ordnance Department, and the non-commissioned men under the Army Ordnance Corps. In 1918 these two were amalgamated as the Royal Army Ordnance Corps. In 1965 the Royal Army Ordnance Corps assumed the supply functions of the Royal Army Service Corps when the latter was revised as the Royal Corps of Transport.

Corps of Royal Electrical and Mechanical Engineers

Colonel-in-Chief

Field-Marshal The Prince Philip Duke of Edinburgh

Colonel Commandant

Major-General P. H. Lee (1986, out of four)

Corps headquarters

Corps Secretariat REME, Isaac Newton Road, Arborfield, Reading, Berkshire.

Corps museum

Corps Secretariat REME, Isaac Newton Road, Arborfield, Reading, Berkshire.

Corps marches

(quick) Lilliburlero, and Auprès de ma Blonde
(slow) Duchess of Kent

Corps motto

none

Nickname

The REME

Uniform

Blue with scarlet piping and blue facings

Corps history

The Corps of Royal Electrical and Mechanical Engineers was created in May 1942 as The Royal Electrical and Mechanical Engineers (using for the most part personnel from the Royal Army Ordnance Corps, the Royal Engineers and the Royal Army Service Corps) to cater for the army's increasingly complex and important electrical and mechanical requirements. In 1949 The Royal Electrical and Mechanical Engineers became the Corps of Royal Electrical and Mechanical Engineers.

Corps of Royal Military Police

Colonel-in-Chief

HM The Queen

Colonel Commandant

General Sir James Glover

Corps headquarters

Rousillon Barracks, Chichester, Sussex.

Corps museum

Rousillon Barracks, Chichester, Sussex.

Corps march

The Watchtower

Corps motto

Exemplo Ducemus (We Lead by Example)

Nickname

The Redcaps

Uniform

Blue with scarlet piping and facings

Corps history

Although a Provost-Marshal was featured in English armies of mediaeval times, it was not until 1661 that a Provost Service was created to ensure the discipline of English forces. An unnamed military police unit was created in 1855, and this became the Corps of Military Mounted Police in 1877, being complemented in 1885 by the Corps of Military Foot Police. The two corps were amalgamated in 1926 as the Corps of Military Police, which became the Corps of Royal Military Police during 1946.

Royal Army Pay Corps

Colonel-in-Chief
none

Colonel Commandant
Major-General J. J. Stibbon (1986, out of two)

Corps headquarters
Worthy Down, Winchester, Hampshire.

Corps museum
none

Corps march
Imperial Echoes

Corps motto
Fide et Fiducia (In Faith and Trust)

Nicknames
The Ink Slingers, The Quill Drivers

Uniform

Blue with primrose yellow facings

Corps history

Up to 1797 regiments had their own civilian paymasters, but in that year commissioned paymasters were introduced, and in 1878 their functions were absorbed into the Army Pay Department when a centralized paymaster service was created. The officers of this department were aided by non-commissioned men who were in 1893 taken under the aegis of the Army Pay Corps. In 1919 a Corps of Military Accountants was formed to deal with the more complex matters of a vastly expanded army, but this was disbanded in 1925. Meanwhile, in 1920 the Army Pay Department and the Army Pay Corps were each granted the prefix 'Royal', and later in the same year were merged as the Royal Army Pay Corps.

Royal Army Veterinary Corps

Colonel-in-Chief

none

Colonel Commandant

Lieutenant-General Sir Brian Kenny

Corps headquarters

Ministry of Defence (AVR), Government Buildings, Worcester Road, Droitwich, Worcestershire.

Corps museum

RAVC Laboratory and Stores, Gallwey Road, Aldershot, Hampshire.

Corps march

arrangement of Drink Puppy Drink and A-Hunting We Will Go

Corps motto

none

Nicknames

The Vets, The Horse Doctors

Uniform

Blue with maroon piping and facings

Corps history

Various veterinary measures were adopted for the British army at the end of the eighteenth century, but it was 1858 before a Veterinary Medical Department (officers) was created, becoming the Army Veterinary Department (officers) in 1881 and the Army Veterinary Corps (officers and other ranks) in 1903. This became the Royal Army Veterinary Corps in 1918.

Small Arms School Corps

Colonel-in-Chief
none

Colonel Commandant
General Sir Roland Guy

Corps headquarters
Depot SASC, Small Arms wing, The School of Infantry, Warminster, Wiltshire.

Corps museum
The Weapons Museum, The School of Infantry, Warminster, Wiltshire.

Corps march
The March of the Bowmen

Corps motto
none

Nicknames
none

Uniform

Blue with Cambridge blue piping and facings

Corps history

The origins of the Small Arms School Corps can be found in the School of Musketry created in 1854 and in 1919 redesignated the Small Arms School. In 1919 a Machine Gun School was also formed, and in 1923 the two became the Corps of Small Arms and Machine Gun Schools. In 1929 the two schools were combined as the Small Arms School Corps.

Military Provost Staff Corps

Colonel-in-Chief

none

Colonel Commandant

Lieutenant-General Sir Norman Arthur

Corps headquarters

Berechurch Hall Camp, Colchester, Essex.

Corps museum

none

Corps march

The Metropolitan

Corps motto

none

Nicknames

none

Uniform

Blue with scarlet piping and facings

Corps history

Formed in 1901 as The Military Prison Staff Corps, this body was redesignated the Military Provost Staff Corps in 1906.

Royal Army Educational Corps

Colonel-in-Chief

HRH The Duchess of Gloucester

Colonel Commandant

Major-General L. Howell (1986, out of two)

Corps headquarters

Eltham Place, Eltham, London.

Corps museum

Eltham Place, Eltham, London.

Corps march

none

Corps motto

none

Nicknames

none

Uniform

Blue with Cambridge blue piping and facings

Corps history

In 1846 the British army decided to centralize educational matters and created the Corps of Army Schoolmasters with a staff of warrant and non-commissioned officers. In 1920 this gave way to the Army Educational Corps, with commissioned and non-commissioned personnel, and in 1946 this became the Royal Army Educational Corps.

Royal Army Dental Corps

Colonel-in-Chief
none

Colonel Commandant
Brigadier G. Smith (1986, out of two)

Corps headquarters
Headquarters and Training Centre RADC, Evelyn Woods Road, Aldershot, Hampshire.

Corps museum
Headquarters and Training Centre RADC, Evelyn Woods Road, Aldershot, Hampshire.

Corps march
Green Facings

Corps motto
Ex Dentibus Ensis (From the Teeth a Sword)

Nickname

none

Uniform

Blue with emerald green piping and facings

Corps history

In 1921 an Army Dental Corps was formed to control the specialized role of dentists who had hitherto served in the Royal Army Medical Corps. The ADC became the Royal Army Dental Corps in 1946.

Royal Pioneer Corps

Colonel-in-Chief
HRH The Duke of Gloucester

Colonel Commandant
Major-General J. J. Stibbon

Corps headquarters
Simpson Barracks, Northampton, Northamptonshire.

Corps museum
Simpson Barracks, Northampton, Northamptonshire.

Corps march
Pioneer Corps

Corps motto
Labor Omnia Vincit (Work Overcomes All)

Nicknames
none

Uniform

Blue with scarlet piping and facings

Corps history

Comprising only combatant soldiers, this corps was raised in 1939 as the Auxiliary Military Pioneer Corps, became the Pioneer Corps in 1940 and received royal patronage in 1946 as the Royal Pioneer Corps.

Intelligence Corps

Colonel-in-Chief
Field-Marshal The Prince Philip Duke of Edinburgh.

Colonel Commandant
Major-General C. R. L. Guthrie

Corps headquarters
Templer Barracks, Ashford, Kent.

Corps museum
Templer Barracks, Ashford, Kent.

Corps march
The Rose and the Laurel

Corps motto
Manui Dat Cognitio Vires (Knowledge gives Force to the Arm)

Nicknames
none

Uniform

Blue with green piping and facings

Corps history

The Intelligence Corps was formed in 1914 but was disbanded in 1929 and then re-formed on an *ad hoc* basis in 1939 as British forces were about to move to France. The Intelligence Corps was formally reconstituted in July 1940 with personnel seconded from other units, but from 1957 the corps has recruited directly.

Army Physical Training Corps

Colonel-in-Chief
none

Colonel Commandant
General Sir Nigel Bagnall

Corps headquarters
HQ and Depot APTC, Army School of Physical Training, Queen's Avenue, Aldershot, Hampshire.

Corps museum
none

Corps march
none

Corps motto
none

Nicknames
none

Uniform

Black with scarlet piping and facings

Corps history

The origins of the Army Physical Training Corps can be found in the Army Gymnastic Staff raised in 1860, and changed in title to the Army Physical Training Staff during 1918. This in turn became the Army Physical Training Corps in 1940.

Army Catering Corps

Colonel-in-Chief
Honorary Major-General HRH The Duchess of Kent

Colonel Commandant
General Sir Geoffrey Howlett (1986, out of two)

Corps headquarters
St Omer Barracks, Aldershot, Hampshire.

Corps museum
none

Corps march
none

Corps motto
We Sustain

Nicknames
none

Uniform

Scarlet with grebe grey piping and facings

Corps history

An Army School of Cookery had been formed in Aldershot before World War I, and in 1941 this became the Army Catering Corps.

Army Legal Corps

Colonel-in-Chief
none

Colonel Commandant
Lieutenant-General Sir David Mostyn

Corps headquarters
ALS1 Ministry of Defence, Empress State Building, Lillie Road, London.

Corps museum
none

Corps march
none

Corps motto
Justitia in Armis (Justice in Arms)

Nicknames
none

Uniform

none

Corps history

In 1948 the Army Legal Services Staff was created as successor to the uniformed branch of the Judge Advocate-General's department, and was restyled the Army Legal Corps in 1978.

Queen Alexandra's Royal Army Nursing Corps

Colonel-in-Chief

HRH The Princess Margaret Countess of Snowdon

Colonel Commandant

Colonel K. Grimshaw

Corps headquarters

The Royal Pavilion, Farnborough Road, Aldershot, Hampshire.

Corps museum

The Royal Pavilion, Farnborough Road, Aldershot, Hampshire.

Corps march

Grey and Scarlet

Corps motto

Sub Cruce Candida (Under the White Cross)

Nicknames

none

Uniform

Dark grey with scarlet facings

Corps history

After the opening of the first British custom-designed army hospital in 1856 it was decided in 1866 that civilian nurses could be used in such institutions, and in 1881 such nurses came under the control of the Army Nursing Service. In 1902 this was revised to become Queen Alexandra's Imperial Military Nursing Service, and from 1907 supplemented by the Territorial Army Nursing Service. In 1949 the two branches were united as Queen Alexandra's Royal Army Nursing Corps.

Women's Royal Army Corps

Commandant-in-Chief
HM Queen Elizabeth The Queen Mother

Controller Commandant
Honorary Major-General HRH The Duchess of Kent

Corps headquarters
Queen Elizabeth Park, Guildford, Surrey.

Corps museum
Queen Elizabeth Park, Guildford, Surrey.

Corps march
Arrangement of Lass of Richmond Hill and Early One Morning

Corps motto
Suaviter in Modo, Fortiter in Re (Gentle in Manner, Resolute in Deed)

Nicknames
none

Uniform

Bottle green and beech brown

Corps history

In 1917 a Women's Army Auxiliary Corps was raised for non-combatant duties in France, and in 1918 this was restyled Queen Mary's Army Auxiliary Corps. In 1919 this was disbanded, but in 1938 an Auxiliary Territorial Service was created, and transformed into the Women's Royal Army Corps during 1949.

The Territorial Army

This book is concerned with Regular army units. However, given the importance of the Territorial Army in British mobilization plans, its units are outlined here for the sake of completeness. The Territorial Army is a capable and well-equipped force, and is currently being upgraded. The following list of Territorial Army units is therefore intended only as a guide to units of regimental size (no order of precedence).

The Duke of Lancaster's Own Yeomanry (now serving in an infantry role)
The Honorable Artillery Company
The Mercian Yeomanry (now serving in an infantry role)
The Queen's Own Yeomanry
The Royal Yeomanry
The Wessex Yeomanry (now serving in an infantry role)

100th (Yeomanry) Field Regiment Royal Artillery (Volunteers)
101st (Northumbrian) Field Regiment Royal Artillery (Volunteers)
102nd (Ulster and Scottish) Air Defence Regiment Royal Artillery (Volunteers)
103rd Lancashire Artillery (Volunteers) Air Defence Regiment Royal Artillery (Volunteers)
104th Air Defence Regiment Royal Artillery (Volunteers)

Royal Monmouthshire Royal Engineers (Militia)
71 (Scottish) Engineer Regiment (Volunteers)
72 Engineer Regiment (Tyne Electrical Engineers) (Volunteers)
73 Engineer Regiment (Volunteers)
74 (Antrim Artillery) Engineer Regiment (Volunteers)

75 Engineer Regiment (Volunteers)
111 Engineer Regiment (Volunteers)

31 (Greater London) Signal Regiment (Volunteers)
32 (Scottish) Signal Regiment (Volunteers)
33 (Lancashire and Cheshire) Signal Regiment (Volunteers) – Liverpool
34 (Northern) Signal Regiment (Volunteers) – Middlesborough
35 (South Midland) Signal Regiment (Volunteers) – Birmingham
36 (Eastern) Signal Regiment (Volunteers) – Wanstead
37 (Wessex and Welsh) Signal Regiment (Volunteers) – Bristol
38 Signal Regiment (Volunteers) – Sheffield
39 (City of London) Signal Regiment (Volunteers) – London
40 (Ulster) Signal Regiment (Volunteers) – Belfast
71 Signal Regiment (Volunteers) – Bromley

1st Battalion 51st Highland Volunteers
2nd Battalion 51st Highland Volunteers
3rd Battalion 51st Highland Volunteers
1st Battalion 52nd Lowland Volunteers
2nd Battalion 52nd Lowland Volunteers

5th (Volunteer) Battalion The Queen's Regiment
6th/7th (Volunteer) Battalion The Queen's Regiment

4th (Volunteer) Battalion The King's Own Royal Border Regiment
5th (Volunteer) Battalion The Royal Regiment of Fusiliers
6th (Volunteer) Battalion The Royal Regiment of Fusiliers
5th (Volunteer) Battalion The Royal Anglian Regiment
6th (Volunteer) Battalion The Royal Anglian Regiment
7th (Volunteer) Battalion The Royal Anglian Regiment

5th (Volunteer) Battalion The Light Infantry
6th (Volunteer) Battalion The Light Infantry
7th (Volunteer) Battalion The Light Infantry

1st Battalion The Yorkshire Volunteers
2nd Battalion The Yorkshire Volunteers
3rd Battalion The Yorkshire Volunteers

4th (Volunteer) Battalion The Royal Irish Rangers (27th [Inniskilling], 83rd and 87th)
5th (Volunteer) Battalion The Royal Irish Rangers (27th [Inniskilling], 83rd and 87th)

1st Battalion The Wessex Regiment (Rifle Volunteers)
2nd Battalion The Wessex Regiment (Rifle Volunteers)

1st Battalion The Mercian Volunteers
2nd Battalion The Mercian Volunteers

3rd (Volunteer) Battalion The Royal Welch Fusiliers
3rd (Volunteer) Battalion The Royal Regiment of Wales (24th/41st Foot)
4th (Volunteer) Battalion The Royal Regiment of Wales (24th/41st Foot)

3rd (Volunteer) Battalion The Worcestershire and Sherwood Foresters Regiment (29th/45th Foot)
5th/8th (Volunteer) Battalion The Queen's Lancashire Regiment
4th (Volunteer) Battalion The Royal Green Jackets

4th (Volunteer) Battalion The Parachute Regiment – Lincoln
10th (Volunteer) Battalion The Parachute Regiment – London
15th (Scottish Volunteer) Battalion The Parachute Regiment

21st Special Air Service Regiment (Artists) (Volunteers)
23rd Special Air Service Regiment (Volunteers)

Index to Regiments and Corps

(Designations since 1900)

(Named regiments and corps are given in alphabetical order.)

ARTILLERY
King's Troop RHA, 65
Royal Horse Artillery, 65
Royal Regiment of Artillery, 63

CAVALRY AND ROYAL ARMOURED CORPS
Blues and Royals, The, 5

Dragoon Guards
Royal Scots (Carabiniers and Greys), 14
1st King's, 12
1st The Queen's, 10
2nd (Queen's Bays), 12
3rd Carabiniers, 15
3rd (Dragoon Guards), 15
4th Royal Irish, 20
4th/7th Royal, 19
5th, 24
5th Royal Inniskilling, 23
6th (Carabiniers), 16
7th Princess Royal's, 20

Dragoons
Inniskillings (6th), 24
Royal Dragoons (1st), 6
Royal North British,
Royal Scots Greys, 15
1st Dragoons, 11
2nd, 17
5th, 24

Household Cavalry, 2

Hussars
Queen's Own, 26
Queen's Royal Irish, 30
Royal, 38
3rd, 27
4th, 31
7th, 27
8th, 31
10th, 39
11th, 39
13th, 43
13th/18th, 42
14th, 46
14th/20th, 45
15th, 50
15th/19th, 49
18th, 43
19th, 50
20th, 46

Lancers
5th, 54
9th, 35
9th/12th, 34
12th, 35
16th, 54
16th/5th, 53
17th, 58
17th/21st, 57
21st, 58

Life Guards, 2
Royal Horse Guards, 6
Royal Tank Corps, 61
Royal Tank Regiment, 60

310

INDEX

CORPS
Army Air Corps, 267
Army Catering Corps, 299
Army Legal Corps, 301
Army Physical Training Corps, 297
Intelligence Corps, 295
Military Provost Staff Corps, 287
Queen Alexandra's Royal Army Nursing Corps, 303
Royal Army Chaplains' Department, 269
Royal Army Dental Corps, 291
Royal Army Educational Corps, 289
Royal Army Medical Corps, 273
Royal Army Ordnance Corps, 275
Royal Army Pay Corps, 281
Royal Army Service Corps, 276
Royal Army Veterinary Corps, 283
Royal Corps of Signals, 68
Royal Corps of Transport, 271
Royal Electrical and Mechanical Engineers, Corps of, 277
Royal Engineers, Corps of, 66
Royal Military Police, Corps of, 279
Royal Pioneer Corps, 293
Small Arms School Corps, 285
Women's Royal Army Corps, 305

FOOT GUARDS
Coldstream Guards, 74
Grenadier Guards, 71
Irish Guards, 80
Scots Guards, 77
Welsh Guards, 82

INFANTRY
Alexandra, Princess of Wales's Own Yorkshire Regiment, 155
Anglian Regiment, The Royal, 122
  1st East, 125
  2nd East, 125
  3rd East, 125
Argyll and Sutherland Highlanders, 241

Bedfordshire and Hertfordshire, 130
Berkshire Regiment, Royal, 225
Black Watch, The, 219
Border Regiment, 106
  The King's Own Royal, 104
Buffs, The, 94

Cambridge, Duke of *see* Middlesex Regiment

Cameron Highlanders, The Queen's Own, 234
Cameronians, The (Scottish Rifles), 178
Cheshire Regiment, 164
Cornwall Light Infantry (32nd), 142

Derbyshire Regiment
Devonshire Regiment, 136
  and Dorset, 134
Dorset Regiment (39th and 54th), 136
Durham Light Infantry, 142

Edinburgh, Duke of, Royal Regiment (Berkshire and Wiltshire), 223
  (7th Gurkha Rifles), 253
Essex Regiment, 130

Fusiliers, The Lancashire, 111
  The Royal (City of London), 111
  The Royal Highland, 158
  The Royal Inniskilling, 183
  The Royal Irish, 183
  The Royal Northumberland, 111
  The Royal Regiment, 109
  The Royal Scots, 160
  The Royal Warwickshire, 111
  The Royal Welch, 167

Gloucestershire Regiment, 188
Gordon Highlanders, The, 238
Green Howards, 155
Green Jackets, 1st, 259
  2nd, 259
  3rd, 259
  The Royal, 257
Gurkha Rifles
  2nd King Edward VII's Own, 249
  6th Queen Elizabeth's Own, 251
  7th Duke of Edinburgh's Own, 253
  10th Princess Mary's Own, 255
Gurkhas, Brigade of, 247

Hampshire Regiment,
  The Royal, 209
Highland
  Light Infantry (City of Glasgow), 160
  Fusiliers, The Royal, 158
  Royal, Regiment of Foot (Black Watch), 219
Highlanders,
  Argyll and Sutherland, 241
  Cameron, The Queen's Own, 234
  Gordon, 238
  Queen's Own, 232

INDEX

Royal (42nd and 73rd), 219
Seaforth, 234
Inniskilling Fusiliers, Royal, 183
Irish Fusiliers, Royal, 183
Rangers, Royal, 182
Rifles, Royal, 184
Kent, Royal Regiment, 94
East (The Buffs), 94
West, 94
King's Own Royal Border Regiment, 104
King's Own Royal Regiment (Lancaster), 106
King's Own Scottish Borderers, 175
King's Own Yorkshire Light Infantry, 142
King's Regiment, The, 117
King's Regiment (Liverpool), 19
King's Regiment (Manchester and Liverpool), 119
King's Royal Rifle Corps, 261
King's Shropshire Light Infantry, 142

Lancashire Fusiliers, 111
Lancashire Regiment
East, 200
North, 204
(Prince of Wales's Volunteers), 200
The Queen's, 198
South, 200
Lancaster, The King's Own Royal Regiment, 106
Leicestershire Regiment, 132
The Royal, 132
Light Infantry, The, 139
Lincolnshire Regiment,
The Royal, 127
Liverpool, The King's Regiment, 119
London, City of, Regiment (Royal Fusiliers), 111
Loyal Regiment (North Lancashire), 200

Manchester Regiment, 119
and Liverpool Regiment, 119
Middlesex Regiment (Duke of Cambridge's Own), 94
East, 94
West, 94

Norfolk, Royal Regiment, 125
Northamptonshire Regiment, 127
Northumberland Fusiliers, Royal, 111

Oxfordshire Light Infantry, 260
and Buckinghamshire Light Infantry, 260

Parachute Regiment, 245
Prince of Wales's Own Regiment of Yorkshire, 150

Queen's Lancashire Regiment, 198
Queen's Own Buffs, 94
Queen's Own Cameron Highlanders, 234
Queen's Own Highlanders, 232
Queen's Own Royal West Kent, 94
Queen's Regiment, The, 91
Queen's Royal Regiment (West Surrey), 94
Queen's Royal Surrey Regiment, 94

Rifle Brigade, 263
Rifle Corps, The King's Royal, 261
Rifles (*see also* 'Gurkha')
Royal Irish, 184
Royal Ulster, 183
Scottish, 178
Royal Anglian Regiment, 122
Royal Berkshire Regiment, The, 225
Royal Fusiliers, 111
Royal Green Jackets, 257
Royal Hampshire, 209
Royal Highland Fusiliers, 158
Royal Highland Regiment, 219
Royal Inniskilling Fusiliers, 183
Royal Irish Fusiliers, 183
Royal Irish Rangers, 181
Royal Irish Rifles, 184
Royal Regiment of Fusiliers, 109
Royal Regiment of Wales, 170
Royal Scots, The, 88
Royal Scots Fusiliers, 160
Royal Sussex, 94
Royal Ulster Rifles, 183
Royal Warwickshire (Fusiliers), 111
Royal Welch Fusiliers, 167
Royal West Kent Regiment, 94

Scots Fusiliers, Royal, 160
Scots, The Royal, 88
Scottish Borderers, King's Own, 175
Scottish Rifles, 178
Seaforth Highlanders, 234
and Camerons, 234
Sherwood Foresters, 194
Shropshire Light Infantry, King's, 142
Somerset Light Infantry, 142

INDEX

and Cornwall Light Infantry, 142
South Wales Borderers, 172
Special Air Service Regiment, 265
Staffordshire Regiment (The Prince of Wales's), 213
  North, 215
  South, 215
Suffolk Regiment, 125
Surrey Regiment
  East, 94
  Queen's Royal, 94
  West, 94
Sussex Regiment
  Royal, 94

Ulster Rifles, Royal, 183

Warwickshire Fusiliers, Royal, 111

Welch Regiment, 172
  Royal, Fusiliers, 167
Wellington's (Duke of) Regiment, 206
Wiltshire Regiment, (Duke of Edinburgh's), 225
Worcestershire Regiment, 194
  and Sherwood Foresters Regiment, 192

York and Lancaster Regiment, 229
Yorkshire Light Infantry, King's Own, 142
Yorkshire Regiment, Alexandra Princess of Wales's Own (Green Howards), 155
Yorkshire Regiment, East, 152
  The Prince of Wales's Own, 150
  West, 152